# BIGFO(
# NATION

# The History of Sasquatch in North America

Adventures Unlimited Press

# BIGFOOT NATION

David Hatcher Childress

Adventures Unlimited Press

**Bigfoot Nation**

ISBN: 978-1-939149-96-1

Published by:
Adventures Unlimited Press
One Adventure Place
Kempton, Illinois  60946  USA
auphq@frontiernet.net


AdventuresUnlimitedPress.com


Additional Illustrations by Chas Berlin

Have you seen this man?

Thanks to all sorts of people who abide in Bigfoot Nation including:

Peter Guttilla, Colin and Janet Bord, John Green, Christopher Murphy, Thomas Steenburg, Loren Coleman, Robert Robinson, J. Robert Alley, David Paulides, Craig Woolheater, Chas Berlin, David Hancock, Grover Krantz, Jeff Meldrum, Rene Dahinden, Roger Patterson, and the whole host of bigfoot researchers out there—there are many of you and I cannot possibly name you all. Please look through the bibliography, which I tried to make as thorough as possible, to find the many other bigfoot researchers over the years. And to the many other researchers— old and new—keep on hiking down those lost trails of Bigfoot Nation, but keep your distance.

# BIGFOOT NATION

## The History of Sasquatch in North America

# TABLE OF CONTENTS

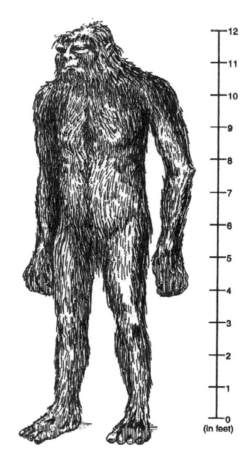

Have you seen this man?

# CHAPTER 1

# Introduction to Bigfoot Nation

When we remember that we are all mad,
the mysteries disappear and life stands explained.
—*Mark Twain*

᛭ —᚜— ᛭

Yes, Bigfoot Nation. Its time has come. It is time that we acknowledged the reality around us. It is impossible to turn this Holodeck off, so we might as well see the shadow nation that is all around us. It is Bigfoot Nation, lurking in the deep woods, on the edge of lonesome highways and logging roads, sometimes dumpster diving on the edge of town—peeking in windows to see what might be happening inside.

This is the fascinating—and frightening—world of Bigfoot Nation. Though there is the occasional report of bigfoot in northern Mexico, North American bigfoot seems to be confined to the United States and Canada. And except from the most extreme Arctic and desert environments in these states and territories, bigfoot reports continue to come in from all over the place. Bigfoot Nation stretches from Alaska, the Yukon and British Columbia to the swamps of Florida. From the berry fields of Nova Scotia, Quebec, and Maine to the mountains of Missouri and Arkansas to California and Oregon. No town, county or state is outside of Bigfoot Nation. Like coyotes, bigfoot is in every state and on the outskirts of even the largest cities.

My early introduction to the subject of bigfoot was in Durango, Colorado in 1967. I was in junior high school at the time and a lecture was given one evening by the famous California bigfoot hunter Roger Patterson. This was a year or so before he was to take his now-famous 16mm film footage of a female sasquatch walking briefly across a field in northern California. He was promoting his new book, *Do Abominable Snowmen of America Really Exist?*[16]

I enjoyed his slides and lecture. He presented a slide of the sasquatch photo printed in the *San Francisco Chronicle* on December 7, 1965, and various other evidence that America did indeed have its own abominable snowman. Patterson even played a reel-to-reel tape recording that featured the rather frightening call of a bigfoot late at night in some remote mountain campground. It was a bit sensational, but it stuck in the memory, to say the least. I bought a copy of Patterson's book, only $1.95 back in 1967, and my search for bigfoot had begun.

Over the years I bought other cryptozoology books, including Bernard Heuvelmans' classic *On the Track of Unknown Animals*[32] and went on the occasional investigative trip in search of cryptids. I amassed a huge library on bigfoot and other aspects of cryptozoology. I was surprised at how common bigfoot was across the United States. As we shall see, reports of hairy wild men and bigfoot originally came from the Midwest and Eastern portions of the country. I began to meet people who told me of their encounters with bigfoot. In most cases, people who meet bigfoot are utterly terrified, and in many cases it is a life-changing experience. Many do not talk about their encounter until some time has passed and they have found someone that they think they can share their story with who will not be skeptical of the episode. Indeed, as you read this book and the many incidents that I chronicle over more than 200 years, you will see that many witnesses are police officers. Except on Indian Reservations, most police are reluctant to discuss bigfoot for fear of ridicule, but some officers still file reports that mention the hairy critter.

Throughout this book I will not capitalize bigfoot or sasquatch unless it is part of a title or headline. Just like bear, cougar or unicorn, I feel that we do not need to capitalize the word for bigfoot. Also, the term bigfoot is both singular and plural throughout this book although some books have used the word bigfeet as a plural form of bigfoot. Similarly, sasquatch does not need to be capitalized and is also singular and plural.

The subject of Bigfoot Nation is one of a nation in the shadows. This book will take a historical look at the discovery and interaction between bigfoot and European/American pioneers as the settlement of the United States and Canada began on the east coast and moved west. American Indians had already interacted with sasquatch and even today most Native Americans completely believe in bigfoot. Native Americans have many legends and traditions concerning bigfoot, but they generally avoid the creatures and consider them dangerous. In the past, most Native Americans lived in group settings and this offered protection from many things, such as weather, famine and wild animals—including bigfoot.

As settlers moved westward through the Ohio Valley into Illinois and the West, there were more lonely farms and homesteads. Farming was the main occupation of Americans in the 1800s and where a farmstead could be carved out from the surrounding prairie or forest, there would be a farm. Forests were cleared and new animals appeared on the land: chickens, pigs, goats, sheep, cows and horses. Orchards were planted and gardens grew a wide range of vegetables. Bigfoot was losing his deep forests and swamps, but there were new foods to plunder—bigfoot has often been seen around orchards and berry patches, gorging on the ripe and plentiful food.

But also coming with these farmers and ranchers were lawmen, doctors, teachers and newsmen. These newsmen relied on local and national news to sell papers and get local advertising. It is with the advent of these newspapers, as well as travel and historical books, that we get the important early stories of contact with bigfoot starting in the early 1800s, and the press continues to keep it alive up to this very time.

The early reports of bigfoot called him wildman or grassman. Later he would be called swamp booger and skunk ape. In some ways he was the boogeyman. While in Tibet, Mongolia, Nepal and Bhutan they had various specific names for a similar creature, now typically called a yeti, in North America there was no name for this creature. Such descriptors as "the big people," or sasquatch and other names were used by the locals until October 2, 1958, when a road construction worker named Jerry Crew found unusually large footprints around his bulldozer on a road being constructed in Bluff Creek, California.

Jay Crew was part of a team cutting a road in the wild northern California area near the Oregon border where the Hoopa Indian Reservation is located. Thick forests with streams full of salmon are contained in a large area of wilderness and remote logging locations. On that October day, Jay Crew noticed a very clear footprint in the mud along the side of the road in that rainy part of northern California. But, he had seen these footprints before and this time he was prepared to make a plaster cast of the mysterious footprint.

He then reported the find, along with a photo of himself holding his first-of-a-kind plaster cast of a bigfoot footprint. In the story, Crew called the maker of the footprint "bigfoot." The Associated Press picked up the story along with Crew holding his plaster cast and the name was suddenly in the vernacular. So, since October 1958 the word bigfoot has been used to describe a creature that lurks among us—a missing link—something similar to us, but different. Something so wild and dangerous that we must not speak of its existence.

As mentioned above, in Asia they were calling similar creatures yetis, almas, or abominable snowmen. Now in North America we call them bigfoot, sasquatch, swamp apes or the grassman. In certain areas of Canada and the USA the local bigfoot will be called by specific local names, such as the Mogollon Monster for Arizona's bigfoot, or the Du Pont Monster for the various bigfoot known to haunt the Du Pont chemical plant near Seneca, Illinois. One famous bigfoot in North Carolina is called Knobby after a mountain he is frequently seen at. California bigfoot researcher and retired policeman David Paulides, now a resident of Colorado, notes in his books that the name "devil" often appears in the name of state parks, caverns, hollows and such. Many of these areas have had incidents of bigfoot activity or unexplained disappearances that may also involve bigfoot.[40]

Fortean author Jim Brandon in his book *Weird America*[17] suggested as much. He said authors have long made a case, especially in the United States, that associating the descriptive term "devil" with any cave, lake, or geographical area, meant that bigfoot sightings had occurred or that there were unexplained deaths or disappearances in the area.

So, we might conclude here that Bigfoot Nation is also Devil's Nation: Devil's Hole; Devil's Lake; Devil's Hollow; Devil's Creek; Devil's Bend—got one in your area?

Bigfoot is around us every day in commercials for fast food outlets, beef jerky and just about every other endorsement that can be imagined. Bigfoot Nation is not getting any money from these amusing campaigns, nor do they desire any. It is a simple fact that bigfoot—and his friends, whoever they may be—do not use or need "money"—nor do they understand it. Many modern humans do not understand money either, and I am probably one of them.

Bigfoot, however, cannot use money but doesn't mind a candy bar, peanut butter jar, or other tasty snack that is different from his usual fare of god-knows-what.

Those trying to contact bigfoot often open a jar of peanut butter, or a Snickers bar, and hang them by a string from a lower branch of a pine tree. The open jar of peanut butter is tied with a string and hung from the branch so that it is nine or ten feet off the ground. The idea is that only bigfoot, or a very large bear, could reach the open jar. Small birds might be able to get at the mashed peanuts at the top of the open jar, but usually the jar is empty within a few days, as expected, and it seems that bigfoot is enjoying this treat—which is ultimately a trap.

Bigfoot Nation, alarming as it seems, surrounds us. It is everywhere. Swamps, river grasslands, forests, and even desert areas—have reported bigfoot as lurking on the edges of civilization. Ultimately the old males are forced out to become dumpster divers. These are probably the reports of white-haired bigfoot near cities and highways, often reported by truck drivers.

With this book I will try to create a chronological timeline for Bigfoot Nation starting in the early 1800s. After that we will look at bigfoot reports from 1900 to 1950 and then examine bigfoot reports from after WWII (1950) to the Millennium. This

**15**

*Introduction*

is the period where bigfoot got his name coined and the elusive creatures entered popular culture in the form of magazine articles, movies, books and television. A movie named *Bigfoot* was shown at drive-in theaters around the country in 1971. There is a popular mini-mart chain in Indiana and surrounding states called Bigfoot. From beef jerky to parkas to computer software, the bigfoot brand is everywhere—but where is bigfoot?

I have gathered information from a variety of sources and fortunately I have a very large library of bigfoot, yeti and sasquatch books. I give my sincere thanks to all of those researchers and writers who have written books on bigfoot. There are too many to list here but they can all be found in the bibliography at the end of this book.

So, let us proceed to the early history of Bigfoot Nation, a history that includes an American President and some bizarre news stories.

The *San Francisco Chronicle* featured an article on bigfoot in 1965.

An early American meets one of the giants of the forest.

# CHAPTER 2

# 1800 to 1899
# The Wild Men of the Frontier

Behold, Esau my brother is a hairy man,
And I am a smooth man.
—*Genesis 27:11*

Probably the earliest known report of bigfoot comes from the Canadian Rockies. The incident occurred in Jasper, Alberta in 1811 when a British fur trader and explorer named David Thompson encountered giant footprints in the Athabasca River area. Said Thompson in his diary published by the *Oregon Historical Quarterly*, Number 15 (March-June 1914):

> I now recur to what I have already noticed in the early part of last winter, when proceeding up the Athabasca River …we came to the track of a large animal, which measured fourteen inches in length by eight inches in breadth by a tape line. As the snow was about six inches in depth the track was well defined, and we could see it for a full hundred yards from us, this animal was proceeding from north to south. We did not attempt to follow it, we had not time for it, and the Hunters, eager as they are to follow and shoot every animal, made no attempt to follow this beast, for what could the balls of our fowling guns do against such an animal? Reports from old times had made the head branches of this River, and the Mountains in the

vicinity the abode of one, or more, very large animals, to which I never appeared to give credence; for these reports appeared to arise from that fondness for the marvelous so common to mankind: but the sight of the track of that large a beast staggered me, and I often thought of it, yet never could bring myself to believe such an animal existed, but thought it might be the track of some Monster Bear.

### 1818 Report of a Wild Man of the Woods

The earliest newspaper report of bigfoot can be found Colin and Janet Bord's 1982 book *The Bigfoot Casebook.*[3] The article is from the *Exeter Watchman* dated September 22, 1818. It concerns a bigfoot being seen around the town of Ellisburgh near Sacket's Harbor which is on Lake Ontario in the very northwest section of Upstate New York. The story is dated September 6 from Sacket's Harbor and had the headline: "ANOTHER WONDER." The article went on to say:

Report says, that in the vicinity of Ellisburgh, was seen on the 30th. By a gentleman of unquestionable veracity, an animal resembling the Wild Man of the Woods. It is stated that he came from the woods within a few rods of this gentleman—that he stood and looked at him and then took his flight in a direction which gave a perfect view of him for some time. He is described as bending forward when running—hairy, and the heel of the foot narrow, spreading at the toes. Hundreds of persons have been in pursuit for several days, but nothing further is heard or seen of him.

The frequent and positive manner in which this story comes, induces us believe it. We wish not to impeach the veracity of this highly favored gentleman—yet, it is proper that such naturally improbable accounts should be established by the mouth, of at least two direct eyewitnesses to entitle them to credit.[3]

### 1839 Article about Bigfoot in Wisconsin

A report from 1839 is from December in La Porte County, Indiana. There a "wild child" was seen repeatedly around Fish Lake and was reported in the *Michigan City Gazette* that said, "It is reported to be about four feet high and covered with a coat of light chestnut-colored hair. It runs with great velocity, and when pursued, as has often been the case, it sets up the most frightening and hideous yells, and seems to make efforts at speaking."[11]

Another early report comes from 1839 concerning Wisconsin. The highly detailed story was reported in the *Boston Daily Times* on April 1, 1839. The article was sent to *Cryptomundo* by Scott McClean, who wondered if it was just a coincidence that the bizarre story was published on April Fool's Day. Still, the story has a ring of authenticity to it. The story is of a lumber steamship that goes up the Mississippi to Prairie Du Chien in Wisconsin and then continues north to what is now known as the Minnesota River, but was called the Saint Peters River back then. While spending time at this northerly timber camp the lumbermen encounter—and capture—a bigfoot. The article was entitled, "When Will Wonders Cease?"

Said the article:

> Robert Lincoln, Esq., Agent of the New York Western Lumber Company, has just returned from the Saint Peters river, near the head of steamship navigation, on the upper Mississippi, bringing with him a living American Ourang Outang, or Wild Man of the Woods, with two small cubs, supposed to be about three months old. Mr. Lincoln informs us that he went out to the north-west as Agent of the New York Lumber Company, in July last, with a view to establish extensive saw-mills, on the pine lands near the Falls of Saint

An 1820 drawing of a "cannibal monster" by David Cusick. The hairy monster is watching a woman roasting acorns and frightened away thinking she is eating hot coals.

Anthony; and he has given us a detail of the operations of the company, and the circumstances which lead to the capture of the extraordinary creatures mentioned above.

Those who are acquainted with the leading features of the Valley of the Mississippi, are aware that there is little or no pine timber throughout the States of Illinois and Missouri, or in the extensive territories of Wisconsin and Iowa. The inhabitants of that region are obliged to use oak and walnut for common building purposes, and the labor of working such materials is very great. The greatest portion of the pine timber that finds its way into the upper part of the Valley, is floated down the Ohio, and from thence carried up the Mississippi and Illinois rivers by steamboats. The most ordinary kind of pine timber is worth $60 per thousand, in any part of Illinois or the territories; in New England the same quality sells for about half that sum. There are some very extensive and immensely valuable pine lands near the Falls of Saint Anthony, on the Upper Mississippi; but until recently they have been in the possession of the Sac and Fox Indians. In the summer of 1838, a treaty was ratified with these Indians, by which they ceded the whole of their pine lands to the United States. The ceremonies of this treaty were performed at Fort Snelling, about the first of July last. Capt. Marryatt, the famous English novelist, was then on the Upper Mississippi, and was present to witness the war dances on this occasion, which, it is said, were conducted with unusual splendor. He also spent several days among the Indians, and by the assistance of the American officers at Fort Snelling, obtained a large collection of ornaments and curiosities.

Some shrewd men at Albany and New York who knew what the treaty referred to, was about to be ratified, and who were aware, also, of the value of the timber, formed a company, with a substantial capital, and engaged a large number of enterprising mechanics and laborers to go out and establish saw-mills for cutting timber on the Saint Peters. They rightly supposed that the land would not "come into market," as the phrase is, for several years, as it is worth but little except for timber. Those who wish to obtain land for cultivation, go into the more fertile parts of the territories. Companies may therefore "claim" land, establish mills, and cut off the timber where ever they can find it, without fee or license. The timber may then be floated down the Mississippi in rafts, for a mere trifle, and sold at the highest prices any where on the river.

The New York Company sent out their expedition in July last. The workmen and laborers with the principal part of the machinery went by way of New Orleans, and at that city they chartered a steamboat and proceeded up the Mississippi. The whole business was under the direction of Mr. Lincoln. They had on board all the necessary tools and saws, together with the apparatus for a gristmill, oxen, horses, cows, a good stock of provisions, arms, ammunition, &c. &c. They passed directly up the river, only stopping to take in wood and water, until they reached Prairie Du Chien, at the mouth of the Wisconsin. Here they put their animals on shore, and remained two days.

On the third day they re-embarked and finally reached the Saint Peters in safety. Their enterprise proved highly successful. They found the timber of the first quality, and the facilities for building mills much greater than they anticipated. The work went on very prosperously, and in a few months Mr. Lincoln had the satisfaction of launching his rafts on the headwaters of the Mississippi! They continued to prosecute their labors vigorously, until winter set in, when a part of the workmen started for Saint Louis, and a part of them remained to superintend the cutting of timber.

During the winter, Mr. Lincoln and several of the workmen made frequent excursions in pursuit of game, which was very abundant, and their camp was one continued scene of festivity. The Indians brought in large quantities of furs, which Mr. Lincoln purchased for a mere trifle, and lined his cabins with them throughout, which rendered his rude huts very warm and comfortable. The whole party were as hearty as bucks, and appeared to enjoy themselves exceedingly.

About the 15th of January, two of the carpenters who had been out in pursuit of a gang of wolves that had proved very troublesome, came into the camp and reported that they had seen a huge monster in the forest, on a branch of the Mississippi, having the form of a man, but much taller and stouter, covered with long hair, and of a frightful aspect. They stated that when first seen, he was standing on a large log, looking directly at them and the moment they raised their muskets, he darted into the thicket and disappeared. They saw him again in about half an hour, apparently watching them, and when they turned towards him he again disappeared. Mr. Lincoln was at first disposed to think lightly of this matter, believing that the men might have been mistaken about the size and height of the object, or supposing it might have been a trick of the Indians to frighten them.

He was informed, however, by some of the natives, that such a being had often been seen on the St. Peters, and near the Falls of the Mississippi, and they proposed to guide a party of the workmen to a bluff where it was thought he might be found. The men were all ready for an adventure, and arming themselves with rifles and hunting-knives, they started for the bluff under the direction of Mr. Lincoln and the Indian guides. On the way they were joined by several of the natives, and the whole party numbered twenty-three.

They arrived at the bluff late on the afternoon of the 21st of January, and encamped in a cave or grotto, at the foot of the hill. Early the next morning, two of the Indians were sent out to reconnoiter, and in about an hour returned, and said they had seen the wild man, on the other side of the hill. The whole party immediately prepared for the pursuit. Mr. Lincoln gave positive orders to the men, not to fire upon him unless it should be necessary in self-defense, as he wished, if possible, to take him alive. The Indians stated that although a very powerful creature, he was believed to be perfectly harmless, as he always fled at the approach of men. While Mr. Lincoln was giving his men their instructions, the wild man appeared in sight. He ordered them to remain perfectly quiet, and taking out his pocket-glass surveyed him minutely. He appeared to be about eight or nine feet high, very athletic, and more like a beast standing erect than a man. After satisfying himself with regard to the character of the creature, Mr. Lincoln ordered his men to advance. The Indians had provided themselves with ropes, prepared to catch wild horses, with which they hoped to ensnare and bind the creature, without maiming him.

The instant the company moved towards the wild man, he sprung forward with a loud and frightful yell, which made the forest ring; the Indians followed close upon him, and Mr. Lincoln and his men brought up the rear. The pursuit was continued for nearly an hour, now gaining upon the object of their chase, and now almost losing sight of him. The trees, however, were quite open, and free from underbrush, which enabled them to make their way very rapidly. Whenever they came very near him, he started forward again with a yell, and appeared to increase his speed. He finally darted into a thicket, and although they followed close and made much search, they were unable to find him.

They then began to retrace their steps towards the place of encampment, and when within about a mile of the cavern, the wild man crossed their path, within twenty rods of the main body of the party. They immediately gave chase again, and accidentally drove the creature from the forest into an open field or prairie.

The monster appeared to be much frightened at his situation, and leaped forward, howling hideously. At length he suddenly stopped and turned upon his pursuers. Mr. Lincoln was then in the advance. Fearing that he might attack them, or return to the woods and escape, he fired upon him and lodged a charge of buck-shot in the calf of his leg. He fell immediately, and the Indians sprang forward and threw their ropes over his head, arms and legs, and with much effort succeeded in binding him fast. He struggled, however, most desperately, gnashed his teeth, and howled in a frightful manner. They then formed a sort of litter of branches and limbs of trees, and placing him upon it, carried him to the encampment. A watch was then placed over him,

**25**

and every effort made that could be devised to keep him quiet, but he continued to howl most piteously all night. Towards morning two cubs, about three-feet high, and very similar to the large monster, came into the camp, and were taken without resistance. As soon as the monster saw them he became very furious, gnashed his teeth, and howled, and thrashed about, until he burst several of the cords, and came very near effecting his escape. But he was bound anew, and after that was kept most carefully watched and guarded. The next day he was placed on the litter and carried down to the mills on the Saint Peters.

For two or three days, Mr. Lincoln says, he refused to eat or drink, or take any kind of food, but continued to howl at intervals for an hour at a time. At length, however, he began to eat, but from that time his howls ceased, and he has remained stupid and sullen ever since. The cubs took food very readily, and became quite active and playful. Mr. Lincoln is a native of Boston, and some of the workmen engaged at his mills are from this city. He arrived here [in Boston] Saturday afternoon in the brig *St. Charles*, Stewart, master, from New Orleans, with the wild man and the cubs, and they were all removed from the vessel that evening. By invitation of Mr. Lincoln, who is an old acquaintance, we went down to his rooms to examine this monster. He is a horrid looking creature, and reminds us very strongly of the fabled satyrs, as we have pictured them to our own mind. He is about eight feet three inches high, when standing erect, and his frame is of giant proportions in every part. His legs are not straight, but like those of the dog and other four-footed animals, and his whole body is covered with a hide very much like that of a cow. His arms are very large and long, and ill-proportioned.

It does not appear from his manner that he has ever walked upon "all fours." The fingers and toes are mere bunches, armed with stout claws. His head is covered with thick, coarse, black hair, like the mane of a horse. The appearance of his countenance, if such it may be called, is very disgusting nay, almost horrible.

**26**

It is covered with a thinner and lighter coat of hair than the rest of the body; there is no appearance of eye-brows or nose; the mouth is very large and wide, and similar to that of a baboon. His eyes are quite dull and heavy, and there is no indication of cunning or activity about them. Mr. Lincoln says he is beyond dispute carnivorous, as he universally rejects bread and vegetables, and eats flesh with great avidity. He thinks he is of the ourang outang species: but from what little we have seen, we are inclined to consider him a wild animal, somewhat resembling a man. He is, to say the least, one of the most extraordinary creatures that has ever been brought before the public, from any part of the earth, or the waters under the earth, and we believe will prove a difficult puzzle to the scientific. He lies down like a brute, and does not appear to possess more instinct than common domestic animals. He is now quite tame and quiet, and is only confined by a stout chain attached to his legs.

This is the first creature of the kind, we believe, ever found on this continent. It was to be expected, however, that in penetrating the remote recesses of the new world, monsters would be found, and great natural curiosities brought to light; and it has been a matter of surprise to many that so little of the marvelous has ever been discovered. But we cannot tell what the wilds of the far Northwest, the shores of Lake Superior, the regions of the Rocky Mountains, and the vast territory of the Oregon, may yet bring forth.

It is Mr. Lincoln's intention to submit these animals to the inspection of the scientific for a few days, in order to ascertain what they are, and after that to dispose of them to some persons for exhibition. Mr. Lincoln himself will return to the Saint Peters in the course of two or three weeks.

P. S. Mr. Lincoln informs us that he will exhibit the Wild Man and his cubs, gratuitously, this forenoon, in the rear of No. 9 Elm Street. We presume our citizens will not be slow to take advantage of this offer.

This astonishing story was to foreshadow hundreds, if not thousands, of similar stories to be printed in newspapers in the US and Canada for the next 180 years. Like other captured apemen, we will probably never know what happened to this poor creature. What we do know is that this is not the last story of its kind—these creatures were to be spotted throughout the Ohio and Mississippi River valleys.

## 1847: Mount St. Helens a Forbidden Area

An explorer in the Pacific Northwest, the artist Paul Kane, comments on a strange creature in his book, *The Wanderings of an Artist.* His entry for March 26, 1847 reads:

> When we arrived at the mouth of the Kattlepoutal River, 36 miles from Vancouver [Washington], I stopped to make a sketch of the volcano, Mt. St. Helens, distant, I suppose, about 30 or 40 miles. This mountain has never been visited by either whites or Indians; the latter assert that it is inhabited by a race of beings of a different species, who are cannibals, whom they hold in great dread …these superstitions are taken from a man, who they say, went into the mountain with another, and escaped the fate of his companion, who was eaten by the "skoocooms," or "evil genii." I offered a considerable bribe to any Indian who would accompany me in its exploration but could not find one hardy enough to venture there.[21]

It would seem that this mysterious and feared race of skoocooms is part of Bigfoot Nation. Mount St. Helens is an area where many bigfoot have been reported.

## 1851: Two Hunters See Bigfoot in Arkansas

Colin and Janet Bord report that two hunters in Greene County, Arkansas saw a herd of cattle that was being chased by a bigfoot. They watched the creature for some time which was "an animal bearing the unmistakable likeness of humanity. He was of gigantic stature, the body being covered with hair and head with long locks that fairly enveloped the neck and shoulders."[3]

A man named John Weeks recalled how his grandfather told him about being a gold prospector in California's Mount Shasta area in the 1850s. Said Weeks:

> My grandfather prospected for gold in the eighteen
> fifties throughout the region described as being the home
> of the Snowman. Upon grandfather's return from to the
> East he told stories of seeing hairy giants in the vicinity of
> Mount Shasta. These monsters had long arms but short legs.
> One of them picked up a 20-foot section of a sluiceway and
> smashed it to bits against a tree.
>
> When grandfather told us these stories, we didn't believe
> him at all. Now, after reading your article, it turns out he
> wasn't as big a liar as we youngsters thought he was.[3]

## 1868 Report of an Ape Man in Alabama

An early bigfoot/skunk ape report came from Alabama in 1868. Chad Arment, author of *Historical Bigfoot*, reproduces a fascinating story from 1868 about a giant wild apeman that was seen near Meadville, in Franklin County, Alabama where men with hunting dogs:

> …discovered the tracks of the game in some miry
> places, which appeared similar to the track of a human foot;
> and they observed, also, that the toes of one foot turned
> backward. On coming up with the dogs, who were now
> baying, they beheld a frightful looking creature, of about
> the average height of man, but with far greater muscular
> development, standing menacingly a few yards in front of
> the dogs. It had long, coarse hair flowing from its head and
> reaching near its knees; its entire body, also, seemed to be
> covered with hair of two or three inches' length, which was
> of a dark brown color. From its upper jaw projected two
> very large tusks, several inches long. …it fled toward the
> Mississippi River, and was not overtaken again until within
> a few yards of the bank. When the party came up with the
> dogs the second time, the monster was standing erect before
> them, none of them having yet dared to clinch with it. But
> when the dogs were urged by their masters, they endeavored
> to seize it, when it reached forward and grabbed one them,

and taking it in its hands, pressed it against its trunk, which pierced it through and killed it instantly. Becoming alarmed at this display of strength, the hunters fired several shots at the creature, which caused it to leap into the river... after sinking and rising several times, it swam to the Louisiana shore and disappeared.[44]

Arment says that this story came from the *Daily Herald* of Dubuque, Iowa for June 27, 1868, and we see that we might conclude from this account that bigfoot is a good swimmer! Indeed, the common southern terms of grassman and swamp ape indicate that these creatures are semi-aquatic apemen who are good swimmers and can live in swamps and remote river valleys that contain dense forests and brush. The large tusks on this bigfoot, from the upper jaw, are unexplained and this is not something that is typically reported. They would seem to be describing large canine teeth and perhaps the bigfoot was missing other teeth.

### 1869: A Gorilla in Ohio

Another early bigfoot incident occurred in Ohio and was reported in the *Minnesota Weekly Record* on Saturday, January 23, 1869. The title of the story was "A Gorilla in Ohio." The first gorilla was captured in Liberia, Africa in 1847 and the word came into the English language at that time. Said the 1869 article:

Gallipolis [Ohio] is excited over a wild man, who is reported to haunt the woods near that city. He goes naked, is covered with hair, is gigantic in height, and "his eyes start from their sockets." A carriage, containing a man and daughter, was attacked by him a few days ago. He is said to have bounded at the father, catching him in a grip like that of a vice, hurling him to the earth, falling on him and endeavoring to bite and to scratch like a wild animal. The struggle was long and fearful, rolling and wallowing in the deep mud, [half] suffocated, sometimes beneath his adversary, whose burning and maniac eyes glared into his own with murderous and savage intensity. Just as he was about to become exhausted from his exertions, his daughter, taking courage at the imminent danger of her parent, snatched up a rock and hurling it at the head of her father's would be murderer, was fortunate enough to put an end to the struggle by striking him somewhere about the ear. The creature was not stunned, but feeling unequal to further exertion, slowly got up and retired into the neighboring copse that skirted the road.[44]

It is interesting to note that this incident took place in Ohio but the newspaper clipping that we have of the story comes from a Minnesota newspaper. This shows us how newspapers were cropping up all over the place after the Civil War and that there were almost certainly newspapers in Ohio at this time that also carried this story. Many old newspapers no longer exist and often records of old issues are lost in fires and floods.

We also see with this story that until the name "bigfoot" came along in 1958, people struggled for a name for the creature they encountered. Gorilla is still used to occasionally describe bigfoot sightings (such as, "I took this picture of a gorilla in our back yard…").

Also, according to Janet and Colin Bord, in 1869 in the Arcadia Valley of northwest Arkansas a bigfoot was seen repeatedly and it approached cabins, especially when the men were gone and only women and children were around. It was described as a "wild man, gorilla, or 'what is it?'" At one point over sixty of the local citizens got together to hunt the animal, which they called Old Sheff, and it disappeared for some days but then returned.

The Bords also chronicle another incident in 1869. A letter written by a man from Grayson, California to the Antioch *Ledger* says he witnessed a bigfoot playing with the sticks in his campfire. He was in an area called Orestimba Creek, about 20 miles north of Grayson, and had seen large footprints around his campsite. He was determined to see who or what it was that was visiting his camp while he was gone. He hid in some bushes nearby and waited. Said the man in his letter to the newspaper:

Suddenly I was surprised by a shrill whistle such as boys produce with two fingers under their tongues, and turning quickly, I ejaculated, "Good God!" as I saw the object of my solicitude standing beside the fire, erect, and looking suspiciously around. It was the image of a man, but it could not have been human.

I was never so benumbed with astonishment before. The creature, whatever it was, stood fully five feet high, and disproportionately broad and square at the fore shoulders, with arms of great length. The legs were very short and body long. The head was small compared with the rest of the creature, and appeared to be set upon his shoulders without a neck. The whole was covered with dark brown and cinnamon colored hair, quite long on some parts, that on the head standing in a shock and growing close down to the eyes, like a Digger Indian's.

As I looked he threw his head back and whistled again, and then stopped and grabbed a stick from the fire. This he swung around, until the fire on the end had gone out, when he repeated the maneuver. I was dumb, almost and could only look. Fifteen minutes I sat and watched him as he whistled and scattered my fire about. I could easily have put a bullet through this head, but why should I kill him? Having amused himself, apparently, as he desired, with my fire, he started to go, and having gone a short distance he returned, and was joined by another—a female, unmistakably—when both turned and walked past me, within twenty yards of where I sat, and disappeared in the brush.[3]

It is unusual for bigfoot to play with a camp fire and hold a burning torch. In this case the bigfoot was curious about the fire, but had no use for it. In another incident, also from 1869, a bigfoot—or wild man—was seen carrying a club:

…A large party, armed and equipped, lately started in pursuit of "it," and one night a splendid view was obtained of the object which, it was concluded, had once been a white man, but was now covered with a coat of fine, long, hair, carried a club in the right hand and in the left a rabbit. The moment it caught sight of the party, as the moon shone out, it dashed past the camp "with the scream like the roar of a lion," brandished the huge club and attacked the horses in a perfect frenzy of madness.

The savage bloodhounds which the party had brought along refused to pursue the object; and so the party hastily raised a log rampart for self-defense; but instead of making attack, the object merely uttered the most terrible cries through the night, and in the morning disappeared. It was evident, however, from the footprints, that the object would require a "pair of No. 9 shoes," and this is all we know. The party could have shot it on first seeing it, but failed to do so.[3]

It is interesting that the bigfoot carried a club. This is rarely seen in bigfoot reports, but there are other incidents where a bigfoot was carrying a club. Also, it commonly believed that uses a club or tree branch to make loud knocks against a tree.[71] That the bloodhounds refused to follow or attack the creature is very standard in bigfoot reports, though there are incidents when dogs have engaged a bigfoot.

## 1871: Woman Kidnapped by Sasquatch

One of the few abduction stories involving sasquatch happened in 1871 on the Chehalis Reservation in northern British Columbia, an area of many bigfoot reports. In that year Serephine Long was abducted while collecting cedar roots in the forest and was returned one year later in 1872. She said that one of the hairy giants that inhabited the region grabbed her and smeared tree sap on her eyes so she could not see where he was taking her. He took her to a cave somewhere where the sasquatch forced her to live with him and his elderly parents. "They fed me well," she reportedly said.

She convinced the bigfoot to take her back to her village and the bigfoot again took tree sap and put it on her eyelids so she could not see and took her to the vicinity of the village. She finally arrived back after one year missing and collapsed of exhaustion. She was put in a bed and that same night gave birth, but the infant died a few hours later. Interviewed in 1925 she said that she was

Serephine Long in about 1941 at the age of 87.

glad the baby had died and she hoped she would never see the hairy giant again.[7]

## 1877: A Wild Man at the Smithsonian Institution

A newspaper report from the Washington, D.C. newspaper *The Daily Telegram* had an astonishing report on April 9, 1877 on its first page about a live "wild man" who was on display at the Smithsonian Institution. This newspaper report was dug up by bigfoot researcher Joe Fex and carried several headlines. The headlines started with "EXTRA: THE WILD MAN AT THE SMITHSONIAN." The second headline read, "HIS SAVAGE

ATTACK UPON A YOUNG LADY," and finally, "HER CLOTHING IN RIBBONS," "HE WILL BE INCARCERATED IN AN IRON CAGE TO-DAY." The brief story went on to say:

Among the curiosities from the Centennial, received by, and now on exhibition at the Smithsonian Institution, is a specimen of "Wild Man" who, although perfectly tame and

The Washington, DC story in *The Daily Telegraph* for April 3, 1977.
Thanks to Joe Fex and APE-X Research.

35

subdued at Philadelphia, now has become unmanageable to such an extent that an iron cage had to be procured to prevent him from injuring people. The savage attack he made upon a young lady, some several days ago tearing her clothing in ribbons and bruising her severely before she could be rescued, was the principal reason a cage was ordered for him, and since the assault on the young lady eight men have alternately kept watch over him, night and day. The cage arrived at the Smithsonian on Saturday, and workmen were engaged yesterday (Sunday), in placing it into position. The creature will be incarcerated in it some time to-day.

So, here we have some pretty startling facts that can be identified directly from the article and by inference. These facts would be:

1. This would seem to be the first documented attack on a woman by a bigfoot. Bigfoot is attracted to human females and is generally not afraid of women or small children.

2. He had been "subdued" in Philadelphia but was apparently from somewhere else.

3. He had been brought to Washington, D.C. to be exhibited for the 1877 centennial celebrations.

4. In April of 1877 the Smithsonian Institution was in possession of a bigfoot and it was being exhibited in an iron cage.

5. This story of a captured bigfoot—in our nation's capital no less—is now part of a cover-up and conspiracy to keep the existence of bigfoot a secret. If bigfoot doesn't exist, then it would be impossible for him to have been on display in an iron cage in April of 1877.

Indeed, we have the first stark evidence with this story that—at least at one time—the various authorities in Washington were aware that rural America contained "wild men," what we would call bigfoot today.

What happened to this wild man in possession of the Smithsonian? One has to imagine that there would be another article or two out there a few days later on the subject. However, it would appear that talk of the wild man in an iron cage ceased and this creature disappeared from history. No scientific papers were written about this curious subject, despite the fact that he was being held at a prestigious museum. Is it possible that somewhere in the depths of the Smithsonian there is a whole file on this wild man? Perhaps his skeleton is preserved and on display, for the special eyes of only a few.

That is probably the most disturbing part of this news story, that some sort of cover-up is involved and like some post-Civil War *X-Files*, we have the government (or elements within) withholding information from the public at large. Is it because the reality of bigfoot is just too frightening? Was this an early effort to suppress any knowledge of Bigfoot Nation?

### 1879: Hunter Shoot Wild Man in Vermont
The Bord's also give us a curious story from the Green Mountains of Vermont where two hunters encountered a wild man in October of 1879 south of Williamstown. They described the creature as:

> …about five feet high, resembling a man in form and movements but covered all over with bright red hair, and having a long straggling beard, and with very wild eyes. When first seen, the creature sprang from behind a rocky cliff, and started for the woods near by, when, mistaking it for a bear or other wild animal, one of the men fired, and, it is thought, wounded it, for with fierce cries of pain and rage, it turned on its assailants driving them before it at high speed. They lost their guns and ammunition in their fight and dared not return for fear of encountering the strange being.[3]

### 1883: Female Bigfoot Seen in Indiana
A newspaper article from Lafayette, Indiana said that in July of 1883 a woman named Mrs. Frank Coffman was passing through the woods when she saw a strange creature eating sassafras bark. It was "female in contour, with long black hair blowing in the wind. Short gray hair covered its body." It was chased through the woods by a 100-man hunting party, where it was seen swinging from bushes

to tree branches with ease. It finally reached a swamp where it disappeared.[11]

### 1884: Jacko the Ape Boy

A sasquatch was supposedly killed at a railway camp north of the town of Spuzzum in British Columbia around the year 1883 or 1884. The creature had been stealing from the meat store so some cowboys waited for him to enter the camp and lassoed him around the neck. With one end tied to a post, the sasquatch jumped and broke his neck. As the men later stood around looking at the dead monster Chief Petek arrived and claimed the body of the sasquatch, saying that his tribe had great respect for these creatures and he wanted to give it a proper burial. The chief then reportedly buried the sasquatch somewhere near Spuzzum.

The amazing story of Jacko was first told by Ivan T. Sanderson in his book *Abominable Snowmen: Legend Come to Life*.[9] Jacko was said to be a smallish apelike creature captured near Yale, British Columbia in June 1884. Yale is just south of Spuzzum,

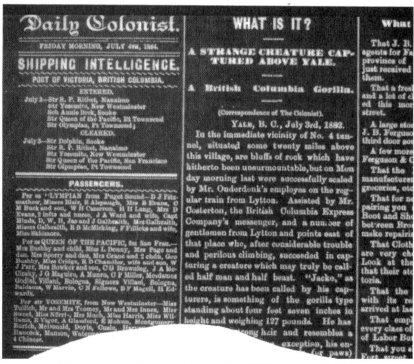

An 1884 newspaper article about Jacko. The 1882 date is probably a typo.

from the previous story. Jacko allegedly had been found injured on a railway line near Yale, having fallen off of a cliff. He was "of the gorilla-type" though standing only four feet seven inches tall and weighing 127 pounds. He was covered in glossy hair about an inch long.

Jacko was taken to the town of Yale tied up in the baggage car. He was exhibited, supposedly, in the local jail, and stories to this effect did appear in local newspapers, such as the *Mainland Guardian* of New Westminster on July 9, 1884. However, cryptozoologists John Green, Loren Coleman and others think that this event may have been more of a newspaper hoax, as were common at the time, than a genuine tale of a young sasquatch who was held in the hoosegow of a remote frontier town.

Still, one wonders about the great detail in the Jacko story, too long to be told here, but one that includes many names of railway men and information about his "keeper," a man named George Tilbury. John Green felt that the newspapers had been somehow duped into printing the stories. In one of the later newspaper stories, 200 people came to the local jail to view Jacko but only saw a half naked human who was in the jail on some petty charge.

Jacko bound inside the baggage car in 1884. (Duncan Hopkins)

A rumor exists that Jacko had been earlier placed on a train going back east where he was to end up in a circus show. Jacko, if he ever existed, vanished without a trace.

A short book on Jacko was published in 2011 by Christopher L. Murphy entitled *Yale & the Strange Story of Jacko the Ape-Boy*. Perhaps Jacko was a prisoner of war in the struggle with Bigfoot Nation.

## 1885: Wild Man Seen Eating Deer Flesh

A newspaper article in 1885 tells of a wild man being seen around the town of Lebanon, Oregon. A man named Mackentire had seen the wild man earlier in the year and then a Mr. Fitzgerald and others saw the wild man, covered in hair, eating the raw flesh off of a dead deer that he had apparently killed. He fled when the Fitzgerald party spotted him. A hunting party was to be organized, the article said, to find the "unfortunate man [who] was lost became deranged and has managed to find means of subsistence while wandering about in the mountains, probably finding shelter in some cave."[3]

## 1891: Bigfoot Kills Dog in Michigan

A brief newspaper article from October of 1891 tells us what typically happens to dogs that attack bigfoot. The location is northern Michigan, north of Lansing in rural Gladwin County. Says the article:

> George W. Frost and W. W. Vivian, both reputable citizens, report having seen a wild man near the Tittabawassee River, in Gladwin County. The man was nude, covered with hair, and was a giant in proportions. According to their stories he must have been at least seven feet high, his arms reaching below his knees, and with hands twice the usual size. Mr. Vivian set his bull dog on the crazy man, and with one mighty stroke of his monstrous hand he felled the dog dead. His jumps were measured and found to be from 20 to 23 feet.[3]

※ —⁓— ※

## 1893: Teddy Roosevelt and Bigfoot

One of the earliest known bigfoot stories was told by the future American President Teddy Roosevelt in his early hunting book, *The Wilderness Hunter,* published in 1893. In one chapter, Roosevelt shares a bigfoot tale involving a German fur trapper he calls "Bauman," who was trapping with a friend near the Salmon River in the Bitterroot Mountains along the Idaho and Montana border sometime in the 1880s.

This is the story that Roosevelt told in his book:

> I have heard but few ghost stories while living on the frontier, and a few were of a perfectly commonplace and conventional type.
>
> But I once listened to a goblin story which rather impressed me. It was told by a grizzled, weather-beaten old mountain hunter, named Bauman who was born and had passed all his life on the frontier. He must have believed what he said, for he could hardly repress a shudder at certain points of the tale; but he was of German ancestry, and in childhood had doubtless been saturated with all kinds of ghost and goblin lore, so that fearsome superstitions were latent in his mind; besides, he knew well the stories told by the Indian medicine men in their winter camps, of the snow-walkers, and the specters, and the formless evil beings that haunt the forest depths, and dog and waylay the lonely wanderer who after nightfall passes through the regions where they lurk; and it may be that when overcome by the horror of the fate that befell his friend, and when oppressed by the awful dread of the unknown, he grew to attribute, both at the time and still more in remembrance, weird and elfin traits to what was merely some abnormally wicked and cunning

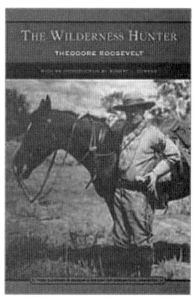

wild beast; but whether this was so or not, no man can say.

When the event occurred Bauman was still a young man, and was trapping with a partner among the mountains dividing the forks of the Salmon from the head of Wisdom River. Not having had much luck, he and his partner determined to go up into a particularly wild and lonely pass through which ran a small stream said to contain many beaver. The pass has an evil reputation because the year before a solitary hunter who had wandered into it was there slain, seemingly by a wild beast, the half-eaten remains being afterwards found by some mining prospectors who had passed his camp only the night before.

The memory of this event, however, weighed very lightly with the two trappers, who were as adventurous and hardy as others of their kind. They took their two lean mountain ponies to the foot of the pass, where they left them in an open beaver meadow, the rocky timber-clad ground being from thence onwards impracticable for horses. They then struck out on foot through the vast, gloomy forest, and in about four hours reached a little open glade where they concluded to camp, as signs of game were plenty.

There was still an hour or two of daylight left, and after building a brush lean-to and throwing down and opening their packs, they started up stream. The country was very dense and hard to travel through, as there was much down timber, although here and there the somber woodland was broken by small glades of mountain grass.

At dusk they again reached camp. The glade in which it was pitched was not many yards wide, the tall, close-set pines and firs rising round it like a wall. On one side was a little stream, beyond which rose the steep mountain-slopes, covered with the unbroken growth of the evergreen forest.

They were surprised to find that during their short absence something, apparently a bear, had visited their camp, and had rummaged about among their things, scattering the contents of their packs, and in sheer wantonness destroying their lean-to. The footprints of the beast were quite plain, but at first they paid no particular heed to them, busying themselves with rebuilding the lean-to, laying out their beds and stores, and lighting the fire.

While Bauman was making ready supper, it being already dark, his companion began to examine the tracks more closely, and soon took a brand from the fire to follow them up, where the intruder had walked along a game trail after leaving the camp. When the brand flickered out, he returned and took another, repeating his inspection of the footprints very closely. Coming back to the fire, he stood by it a minute or two, peering out into the darkness and suddenly remarked, "Bauman, that bear has been walking on two legs." Bauman laughed at this, but his partner insisted

A photograph of Teddy Roosevelt in 1885.

**43**

that he was right, and upon again examining the tracks with a torch, they certainly did seem to be made by but two paws, or feet. However, it was too dark to make sure. After discussing whether the footprints could possibly be those of a human being, and coming to the conclusion that they could not be, the two men rolled up in their blankets and went to sleep under the lean-to.

At midnight Bauman was awakened by some noise and sat up in his blankets. As he did so his nostrils were struck by a strong, wild-beast odor, and he caught the loom of a great body in the darkness at the mouth of the lean-to. Grasping his rifle, he fired at the vague, threatening shadow, but must have missed, for immediately afterwards he heard the smashing of the underwood as the thing, whatever it was, rushed off into the impenetrable blackness of the forest and the night.

After this the two men slept but little, sitting up by the rekindled fire, but they heard nothing more.

In the morning they started out to look at the few traps they had set the previous evening and to put out new ones. By an unspoken agreement they kept together all day, and returned to camp towards evening.

On nearing it they saw, hardly to their astonishment, that the lean-to had been again torn down.

The visitor of the preceding day had returned, and in wanton malice had tossed about their camp kit and bedding, and destroyed the shanty. The ground was marked up by its tracks, and on leaving the camp it had gone along the soft earth by the brook, where the footprints were as plain as if on snow, and, after a careful scrutiny of the trail, it certainly did seem as if, whatever the thing was, it had walked off on but two legs.

The men, thoroughly uneasy, gathered a great heap of dead logs, and kept up a roaring fire throughout the night, one or the other sitting on guard for most of the time. About midnight the thing came down through the forest opposite, across the brook, and stayed there on the hillside for nearly an hour. They could hear the branches crackle as it moved about, and several times it uttered a harsh, grating, long-drawn moan, a peculiarly sinister sound. Yet it did not venture near the fire.

In the morning the two trappers, after discussing the strange events of the last thirty-six hours, decided that they would shoulder their packs and leave the valley that afternoon. They were the more ready to do this because in spite of seeing a good deal of game sign they had caught very little fur. However, it was necessary first to go along the line of their traps and gather them, and this they started out to do.

All the morning they kept together, picking up trap after trap, each one empty. On first leaving camp they had the disagreeable sensation of being followed. In the dense spruce thickets they occasionally heard a branch snap after they had passed; and now and then there were slight rustling noises among the small pines to one side of them.

At noon they were back within a couple of miles of camp. In the high, bright sunlight their fears seemed absurd to the two armed men, accustomed as they were, through the long years of lonely wandering in the wilderness to face every kind of danger from man, brute, or element. There were still three beaver traps to collect from a little pond in a wide ravine nearby. Bauman volunteered to gather these and bring them in, while his companion went ahead to camp and made ready the packs.

On reaching the pond, Bauman found three beaver in the traps, one of which had been pulled loose and carried into the beaver house. He took several hours securing and preparing the beaver, and when he started homewards he marked with some uneasiness how low the sun was getting. As he hurried towards camp, under the tall trees, the silence and desolation of the forest weighed on him. His feet made no sound on the pine needles, and the slanting sunrays, striking through among the straight trunks, made a gray twilight in which objects at a distance glimmered indistinctly. There was nothing to break the ghostly stillness which, when there is no breeze, always broods over these somber primeval forests.

At last he came to the edge of the little glade where the camp lay, and shouted as he approached it, but got no answer. The campfire had gone out, though the thin blue smoke was still curling upwards. Near it lay the packs, wrapped and arranged.

At first Bauman could see nobody; nor did he receive an answer to his call. Stepping forward he again shouted, and as he did so his eye fell on the body of his friend, stretched beside the trunk of a great fallen spruce. Rushing towards it the horrified trapper found that the body was still warm, but that the neck was broken, while there were four great fang marks in the throat.

The footprints of the unknown beast-creature, printed deep in the soft soil, told the whole story.

The unfortunate man, having finished his packing, sat down on the spruce log with his face to the fire, and his back to the dense woods, to wait for his companion. While thus waiting, his monstrous assailant, which must have been lurking nearby in the woods, waiting for a chance to catch one of the adventurers unprepared, came silently up from behind, walking with long, noiseless steps, and seemingly still on two legs. Evidently unheard, it reached the man, and broke his neck by wrenching his head back with its forepaws, while it buried its teeth in his throat. It had not eaten the body, but apparently had romped and gambolled round it in uncouth, ferocious glee, occasionally rolling over and over it; and had then fled back into the soundless depths of the woods.

Bauman, utterly unnerved, and believing that the creature with which he had to deal was something either half human or half devil, some great goblin-beast, abandoned everything but his rifle and struck off at speed down the pass, not halting until he reached the beaver meadows where the hobbled ponies were still grazing. Mounting, he rode onwards through the night, until far beyond the reach of pursuit.

Teddy Roosevelt, one of America's most popular presidents, was known for his adventurous outdoor spirit and honesty. It would seem that the reality of bigfoot and the early stories pertaining to the wild apeman would be given a great deal of credibility if President Teddy Roosevelt was a believer in the elusive and dangerous creature.

### 1894: Man-Beast Stealing Chickens in Kentucky

A newspaper report from Dover, New Jersey on January 8, 1894 said that there was a wild man in the woods near Mine Hill. The wild man was hairy and naked, nearly six feet tall and had tried to get into some of the homes, apparently in search of food. A hunting party was organized to find the creature but nothing was found.[3]

In May of 1894 there were reports coming out of Deep Creek, Kentucky, that a "man-beast" had been seen in the area and that chickens, eggs, young pigs and lambs had been missing from farms. A man named Joseph Ewalt had seen the creature and described it as having "great long white hair hanging down from his head and face that was coarse as a horse's mane. His legs were covered with hair and the only article of clothing he wore was a piece of sheepskin over the lower portion of his body, reaching nearly for his knees. He said a light came from his eyes and mouth similar to fire."

Men in the area decided to try to catch the creature and started keeping an eye out for it. Then, one morning Eph Boston and his sons saw it making for their barn. They said it was a man-beast with clawed feet and cat-like hands. Soon it came rushing out of the barn grasping three chickens. Tom Boston shot at the creature but it continued to run and went into a nearby cave. They got their neighbors and entered the first part of the cave where they saw bones, feathers and such. Then they heard an "unearthly yell" and quickly retreated. All efforts to catch the beast failed, including smoking it out of the cave.

### 1897: Gorilla-like Creature in Ohio

In late April, 1897 a man near Sailor, Indiana shot a bigfoot. Two farmers, Adam Gardner and Ed Swinehart, saw a hair-covered,

**47**

man-sized "beast" walking on its hind legs. When it saw them approaching, it made for thick woods and they shot at it. It dropped onto all fours and bounded away.[11]

Also in late April a "wild man" was seen in the woods near Stout, Ohio. After it was alleged that the wild man had attacked a boy, a party of thirty men went searching for the creature. One witness said it was very tall, nearly naked and could run like a deer. Another witness said that it wore a pair of tattered pants.[3] It is likely that these witnesses were not expecting the "wild man" to be completely covered in hair, they mistook the matted hair for tattered pants. On the other hand, maybe it was a pair of tattered pants as there have been other reports of bigfoot "wearing" something like pants or a belt.

Christopher Murphy, Joedy Cook and George Clappison record a number of interesting incidents in the Midwest in their book *Bigfoot Encounters in Ohio: Quest for the Grassman.*[66] They report that on May 26, 1897 near Rome, Ohio in the very south of the state, Charles Lukins and Bob Forner claimed that they encountered a wild man while cutting timber out of town. After struggling with the "gorilla-like creature" they were able to drive it into retreat among the cliffs. They called the creature a "terror" and said it was about six feet tall. This report came from the *Cleveland Plain Dealer*, May 27, 1897.

The authors also chronicle several other events in 1897, such as farmers around Logan, Ohio reporting in May that a strange animal had appeared in the vicinity and numerous sheep had disappeared. Several old pioneers who heard the beast crying at night thought it was a panther. They hunted for the strange animal but failed to kill or capture it.[66]

In the summer of 1897 a native American from Tulelake, in northeastern Siskiyou County, California, nearly on the border with Oregon, became friends with a bigfoot. The witness said that on a summer evening he saw what at first looked like a tall bush ahead of him on the trail. Then he caught a strong, musky odor and realized the bush was alive and that it was a creature with eyes and thick, coarse hair. The creature made a noise and the man laid down his line of fish as a gesture of friendship. The creature took the fish and went into the trees where it made a long, low call. A few weeks later the man heard the strange noise outside his cabin and found a pile of fresh deerskins left by the door. Then he heard the strange bigfoot call in the trees. Sometimes other things were left as well, like wild fruits and berries.[3]

As the year 1900 was coming up the world was changing fast. There was now electricity in many cities and motorcars were starting to ply the roads along with buggies and carriages. The train network had expanded considerably throughout the West and Midwest. Settlers were clearing more land and moving into even the most isolated areas of the mountain west. There were big changes coming for Bigfoot Nation.

A stamp commemorating sasquatch issued by Canada in 1990.

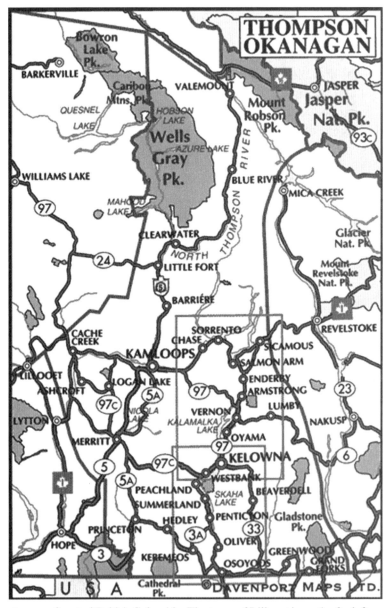

A map of central British Columbia. The town of Lillooet is on the far left.

# CHAPTER 3

# 1894:
# The Oldest Bigfoot Photo

Scientists believe he's a missing link,
Some people think that he's extinct,
Others say something from the battle green,
But, listen to bigfoot's mournful scream.
—*Bigfoot*, Don Jones

There is an astonishing photo from Canada taken in 1894 which would seem to be the oldest known photograph of bigfoot. Craig Woolheater posted the photo on his blog at Cryptomundo. com on November 16, 2006. The photo had originally been sent to Tom Biscardi by Lyle Billett of Victoria, Canada.

Fellow Cryptomundo blogger Loren Coleman found the photo on Woolheater's website and posted it again, where I saw it. The photo also appears in the updated version of the 1982 book *Bigfoot Casebook* by Colin and Janet Bord.[4]

It is said that a picture tells a thousand words, and this photo says a lot. It does not seem to be a fake. The photo is cracked from a fold in the upper quarter. A sasquatch is lying on snow with its arms in front so the hairy hands can be seen. The face is hairy but not very detailed. Snowshoes can be seen at the left edge of the photo. There seems to be a fence and a building on the right side, just beneath the crack. The feet of the dead sasquatch are not seen, cropped out of the right side of the photo.

The story that this photo tells us is that in 1894 in the wilds of western Canada some trappers and mountain men encountered a bigfoot and shot him. It may have happened near their cabin. They took a photograph of it. But there is more: the photo had some writing on the back of it, maybe in the hand of Lyle Billett.

The back of the photo bore this text:

Year 1894
Yalikom River Around Lilliott B.C.
Forestry-Hudsonbay Co.
They took the picture and the Guy that was in the picture went
& stole them back from the forestry records (hudsonbay co.) I
believe his last name was Holiday (Don't know the first name)
Never took all pictures (only one) and took pictures of the rest.
(Glass Plate Photography)

This is very interesting information and confirms what some
have suspected for many years: there is something of a cover-
up going on concerning evidence of bigfoot. We now get a more
complete story: There was more than one photo and someone
named Holiday apparently took the photos, or was pictured in one
or more of them. He went to the forestry records of the Hudson's
Bay Company where he "stole back" one of the photos—the
number of photos taken of the bigfoot is not known. We might
guess that there were four or five original, glass plate photos.

So, some trappers shot and killed a bigfoot in 1894, and they
worked for the Hudson's Bay Company, Canada's earliest trading
company, founded in 1670. The Hudson's Bay Company is no
ordinary company; it was the de facto government in large parts of
North America before European states or the United States were
able to lay claim to areas in this vast domain. Today it is one of the

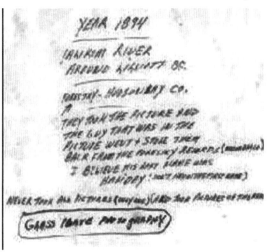

Writing on the back of the photo from Lillooet, British Columbia.

oldest operating companies in the world. Begun as a fur trading company on the Hudson Bay, it now has its headquarters in the Simpson Tower in Toronto. At one point the Hudson's Bay Company had its own country of a sort, called Rupert's Land. At that time, the Hudson's Bay Company was one of the largest landowners of the world, with approximately 15% of the land mass of North America. Rupert's Land consisted of lands that were in the Hudson Bay drainage system—basically the land surrounding

The 1894 photo taken at Lillooet, British Columbia.

A close-up 1894 photo taken at Lillooet, British Columbia.

any rivers that drained into the Hudson Bay. It was named after the first governor of the company, Prince Rupert of the Rhine, who was a nephew of Britain's King Charles I. The governor and the Company of Adventurers of England Trading comprised the original group that chartered the Hudson's Bay Company.

Rupert's Land and the Hudson's Bay Company had their headquarters at the York Factory, a town and fort along the Hayes River leading into Hudson Bay. Once the capital of Rupert's Land, it was closed down by the company in 1957.

The Hudson's Bay Company nominally owned Rupert's Land for 200 years, until about 1870, some 24 years before this photo was allegedly taken—and suppressed. Still, the Hudson's Bay Company was very powerful in 1894 and remains a major fixture in the Canadian economy today as the owner of many of Canada's retail chains such as The Bay, Zellers, Fields and Home Outfitters. The company has archives, located in Winnipeg, Manitoba, said to be a collection of the company's records and maps—does it include some bigfoot photos? That is what the writing scribbled on this bigfoot photo suggests.

One has to wonder, if this photo is genuine, why it was not published many years ago, and featured in every

**HUDSON'S BAY CO.**

bigfoot book written since 1894? Here we have what seems to be some pretty solid evidence of bigfoot-sasquatch that is just what the scientific community says they are looking for. In fact, these folks from the Hudson's Bay Company not only have some photos of a dead bigfoot, at one time (say the photos) they actually had a dead bigfoot! We are talking here about bigfoot steaks, bigfoot fur, a bigfoot head, bigfoot paws and all that.

Since the Hudson's Bay Company specialized in dead animals and their fur, one would think that this animal—whatever it was—was carefully skinned and preserved. Was its head mounted and displayed in the den of some chairman of the company? That seems far-fetched today, but perhaps back in 1894 it might have been seen, perhaps surrounded by some secrecy, in some Canadian or British aristocrat's personal collection.

Because of my interest in bigfoot and other hidden animals, I've often been asked the question, "Why isn't there more evidence for bigfoot than just stories? Where are the photos and where are

A map of Rupert's Land.

the dead bodies that must have been found over the years?"

I have typically said in answer to these questions, that one does not see a dead bear or mountain lion on the trail when walking through the Rocky Mountains or the Pacific Northwest. Though these animals are known to exist, one rarely sees them at all and

A sign for Lillooet, British Columbia.

never a dead one just lying there in the forest. The carcass would only be there for a few hours, days or weeks, and many animals that are about to die (of old age or disease) go off somewhere very far out of the way.

But now we have another explanation. One that is startling to the researcher and the skeptic alike—that evidence of bigfoot, including good photos and preserved bodies, has been gathered but kept a secret. "But why?" you ask. Why wouldn't the Hudson's Bay Company just publish its photos and display a mummified bigfoot to gawking tourists in Toronto? Why would the Canadian government (or American or British) suppress evidence of bigfoot? Don't we live in a transparent society where everything that exists—and there are clear photos and bodies of—would be shown to the interested viewers around the world? Or do we live in world where some things are suppressed, including evidence of bigfoot? Add to the suppression of real bigfoot evidence some hoax bigfoot cases that everyone can laugh at, and you have a subject that appears to be just fantasy and tall tales. Some things are just too shocking to the status quo—strange mutations or missing links that make us question traditional religious beliefs or the tenets of mankind's sacred pillars of science and reason. If all the experts and scholars have been so wrong for decades, what are we supposed to believe from them?

In the case of this photo, part of a series apparently, a professional photographer must have been involved. Photography, until recently, was expensive and rare; it required professional photographers with expensive, heavy equipment. Having a photograph taken in 1894 was a big deal, glass plate photography being very time consuming for each individual photo. Taking such photos in the wilderness would have been quite an endeavor. Photography for the common man took many decades to reach even the Kodak Brownie and Instamatic periods of the 1940s and 1960s. Then, finally, common folk could have a simple camera with them to take photos when they were on long camping trips and hikes in remote mountain areas.

This is one of the great hopes of the current digital photo revolution, especially because cameras (even video cameras), are now part of most mobile phones that are in the possession of more and more people everyday. In theory, the sheer number of cell phone cameras in use today should result in more bigfoot, ghost and anomalous photos being snapped than ever before.

Also, what of this location in British Columbia? I found that if I searched the Internet for the Yalikom River, as written on the back of the photo, what I found was the Yalakom River which is a tributary to the Bridge River which is a principal tributary to the Fraser River, a major part of Rupert's Land territory. Plus, I was able to find out that the Yalakom River enters the Bridge River near the town of Lilooet, which is apparently the town mentioned as Lilliott.

Lilooet is apparently one of the oldest towns in North America. It is so old that its age is not known. It is considered to be one of the oldest continuously inhabited locations in North America, reckoned by archaeologists to have been inhabited for several thousand years. The town attracted large seasonal and permanent populations of native peoples because of the confluence of several main streams with the Fraser, and also because of a rock-shelf just above the confluence of the Bridge River that is an obstacle to the annual migration of salmon—an abundant food source.

Did this salmon-shelf cause the downfall of our unfortunate sasquatch, shot by a trapper in the employ of the Hudson's Bay Company? According

A mixed-blood fur trapper, 1870.

to the information on Lilooet this natural shelf along the riverbed is an important salmon station on the Fraser-Bridge-Yalakom River:

> This rock shelf, known in gold rush times as the Lower Fountain, was reputedly made by the trickster Coyote, leaping back and forth across the river to create platforms for people to catch and dry fish on. This location, named Sat' or Setl in the native language and known as the Bridge River Rapids or Six Mile in English, is the busiest fishing site on the Fraser above its mouth and there are numerous drying racks scattered around the banks of the river canyon around it.

We now have the final scene of the tragic bigfoot in our photograph: he had come to Lilooet (Lilliott as spelled on the backside of the photo) to get some salmon which was known to be plentiful at this spot. While Native Americans who had lived in the area for thousands of years knew not to bother the sasquatch that came to this area of plenty, this poor beast was shot and killed by the Europeans now penetrating the area for the Hudson's Bay Company. What they found shocked them. They shot and killed it. Then they took a photograph of it. Then someone in the company ordered the photo suppressed.

At some point Mr. Holiday decided to get a copy of the photo that he was part of and knew existed. He probably didn't need to physically break into the building to steal the bigfoot photo(s). He was apparently an employee who walked into the building as he typically did, and then went to the files and stole one of the photos and took photographs of the rest. Having a camera to carry and take photos of documents, like photographs in a file, would be unusual at this time, but certainly could have been done.

For anyone involved in such a photo, this incident would have been something that they thought about a lot; the inability to be able to show a friend the "actual" photograph would have been a tremendous rub. Hence the desire to steal a copy of a photograph that one knows exists, but is kept secret by certain powers for their own purposes.

Yes, it seems that a cryptozoology conspiracy exists. Evidence, including photos and bodies, is kept from the press and public at large. It would seem that government and corporate identities are actively covering up evidence of bigfoot. While the governments of Canada and the United States could be trying to protect bigfoot by suppressing evidence of their existence, some countries use the apeman to promote tourism. Countries like Nepal and Bhutan promote "yeti tourism," but still protect the species with national laws.

It seems incredible, but the reality of the sasquatch—the apemen that live on the fringes of civilization—seems hard to deny when faced with what seems to be an overwhelming amount of evidence. Could all of the stories that have come down to us for nearly 200 years in North America be cases of misidentification of bears, or the occasional escaped circus gorilla? Or hoaxes? That, to me, would be very difficult to swallow.

# CHAPTER 4

# The 20th Century Begins 1900 to 1950

Behold, Esau my brother is a hairy man,
And I am a smooth man.
—*Genesis 27:11*

ⁱ̸ —ᴡᴠ— ̸ⁱ

Native Americans have told stories of bigfoot for generations, in which he is given different names, including sasquatch. He is often called a wild man or a giant ape. Many of the earliest bigfoot stories come from Alaska and British Columbia, both large territories with considerable amounts of wilderness areas. Researchers surmise that there are sizeable bigfoot populations along coastal Alaska and British Columbia, as well as inland to the Rocky Mountains. Some of the largest creatures in Bigfoot Nation seem to come from the Pacific Northwest, which includes northern California.

**1900: The Most Hideous Creatures—Neither Men nor Monkeys**

A curious incident occurred at Thomas Bay in coastal Alaska in the spring of 1900. The story is told in a self-published book by Harry Colp of Petersburg, Alaska, *The Strangest Story Ever Told,* and then retold in J. Robert Alley's book *Raincoast Sasquatch.*[12] Thomas Bay is located in the rugged, glacier-studded mountains of the southeast Alaskan panhandle, on the mainland halfway between Petersburg (on Wrangell Island) going north to Juneau. A remote area shrouded in hemlock and cedar, it had long been the subject of rumors of gold to be found for those who went looking.

Harry Colp recounts that he and three others—John, Fred and Charlie—ventured to Thomas Bay in the spring of that year and again in July. On the first trip Charlie encountered a whole troop of smelly sasquatch while on a ridge overlooking a mountain lake, however he had earlier broken his rifle. Charlie is quoted in the book as saying:

> Swarming up the ridge toward me from the lake were the most hideous creatures. I couldn't call them anything but devils, as they were neither men nor monkeys—yet looked like both… their bodies covered with long, coarse hair, except where the cabs and running sores had replaced it. Each one seemed to be reaching out for me and striving to be the first one to get me. The air was full of their cries and the stnech from their sores and bodies made me [feel] faint.
>
> I forgot my broken gun and tried to use it on the first ones, then I threw it at them and turned and ran. God, how did I run! I could feel their hot breath on my back. The smell… was making me sick; while the noises they made, yelling, screaming and breathing, drove me mad…

Running downhill, Charlie managed to get to his canoe and then paddle away from the shore. He paddled along the shore and reached the camp where Colp and the others were waiting. He told the group his story and then left Alaska for good. According to Colp the rest of the group returned, and John and Fred went in search of gold while Colp watched the boat. Fred was attacked by the monsters, almost losing his rifle and becoming incoherent at times, and he and John returned to the boat and went back to Petersburg on Wrangell Island. The three returned again in 1903 and left in fear after having to stay up all night with guns loaded while strange sounds, moaning, branch breaking and foot stomping, occurred around them. Colp returned in 1908 and 1911 and both times he discovered that other lone prospectors had vanished during the time he was gone, leaving their camp supplies and everything. He suspected they had been killed by the smelly monsters.[12]

## 1909: Sasquatch in a Rage

In May of 1909 on a Chehalis Reservation in British Columbia, a local named Peter Williams encountered a sasquatch near a place called Harrison Mills. Williams was chased back to his house by a sasquatch in a rage. The amazing ordeal was described by Williams himself:

I was walking along the foot of the mountain about a mile from the Chehalis Reserve. I thought I heard a noise—something like a grunt nearby. Looking in the direction in which it came, I was startled to see what I took at first sight to be a huge bear crouched upon a boulder twenty or thirty feet away. I raised my rifle to shoot it, but, as I did, the creature stood up and let out a piercing yell. It was a man—a giant, no less than six and one-half feet in height, and covered with hair. He was in a rage and jumped from the boulder to the ground. I fled, but not before I felt his breath upon my cheek. I never ran so fast before or since—through brush and undergrowth toward the Staloo, or Chehalis River, where my dugout was moored. From time to time I looked back over my shoulder. The giant was fast overtaking me—a hundred feet separated us; another look and the distance measured less than fifty—the Chehalis [came in view] and in a moment I [was in] the dugout and shot across the stream to the opposite bank.

The swift river, however, did not in the least daunt the giant, for he began to wade it immediately. I arrived home almost worn out from running and I felt sick. Taking an anxious look around the house, I was relieved to find the wife and children inside. I bolted the door and barricaded it with everything at hand. Then with my rifle ready, I stood near the door and awaited his coming.

If I had not been so excited, I could have easily shot the giant when he began to wade the river. After an anxious waiting of twenty minutes, I heard a noise approaching like the trampling of a horse. I looked though a crack in the old wall. It was the giant. Darkness had not yet set in and I had a good look at him. Except that he was covered with hair

**63**

and twice the bulk of the average man, there was nothing to distinguish him from the rest of us.

He pushed against the wall of the old house with such force that it shook back and forth. The old cedar shook and the timbers creaked and groaned so much under the strain that I was afraid it would fall down and kill us. I whispered to the old woman to take the children under the bed. After prowling and grunting like an animal around the house, he went. We were glad, for the children and the wife were uncomfortable under the bedstead. Next morning I found his tracks in the mud around the house, the biggest either man or beast I had ever seen. The tracks measured twenty-two inches in length, but were narrow in proportion to their length.[29]

## 1915: Sasquatch Eating Huckleberries

British Columbia has many of the early bigfoot reports; it is a large, sparsely populated state with vast forests full of lakes and rivers. In the summer of 1915 near Hope, British Columbia, Charles Flood, a prospector, was with two friends—Donald McRae and Green Hicks—when he saw a sasquatch. The group had crossed an unknown divide in a wilderness area near the Holy Cross Mountains. Said Flood:

> …A mile further up was Cougar Lake. Several years ago a fire swept over many square miles of mountains which resulted in large areas of mountain huckleberry growth. Hicks suddenly stopped us and drew our attention to a large, light brown creature about eight feet high, standing on its hind legs pulling the berry bushes with one hand or paw toward him and putting berries in his mouth with the other hand, or paw. I stood still wondering while McRae and Hicks were arguing. Hicks said, "It's a wild man" and McRae said, "It's a bear." The creature heard us and suddenly disappeared in the brush around 200 yards away. As far as I am concerned the strange creature looked more like a human being, we seen several black and brown bears on the trip, that 'thing' looked altogether different.[7]

## 1919: A Huge Nude Hairy Man

Charlie Victor, who lived near Hatzic, British Columbia said that in the summer of 1919 he had been bathing with friends in a lake and while dressing a "huge nude hairy man" stepped out from a rock where he had apparently been watching Charlie. Victor stated, "He looked at me for a moment, his eyes were so kind looking that I was about to speak to him, when he turned about and walked into the forest."[29]

## 1924: Bigfoot Family Kidnaps Prospector

The year 1924 became a big year for sasquatch encounters. In that year, a Canadian named Albert Ostman claimed he was kidnapped by a sasquatch family, and an American named Fred Beck claimed that he and some friends fought off a small army of sasquatch in a place called Ape Canyon near Mt. St. Helens in Washington state.

Ostman had kept his experience to himself until 1957 when bigfoot reports were making the news in the Pacific Northwest and he decided to tell his story. He claimed that he had been doing construction work in 1924 and needed to take a break, so he decided to look for gold around the head of Toba Inlet in British Columbia. Something kept disturbing his camp late at night and so one night he decided to stay completely dressed inside his sleeping bag, and keep his rifle handy. He fell asleep, however, and late in the night he felt something picking him up. He still had his rifle with him, which he clutched while he was carried for an hour up a steep hill.

Albert Ostman speaking with famous researcher John Green.

**65**

After more ups and downs, he was deposited on the ground, while it was still dark. He claimed that as it got light he could see four bigfoot creatures, two large and two much smaller. This bigfoot family apparently had a young son and daughter, and Ostman speculated that they might have brought him as a suitor to the young female sasquatch.

The young male was about seven feet tall, Ostman said, and probably weighed about 300 pounds. They slept beneath an overhanging rock on dry moss, using moss-filled "blankets" and went out in the daytime to gather grass, shoots, nuts and roots to eat. He never saw them eat any meat.

He eventually made his escape after offering some snuff to the large father sasquatch on occasion. One time, after a few small pinches, the big sasquatch grabbed the whole box of snuff and

Albert Ostman made this drawing of the female sasquatch with a curl of hair.

Albert Ostman being kidnapped by a sasquatch in 1924.

gulped it down. Soon the sasquatch started to become sick and rushed off to get some water. Ostman then grabbed his belongings and ran out of the valley, firing some shots from his rifle as he left to frighten the rest of the family. He was not followed and eventually made his way back to civilization.[29]

In another incident, near Kelso, Washington in July of 1924, Fred Beck and four other gold miners were in a remote log cabin in an area to the east side of Mt. St. Helens, later to become known as Ape Canyon. They said that they encountered a group of four gorilla-men on the mountainside during the daytime, and fired on

**67**

them with a revolver to halt an attack at that time.

One of the huge creatures was believed slain, and the body rolled over a cliff into a deep ravine. The attack resumed after dark. A man named Smith reported to the Cowlitz County Sheriff that the hairy giant apemen pelted their cabin all night with rocks, and danced and screamed until daylight.

The men described the mountain "devils" as being at least seven feet tall and covered with long, black hair. Their arms were long and trailed, the men told the Portland *Oregonian*, which published an article about the encounter.[16]

## 1926: The Word "Sasquatch" is Developed

The word "sasquatch" was basically developed by John W. Burns, a teacher at Harrison Mills on the Chehalis Reservation during this year. Burns anglicized the Chehalis word "Saskehavis" which essentially means "wild man." He was fascinated by the local culture and went on to write some of the earliest articles on sasquatch. He said that the locals knew he was a teacher at the school and would not be skeptical of their stories, so many told him

A photo of Ape Canyon at Mount St. Helens, Oregon.

Fred Beck holding the rifle that he used at Ape Canyon.

things that they would not tell other outsiders. Burns worked on the reservation from 1925 to 1946. Eventually, sasquatch became a household word.[7]

⁙ ⟋⟍⟍⟋ ⁙

**1927: Sasquatch Shows Up at a Picnic**

In September of 1927, William Point and Adaline August were at a hop-pickers picnic near Agassiz, just north of Chilliwack in southern British Columbia when they encountered a bigfoot. Said Point of the incident:

> Adaline August and myself walked to her father's orchard which is about four miles from the hop fields. We were walking on the railroad track and within a short distance of the orchard, when the girl noticed something walking along the track coming toward us. I looked up but paid no attention to it as I thought it was some person on his way to Agassiz. But as he came closer we noticed that

**69**

his appearance was very odd, and on coming still closer we stood still and were astonished—seeing that the creature was naked and covered in hair like an animal. We were almost paralyzed from fear. I picked up two stones with which I intended to hit him if he attempted to molest us, but within 50 feet or so he stood still and looked at us. He was twice as big as the average man, with arms so long that its hands almost touched the ground.

It seemed to me that the eyes were very large and the lower part of his face, gave the creature such a frightful appearance that I ran away as fast as I could. After a minute or two I looked back and saw that he resumed his journey. The girl had fled before I left, and she ran so fast that I did not overtake her until I was close to Agassiz, where we told the story of our adventure to the Indians who were still enjoying themselves. Old Indians who were present said: the wild man was no doubt a sasquatch, a tribe of hairy people who they claim have always lived in the mountains—in tunnels and caves.[3]

**1928: Ape is Seen and Shot at Bella Coola**

Several things happened around southern British Columbia in 1928. A woman outside of Lavington was ill in bed and asked her daughter to send away the man standing by the fence of their property. The daughter looked out and saw a tall, bulky and furry creature standing behind a fence post, with its hands resting at the top of the post. The creature left shortly after that and the woman told her daughter that she had seen it farther up the fence line earlier, watching the house.

Then near Bella Coola, BC, a man named George Talleo said he shot at an ape. He said he saw the creature stand up from behind a fallen tree and took a shot at with a small caliber rifle. The creature fell to the ground and Talleo ran from the scene. He said that he had noticed a pile of moss stripped from a rock face that was used to cover a pile of excrement.[7]

**1929: Workmen Discover a 9-Foot Skeleton**

A work crew cutting a trail to a lake near Windermere, BC were reported to have uncovered four extremely large skeletons of what appeared to be men—or sasquatch—in 1928. The skeletons ranged from 6-foot-9-inches tall to an incredible (but not for bigfoot) nine feet tall. Such skeletons are normally given by the Canadian authorities to the local First Nations tribe who then dispose of the remains.[7]

## 1934: Sasquatch Throws Rocks off of Cliff

In March of 1934 it was reported that Tom Cedar of Harrison Mills on the Chehalis Reservation had a frightening encounter with a bigfoot. Cedar was fishing in the Harrison River when his boat was bombarded with huge rocks from the cliffs above the river. He narrowly escaped after one large rock almost hit the boat. He looked up to the cliffs above and saw a huge, hairy man-like creature waving its arms wildly and stamping its feet, clearly agitated by the appearance of Cedar and his boat. The frightened Cedar cut his fishing line and paddled away as fast as he could. Cedar also suspected that the sasquatch had been stealing salmon that he had hung outside to dry, well above where his dogs could reach.

A few nights later Frank Dan reported that he met a sasquatch at Harrison Mills when he went outside to see why his dog wouldn't stop barking. He then saw a "hairy giant" standing there with hair

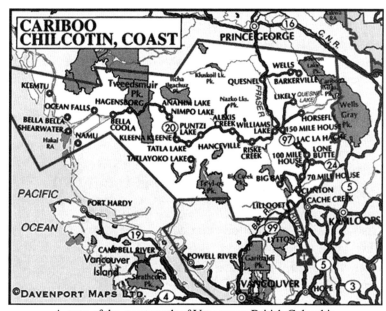

A map of the coast north of Vancouver, British Columbia.

covering it from head to feet except for a small hairless area around the eyes. It was extremely tall with a muscular build and the terrified Dan ran back into the house and bolted the door. The sasquatch walked back into the forest and though Dan was teased about his sighting and fear, bigfoot sightings continued in the area, seemingly a focal point for Bigfoot Nation.

On April 9, 1934, the *Fresno Bee* (Fresno, CA) ran a story entitled "Californians Out to Bag Legendary Sasquatch." The story was about two brothers and medical students at the University of California, J.F. Blakeney and C.K. Blakeney, who were headed to Canada to find sasquatch, probably after seeing the popular feature that appeared on sasquatch in the April 1929 issue of the long-time Canadian magazine *Maclean's*. There appears to be no follow-up article. This seems to be the first official bigfoot expedition.[7]

### 1937: Face to Face with Sasquatch at Abandoned House

In the summer of 1937, Mrs. Jane Patterson, who lived with her husband on a ranch near Osoyoos, BC in the Anarchist Mountain area, encountered a bigfoot. She had wandered over to an old abandoned house on the ranch property to look for rhubarb that she had been told was growing in the garden. As she came up to the house she had to duck under a tree branch and then came face to face with a sasquatch about ten feet away.

Patterson inadvertently said to the creature, "Oh there you are." The sasquatch just blinked its eyes. She backed away and headed for home, hastening her pace when she got away from the house. When she told her husband about the incident he refused to go to the abandoned house with her, stating he did not wish to see a monkey, as Jane had said, "it looked just like a monkey to me!" Three days later he agreed to visit the abandoned house but found nothing.

Also in 1937 Floyd Dillon claimed that he uncovered a nearly 8-foot skeleton with a skull twice the size of a man's skull while digging a trench

# INDIANS FEAR THE SASQUATCH HAVE RETURNED

## Hairy Giants from the Hills Again Terrorize Chehalis as They Used to Long Ago— Visits Recalled.

HARRISON MILLS, March 2.—The fearsome "Sasquatch" have returned. Indian women in the Chehalis reservation are watching their youngsters closely these days, keeping them indoors at night, terrifying them with stories their old folk used to tell, of hairy giants who come down from the mountains and kidnap naughty children.

Men of the tribe are keeping their rifles handy, watching for unusual movements in the forest, and when their dogs bark at night they leap from bed, run to the window and peer out, expectantly. For the Sasquatch have returned.

There is no longer any doubt about it. Suspicions were aroused some time ago that the dreaded wild men of the Chehalis hills were [...]. Frank Dan SAW a Sasquatch! Saw it with his own eyes, clearly. There is no doubt about it now. Ask Frank Dan.

A 1934 article on sasquatch from the Canadian magazine *Macleans*.

behind his house along the Fraser River near Lillooet, BC. He left the bones where they were and reburied them. Later they were dug up and the fragments that were left were sent to the Provincial Museum in Victoria. Dillon also said that the giant seemed to have an 8-inch tail as well, though researchers like Christopher Murphy think that Dillon probably mistook something else for a tail.[29]

## 1941: Sasquatch Chases Mom and Kids

In October of 1941 George and Jeannie Chapman and their family had a frightening experience with bigfoot. They lived in a small, isolated house on the banks of the Fraser River near Agassiz in southern British Columbia. George was a railroad maintenance worker at a small town called Ruby Creek.

One afternoon the three children, ages 5, 7 and 8, were playing

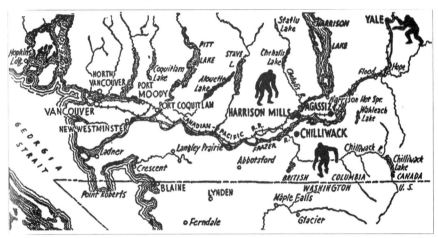

A 1934 map of sasquatch activity from the Lincoln, Nebraska *Sunday Journal & Star*.

in the front yard when one of the children ran into the house shouting that a "big cow is coming out the woods." A dark-haired bigfoot that was nearly eight feet tall was approaching the house as the other children came inside. Jeannie gathered the children and they ran terrified down the railroad tracks in the direction that George would typically walk home. They soon approached him and shouted that a sasquatch was after them.

George gathered other men and they went to the house where they found 16-inch-long footprints leading to a shed where a heavy barrel of smoked fish had been dumped out. The prints led across a field and into the mountains. The huge creature had apparently easily stepped over a fence that was nearly five feet high.

The Chapmans returned to their home but they were continually bothered by howling noises and serious agitation of their dogs, and left again after a week. Another family moved in briefly and left, and ultimately the property was abandoned. A cast was made of one of the footprints.[29]

Later that year, in November 1941 near Harrison Hot Springs it was reported that three canoes full of First Nations people were reported to be fleeing a giant sasquatch terrorizing the village of Port Douglas at the head of Harrison Lake. The occupants said that the sasquatch walked on two legs and was 14 feet tall.[7] This is tall, even for a sasquatch!

Harrison Hot Springs has now dedicated a 1,217-hectare Sasquatch Provincial Park that touches on four lakes, including

**74**

the massive Harrison Lake, which is surrounded by magnificent mountains covered in second-growth deciduous forests. The official Canadian government text on the park has a slightly different explanation for the word sasquatch:

The word sasquatch comes from the Coast Salish word

A 1934 article on sasquatch from the Lincoln, Nebraska *Sunday Journal and Star*.

sasqac, which is the name of a mythical creature that is half-man half-beast and believed to posses an evil spirit and should be avoided. The 60-km long Harrison Lake is famous for its hot springs and was once a part of an early transportation route from the Fraser River to the Cariboo goldfields. Settlement of the area began in 1885 when a bathhouse and hotel was constructed. The historic Harrison Hot Springs Hotel still holds the commercial rights to the hot mineral waters today and continues to be a popular tourism destination. In the early 1900s, logging began around the lake and depleted most of the old-growth forests.

## 1943: Man Attacked by Sasquatch

A deadly incident occurred in 1943 near Ruby, Alaska when a man named John McMire or Mire, also called "The Dutchman" by the local Indians, claimed the he had been attacked by "the bushmen" but his dogs had driven them away. He had lived alone with his dogs in an isolated camp and one night he was attacked. He took his canoe to the nearest village and told his story but died shortly afterward from internal bleeding caused by the attack.[3]

In the summer of 1943 it was reported that an unnamed man from Hope, BC was out berry picking with his wife and others when he strayed from the group. They were about a mile from the small community of Katz when the man was attacked by a sasquatch that came running at him from behind some rocks. The bigfoot hit the man—"hit him in the head, and side, and arms."

The man yelled and others came to his assistance. The sasquatch ran off to pick berries elsewhere. The man's wife reasoned that since the sasquatch was small by sasquatch standards, he had been treated badly as a runt and so was taking out his frustrations on First Nations people. The man was said to have a "crooked arm" until his death in 1955.[21]

## 1947: A Skin-Clad Sasquatch?

A strange encounter was made on Vancouver Island in 1947 when a Mr. and Mrs. Werner were driving on Grouse Mountain. While they were travelling on an old logging road they said they saw two creatures that were naked except had "a skin wrapped around them." Both had shoulder-length hair, but there is no mention of body hair. Probably the skin wrapped around them was their own furry selves.

Both of the sasquatch were barefoot and had "huge feet." The leading bigfoot was about 8 feet tall while the other was about 6 feet tall. They had very bushy eyebrows over very small eyes and wide, flat noses. The taller creature was carrying a stick over its shoulder with what may have been a bag tied to the end. It appeared to be leading the smaller creature, which possibly had its hands tied together. The taller sasquatch was very thin while the smaller one

The 1924 attack in Ape Canyon is seen in this Roger Patterson drawing.

was very broad.[21] Perhaps it was a pregnant bride being led to her new digs, somewhere in Bigfoot Nation.

## 1948: A Bicycle Race

A strange report of a sasquatch racing a bicycle was reported in 1948 on the Chehalis Reservation. Henry Charlie said that he was cycling toward Harrison Mills when saw two unusual creatures come off the hill opposite the Fenn Pretty property. One of the creatures chased him for a distance of more than a mile down Morris Valley Road. He described it as between 7 and 8 feet tall and covered in dark hair, except the face.[29]

Charlie said that the sasquatch had no problem keeping up him as he pedaled as fast as he could down the road. He saw the creature only when he glanced behind himself as he pedaled madly. Eventually it was gone, probably having had some fun—bigfoot style!

## 1949: Horse Stops Because of Bigfoot

In July of 1949 Mrs. G. Mason reported seeing a strange animal near Harrison Hot Springs, a hotbed of bigfoot activity for decades. She was on horseback riding on a bridal trail when her horse balked at going any further. She dismounted and tried to lead the horse forward but it balked again. She then tied the horse up and walked up the trail where she came upon a creature that she thought was a bear.

She approached it and it ran off on all fours and then suddenly stood up and walked into the bush. She said that it had unkempt brown hair and was 7 to 8 feet tall. It was heavily built with medium length arms and did not have a snout like a bear. She returned to her horse which would not continue down the bridal trail until it sensed that the creature was completely out of the area.

Then in the autumn of 1949 a Mr. Hentges reported that he saw what he thought was a gorilla while he was driving down Cluculz Lake near Vanderhoof, BC. Hentges was driving down a highway under construction when he saw what he thought was a gorilla walk across the road in the distance. The creature was walking on two legs with its arms hanging down. When he got to the area where he had seen the giant figure he could not see it and assumed that it was hiding from him in the piles of brush nearby. Alarmed that some gorilla was on the loose, he decided to report it to the police.[29]

The Second World War had actually ended in 1946 but the news of elation in other parts of the country did not reach the denizens of Bigfoot Nation. In fact, it would still be a few more years until the grunts, groans, whistling and screaming—plus other sounds the horrible creature might make—were replaced with a name that everyone could understand: bigfoot.

A rare early photograph of bigfoot said to have been taken in the late 1940s

A curious undated photo from the Internet, likely a fake.

# CHAPTER 5

# The Heyday Years
# 1950 to 1999

Science must begin with myths,
and with the criticism of myths.
—*Sir Karl Popper*

**Bigfoot Encounters in the 1950s**

As more and more humans began to invade the vast forests of Canada and the Pacific Northwest there began to be more stories of loggers on new logging roads finding large footprints in the mud. Thus the term "bigfoot" was coined in 1958 and now pervades the North American culture in nearly every way. From Bigfoot Convenience Stores to Jack Link's beef jerky ads, bigfoot is now a dynamic marketing engine. Bigfoot Nation was marching forward into the modern post-war world. Some people would even devote their entire lives to studying and searching for bigfoot. One of these people was Roger Patterson.

Bigfoot hunter Roger Patterson interviewed Fred Beck in 1966 and included the story in his book *Do Abominable Snowmen of North America Really Exist?*[16] Beck told Patterson about shooting a sasquatch in the Pacific Northwest decades before:

> So we seen him running down this ridge then, and then he took a couple more shots at him. Marion, when he first shot I rushed over there, it was hard going, he said: "Don't run, don't run, Fred, don't run," he said, "he won't go far," he said, "I put three shots through that fool's head, he won't go far."

So we got up the ridge and looked down there he was goin', just jumpin', looked like it'd be twelve, fourteen feet a jump, runnin'. The old man took a couple more shots at him and the old man said, "My God, I don't understand it, I don't understand it, how that fella can get away with them slugs in his head," he says, "I hit him with the other two shots, too."

Regarding that night in their sturdy cabin of pine logs, Beck told Patterson:

When we seen 'em, you know, why we heard that noise—pounding and whistling, at night they come in there and we had a pile of shakes piled up there, big shakes. Our cabin was built out of logs. We didn't have rafters on it, we had good-sized pine logs, you know, for rafters, two-inch shakes, pine shakes. We had them rafters close apart, they was about a foot apart, 'cause he said he wanted to make a roof what'd hold the snow. We made one to hold the snow. Them buggers attacked us, knocked the chinking out on my dad's, on my father-in-law's chest, and had an ax there, he grabbed the ax.

And the old man grabbed the ax and the logs and then he shot on it, right along the ax handle, and he let go of it. And then the fun started! Well, I wanta tell you, pretty near all night long they were on that house, trying to get in, you know. We kept a shootin'. Get up on the house we'd shoot up through the ceiling at them. My God, they made a noise. Sounded like a bunch of horses were running around there. Next day, we'd find tracks, anywhere there was any sand on the rocks, we found tracks of them.[16, 29]

### 1952: Bigfoot Watches Motorist

A motorist driving near Terrace, in northern British Columbia (on the Skeena River where the Kitselas people, a tribe of the Tsimshian Nation, have lived for thousands of years), saw an odd creature standing erect beside the main road to the town in the summer of 1952. The man slowed down and then stopped his car. The bigfoot watched him quietly for a while and then turned and walked into the bush. It turned in the underbrush to look at him again. It was dusk and the man could not see the facial features clearly but he believed it to be a sasquatch. Several other sightings had been made in the area during that same year.[29]

### 1953: A Dark Figure on a Logging Road

Jack Twist was on a camping trip with friends near the Oyster River about 20 miles northwest of Courtenay, British Columbia in September 1953 when, as he walked alone down a logging road, he saw a dark figure several hundred yards away. He thought it was one of his friends and he called out to the figure but did not get an answer. The figure was in front of him and he continued to walk toward it and as he got closer he could see that it was an 8-foot creature covered in dark hair. The bigfoot turned and faced Twist and then turned and walked into the forest.[7]

### 1954: Sasquatch Pass at Chilko Lake Named

An expedition from the Explorers Club with headquarters in New York City and headed by Dr. George Cochran were exploring a route to the Homathko ice fields when they found large human-like footprints in the snow. Similar footprints found in the Himalayas had been in the news and Cochran and his team suspected that they might be the prints of a North American Abominable Snowman. As a result of the discovery the team named the area Sasquatch Pass.[7]

It was observed that footprints in the snow at high altitudes are something of a mystery since such snowy heights have little to do with food gathering. Either the animals are wanting to cross into another forested valley near glaciers such as in the Himalayas or British Columbia, or they may be preserving earlier kill in the frozen areas of a mountain. Dr. Cochran and his team surmised that since wolverines were known to take their kills to snow and bury them to preserve the carcass, sasquatch might be doing the same thing. Bigfoot has been known

to kill a deer and take the hind legs. If some snow was nearby the critter might be preserving his meat stash there for those lean times in Bigfoot Nation.

## 1955: Female Bigfoot Seen in British Columbia

During the 1950s, as more roads were made into the remote forests of the Pacific Northwest, things started to heat up as far as claims of sasquatch encounters. On August 26, 1957 William Roe provided a sworn statement about his encounter with a female sasquatch. Roe, who had worked as a hunter, trapper, and a road worker, was doing a job in British Columbia during October of 1955. One day he hiked five miles up Mica Mountain to explore a deserted mine.

As he was stepping out of a clearing, he saw what he thought was a grizzly bear. When the animal stood up, he realized this was no grizzly bear! The animal, a female sasquatch, was six feet tall, three feet wide, and weighed approximately 300 pounds. Her arms reached almost to her knees, and when she walked she put the heel of her foot down first.

Roe was hiding in some brush and was able to observe the creature from a distance of some 20 feet. He said that he watched, fascinated, as she used her white, even teeth to eat leaves from a nearby bush. Her head was "higher at the back than at the front"; her nose was flat. Only the area around her mouth was bare—the rest of her body was covered in hair, none of which was longer than an inch. The ears looked very much like a human's. The eyes were small and dark, similar to a bear's.

At this point, the animal caught

A drawing of the Roe bigfoot.

Roe's scent and walked back the way she had come, looking over her shoulder as she went. As she disappeared into the bush, Roe heard her make a sound he described as "a kind of a whinny."

Roe said he wanted to find out whether the animal was a vegetarian or whether she consumed meat as well. He searched for and found feces in several places. Upon examination, no hair or insect shells were found. Roe concluded this animal lived solely on vegetation. Most researchers agree however, that these animals probably eat a variety of foods, including fish, fowl, frogs and even deer, plus all kinds of berries, pine cones, wild onions and everything else edible, much like bears.[7]

## 1956: Hairy Creature Grabs Two in Their Sleeping Bags

In May of 1956 near Marshall, Michigan, three friends were sleeping out in the woods when a "huge, hair-covered creature" with green eyes "as big as light bulbs" and smelling "like something rotten" picked up Otto Collins and Philip Williams in their sleeping bags, holding one under each arm. Their companion Herman Williams grabbed his rifle which scared the bigfoot who then dropped the men and ran into the woods.[3]

We don't know if bigfoot was trying to abduct the young men or just trying to scare them, but the encounter certainly terrified the men.

## 1957: Bigfoot Picks Up a Hunter's Deer

In the Autumn of 1957 Gary Joanis and Jim Newall were hunting in the area of Wanoga Butte near Bend, Oregon, and Joanis had just shot a deer. However, before the two could walk over to the dead deer a 9-foot hairy creature came into the clearing, a picked the entire deer up and began to carry it back into the woods under one arm. Joanis was angry that his deer was being stolen and fired repeatedly into the back of the bigfoot with his 30.06 rifle. The bigfoot did not stop walking but made a "strange whistling scream." Joanis and Newall had no choice but to let the bigfoot abscond with their deer.[3]

Bigfoot is known to have been shot on a number of occasions but his thick skin, bones and bulky body make it almost impossible to bring the massive critter down with shots to the upper body. It has been suggested that about the only way to kill a bigfoot is to shoot him through one of his eye sockets.

## 1958: Jerry Crew Coins the Term "Bigfoot"

As related previously, on October 2, 1958, a road construction worker named Jerry Crew found unusually large footprints around his bulldozer on a road being constructed in Bluff Creek, California. Crew noticed a very clear footprint in the mud along the side of the road in

Jerry Crew holds up his cast of a bigfoot.

that rainy part of northern California. He had seen these footprints before and he made a plaster cast of the mysterious footprint. He then reported the find, along with a photo of himself holding his plaster cast of the footprint. In the story Crew called the maker of the footprint "bigfoot," and the name was suddenly in the vernacular.

## 1959: Bigfoot Shot At in Oregon

In October of 1959 at a place called Ten Mile west of Roseburg, Oregon two boys decided to hunt bigfoot at an abandoned sawmill. Wayne Johnson, 12 years old, had seen a bigfoot near the abandoned sawmill and after telling his friend, 17-year-old Walter Stork, the two decided to go back with rifles and shoot the bigfoot. When they got to the abandoned sawmill bigfoot was there waiting for them. The two both fired shots at the bigfoot, Stork with his 30.06 rifle. The bigfoot kept coming at them, but dropped down on his knuckles each time he was shot. The bigfoot had his arms outstretched as if he were herding the boys away. The boys ran and even though the bigfoot could have caught up them, he did not and they later felt that he was essentially shooing them away from the area. Suddenly the bigfoot stopped following them and they did not see where he went. The boys estimated that the bigfoot was almost 14 feet tall, perhaps an exaggeration. Bigfoot has been reported to a height of 15 feet, though any 10- to 12-foot-tall would seem gigantically huge to any normal person. One has to wonder if a bigfoot can really reach the height of 14 or 15 feet, but who knows what the official statistics are in Bigfoot Nation!

A bigfoot investigator named Bob Titmus came to the scene within two days and found some unusual tracks. They were less than 12 inches long but 12 inches wide at the toes, which did not seem very long for a 14-foot bigfoot, though extremely wide. There were no apparent claws on the footprints and in wet ground the prints were an astonishing 13 inches deep. When Titmus tried to make his own footprint in the wet soil he could only make his heel sink as deep as 2 or 3 inches.[3]

Also, sometime in late 1959 a road crew working in the Armstrong area of British Columbia discovered a skeleton of a "man" that was nearly 7 feet tall. The coroner of Lillooet (yes, the place in the 1894 bigfoot photo story), Arthur Phair, was informed of the find and he notified a government official in Victoria. Apparently the skeleton was turned over to the First Nations people of the area for burial. Some speculation is that it was the skeleton of a dead sasquatch.[7] This is an interesting story since a common question that is asked is, "why don't they ever find any bigfoot skeletons?"

### 1960: A Huckleberry Bigfoot in British Columbia

In early August of 1960, well-known Canadian outdoorsman and hunter John Bringsli reported that he had driven up a deserted logging road at Lemmon Creek near Nelson, British Columbia to pick huckleberries when he met a bigfoot. Bringsli said:

> I had just stopped my 1931 coupe on a deserted logging road and walked about 100 yards into the bush. I was picking huckleberries. I had just started to pick berries and was moving slowly through the bush. I had only been there about 15 minutes. For no particular reason, I glanced up and that is when I saw this great beast. It was standing about 50 feet away from me on a slight rise in the ground, staring at me.
> 
> The sight of the animal paralyzed me. It was 7 to 8

feet tall with long legs and short powerful arms with hair covering its body. The first thing I thought was …what a strange looking bear.

It had very wide shoulders and a flat face with ears flat against the side of its head. It looked more like a big hairy ape.

It just stood there staring at me. Arms of the animal were bent slightly, and most astounding was that it had hands… not claws. It was about 8 a.m. and I cold see it very clearly. The most peculiar thing about it was the strange bluish-gray tinge of color of its long hair. It had no neck. Its apelike head appeared to be fastened directly to its shoulders.

When the bigfoot began to move toward him Bringsli ran back to his vehicle and tore out of the area. He returned the next day with some friends and they found footprints that were about 17 inches long.[7]

Bringsli's observation of "short, powerful arms" seems at odds with the typical bigfoot description of having long arms. Perhaps because they were "bent" made them seem to be shorter. Bringsli does not mention a strong odor. The bluish-gray tinge to the hair might indicate that this was an older sasquatch, soon to be dumpster diving in Bigfoot Nation. Bigfoot being encountered in a berry patch is a standard account over the years, and David Paulides in his books chronicles a number of children who have gone mysteriously missing while picking berries with their familes. Some of these children are eventually found, while others turn up dead in strange places, and some are never found. He alludes that bigfoot may be snatching them out of curiosity.[37, 38]

**1961: Bigfoot in the Rearview Mirror**

Sometime in the fall of 1961 Larry Martin and some friends from Alpine, Oregon went into the forest one evening to retrieve a deer that one of them had shot while hunting earlier in the day. When they arrived at the place where the deer had been left, they found that it had been dragged away, plus they heard thrashing noises in the nearby brush. As it was dark, they cautiously looked around with flashlights and were startled when Martin's light illuminated a tall bigfoot only a few feet away. Said Martin, "I knew it wasn't a bear 'cause it had human-like features, you know, it looked like an ape or gorilla or something like that, and it was coming at me."

Martin, nearly six-feet tall, had to shine his flashlight upward into the face of the bigfoot and as he did so his group immediately turned and ran back to the car in fright. The car would not start immediately and Martin could see bigfoot in the rearview mirror walking up to the car. Suddenly, the car started and the group tore down the road; Martin later said, "We got out of there."[3]

## 1962: White-Haired Bigfoot in Oregon

The *Oregon Journal* reported in 1962, in a story entitled "Monster Sightings Rekindle Interest in Mt. St. Helens Hairy Giant Saga," that three persons driving along a remote mountain road east of the Cascade wilderness area said that they saw a 10-foot, white, hairy figure moving rapidly along the roadside. The white-haired sasquatch was caught in the headlights as their car passed, but they were too frightened to turn around to investigate. They apparently reported their sighting to the police.

The *Oregon Journal* also said that a Portland woman and her husband fishing on the Lewis River south of Mt. St. Helens saw a huge beige figure, "bigger than any human," along the bank of the river. As they watched the tall creature, it "moved into a thicket with a lumbering gait."

The article also mentioned that the Clallam Indian tribe of Washington State had traditions of hairy giants on Mt. St. Helens. These hairy giants are called the Selahtik, and are believed to be a tribe of "renegade marauder-like people, who lived like animals in the caves and lava tunnels in the high Cascades."[3]

In June of 1962 Robert Hatfield was woken in the middle of the night by the barking of his dogs at his house just outside of Fort Bragg in northern California. He went outside the front door to investigate and thought he saw the largest bear that he had ever seen: a dark form looking at his barking dogs from the other side of a 6-foot fence. He ran back into the house to wake his brother-in-law Bud Jenkins to show him this gigantic bear. Outside neither of them could see the gigantic animal so Jenkins returned to the house to fetch a flashlight and a gun. Hatfield decided to check around the back of the house and as he rounded the corner he suddenly came "face to chest" with an 8-foot bigfoot. At that point Jenkins said that Hatfield:

> …let out a scream and stepped backwards and as he stepped backwards he fell, so he came into the house on his hands and knees going like mad.
>
> My wife was at this time holding the screen door open for him to come in. I heard the commotion and I ran to the inside door we have here before you step onto the porch, and as he came through the door I saw this large creature going by the window, but I could see neither its lower body nor its head, all I cold see was the upper part of its body through the window there.
>
> When he came in my wife tried to close the door and they got it within about two to for inches of closing and couldn't close it. Something was holding it open. My wife hollered at me and said, "Hurry and get the gun, it's coming through the door!"
>
> Of course by that time I was standing right behind her here in this door leading to the porch, and I said, "Well, let it through and I'll get it."
>
> At that time the pressure went off the door and I shut the door and threw the lock on it. And I walked to the window and put my hand up to the window and looked out, so that I could see out into the yard, because it was still dark, and it was raining, and this creature was standing upright, and I would judge it to be about 8-feet tall and it walked away from the house, back out to this little fence we have, and stepped over the little fence and walked past my car and out towards the main road.[3]

Jenkins judged that the bigfoot must have weighed about 500 pounds, and it always walked upright and had a terrible odor which lingered in the air after the creature had gone. In daylight they searched the yard for footprints and found some four-toed prints that were 16 inches long. On the wall by the house door was found a handprint 11-and-a-half inches long. The two men later said that, while they had been very frightened at the time, the attitude of the creature was one of curiosity rather than aggression.

The Texas oilman and bigfoot hunter Tom Slick made an offer of a one million dollar reward for a sasquatch—dead or alive—while visiting the town of Bella Coola, British Columbia in early 1962. Slick had financed a number of bigfoot and yeti expeditions during the previous decade and was a believer in the creatures. Unfortunately, Slick died when his private plane crashed in Montana on October 6, 1962.[5]

### 1963: Camper Meets Four Bigfoot in British Columbia

In the summer of 1963 a lone camper named Harry Squiness was preparing to get in to his sleeping bag when suddenly his tent flap was opened and a hairy monkey face with human eyes peered in at him. He was camped near a lake in British Columbia called Anahim Lake at a place called Goose Point. Squiness grabbed his flashlight—which failed to work—and he then ran outside the tent and quickly flung some petrol onto his dying campfire which suddenly burst into a big blaze.

In the light of the big flames he could see four bigfoot about 14 feet away, all lying down in the tall grass as if trying to hide. As the firelight revealed them they stood up and walked away into the darkness. Squiness called out, "Hey, what are you doing here? Come back!"

The four bigfoot ignored his calls and silently withdrew to the dark forest. In the morning Squiness searched for footprints in the grass but could only find a huge handprint on a tree trunk. He later showed it to Clayton Mack, a respected Indian hunting guide from Anahim Lake, who confirmed the creature was probably sasquatch.[7]

### 1964: Michigan Berry Pickers Meet Bigfoot

The berry fields around Sister Lakes, Michigan saw the odd bigfoot report, but in June, 1964 there were a series of encounters with a 9-foot bigfoot that was said to lurk in the adjoining swamps. This was a commercial berry operation that hired out-of-state berry pickers at picking time, but this year many were quitting the job because of bigfoot.

Then on June 9, Gordon Brown, a fruit picker from Georgia, was

# Getting into the Monster Act

THE PEOPLE and authorities of the Sister Lakes region in Southwestern Michigan breathed easier Monday, with the crowds of curious and tourists gone and only the "Monster of Sister Lakes" to worry about. But while the weekend crowds were in the area the merchants and roadside establishments were not loath to cash in a bit on the publicity that has followed the first report on the "nine-foot, 500-pound" monster of a week ago. Reid's drive-in restaurant at Sister Lakes enticed tourists with a stuffed monster and offerings of "monster brew" and "monster burgers," above and at right below. A monster trap put in its appearance in front of the home of Dawn Grabemeyer, of rural Dowagiac near Dewey Lake, lower left.

A newspaper article on the 1964 monster hunt in Michigan.

driving near the berry patches at night with his brother when they suddenly saw a bigfoot in the headlights. They stopped the car as the bigfoot disappeared into the woods. They decided to follow its tracks and when they caught up with it they found a 9-foot-tall monster that was a cross between a gorilla and a bear. The two mean hastily retreated to their car and made a quick getaway. Brown later said that he had seen the bigfoot the year before but had been afraid to tell anyone.

The berry farm was part of a farm owned by Evelyn Utrup and her husband John. In the past they had some encounters with bigfoot as it frequently prowled their property. Berries are an important food to bigfoot and, as previously mentioned, berry patches are a spot where bigfoot has been frequently spotted.

Evelyn had seen the bigfoot standing in their yard with the car's headlights on him. She said it had "big bright shining eyes" and that it chased her back into her house with "great thundering feet." She also reported that one of her Alsatian dogs had chased the creature one night and had returned with one eye changed to blue. After a few weeks it changed back to its normal color, brown. What might have caused this?

On June 10 some locals glimpsed the bigfoot and heard some "baby crying" noises. Then on June 11, three 13-year-old girls were walking on a lonely road in nearby Silver Creek Township—in daylight—when they were suddenly confronted by the odorous creature. He stood in front of them on the road and one of the girls, Joyce Smith, immediately fainted. The other girls, Gail and Patsy Clayton, were frozen with fear. After a few terrifying moments the bigfoot lumbered off into the bushes.[3]

This report in the local news turned the quiet community of Sister Lakes in southwest Michigan near Benton Harbor into a veritable circus. Hundreds of monster hunters and sensation seekers descended on Sister Lakes where the local café started selling "monster burgers" and every store in town had a monster sale of some sort with even monster hunting kits being sold for $7.95. It was monster-mania for a while in this part of Michigan but bigfoot wasn't having any part of it and apparently took off for another berry patch with a swamp next to it.

On September 13, 1964 a camper named Benjamin Wilder was

sleeping in his car on a forest road near remote Blue Lake in the northwest corner of California. Wilder was awoken at one a.m. by his car moving. At first he thought it was an earthquake and a rockslide but when he heard no rocks falling he switched on his car's dome light to take a look.

He was shocked to see a large shaggy creature with 3-inch hairs on its chest standing by the driver's door with its two arms on top of the car—shaking it. Wilder shouted at the bigfoot, but it only made "pig-like" noises back. He then sounded the car's horn which scared the bigfoot off and it walked away on two feet over a nearby hill. Wilder never saw the bigfoot's face.

## 1965: Bigfoot Bangs Woman's Head inside Car

In a curious encounter on August 17, 1965, 17-year-old Christine van Acker was driving, with her mother in the passenger's seat, through a wooded area near Monroe in very southeast Michigan, about halfway between Detroit and Toledo, Ohio. The windows of the car were rolled down on that hot August night and as they rounded a bend a large, dark bigfoot stepped out of the forest onto the road.

As in some grade-B horror movie, in her startled terror, Christine meant to accelerate past the creature, but instead stepped on the brake and the car came to a halt and stalled with the motor shutting off. Christine frantically tried to start the car again and suddenly the bigfoot put his huge, hairy hand through the driver's window and grabbed her by the top of her head. Both women were now screaming and bigfoot banged Christine's head against the inside of the car as he suddenly left.

Christine began honking her car horn. Some nearby workmen heard the screams and car horn and came running to the road where they caught a quick glimpse of the 7-foot-tall creature. Christine suffered a black eye and said the creature must have weighed 300 or 400 pounds and had a strong odor about it.

Also in 1965 was an early incident with the Fouke Monster who is featured in the movie *The Legend of Boggy Creek*. A squirrel hunter from Fouke, Arkansas named James Crabtree, only 14-years-old, was out hunting near his home when he was startled to hear horses galloping in panic into a nearby lake. He then heard a dog howling in pain and ran toward it with his loaded shotgun in his hands.

He suddenly came across an 8-foot-tall bigfoot covered in four-inch-long reddish-brown hair. It had long arms and turned to face the boy. The bigfoot began to walk towards Crabtree who then shot it

An early photo of bigfoot taken by Zach Hamilton in northern California and published in *The San Francisco Chronicle* in 1965.

**95**

in the face with his shotgun from an unknown distance. This did not stop the bigfoot from advancing toward the teenager and Crabtree ran back to his house without looking back.[3]

**1966: Bigfoot Grabs Woman through Car Window**

Bigfoot reaching through the car window happened again, but this time in southern California, on the outskirts of Los Angeles and Hollywood! In August of 1966 near the town of Fontana, near Anaheim and the Cleveland National Forest, some boys reported encountering a small bigfoot; one boy said he had been scratched by the creature and had his clothes torn.

Then on August 27 a couple of teenage girls from the area were driving around looking for the monster when they had a shocking encounter with the man himself. The driver, 16-year-old Jerri Mendenhall, had driven up a rough dirt track and was backing the car back to the main road when bigfoot suddenly stepped out of the bushes and grabbed her through the window, which was open on the August evening. Jerri screamed and hit the accelerator back to the main road and bigfoot walked back into the bushes. She described it as having very slimy and matted hair and smelling like "a dead animal."

The ordeal was reported to the police who went to the location and found an unexplained footprint that was 17-inches long and had only two toes. Later Jerri Mendenhall went through a hypnotic session about the incident in which she exhibited "extreme fright."[3]

This is pretty normal with any encounter with bigfoot. Except for small children and autistic adults, most people when they encounter bigfoot go into extreme fright and shock. Even those people who have briefly spotted bigfoot before—say in the headlights of their car—are still very frightened when they come on the powerful creature again, often in a much closer setting. There is a sudden adrenaline rush when you find bigfoot on the side of the road—with him even reaching into your car—as you back up in search of the very monster who is now grabbing you. Hollywood can't make this stuff up (but they will be inspired by it) and it is only normal that a teenage girl would need some counseling concerning the traumatic incident, including hypnotism.

In the summer and fall of 1966 there were several different

*Left*: One of the photos taken in 1894 at Lillooet, British Columbia. *Below*: A close-up 1894 photo taken at Lillooet, British Columbia. *Below Left*: A curious photo of a bigfoot hunter from the Internet, probably a hoax. *Bottom Right*: A stamp featuring a sasquatch issued by the Canadian government.

A photo from 1926 of the giant masks made by the Kwakiutl First Nations people at Alert Bay, British Columbia. The central mask is of D'sonoqua, or Wild Woman of the Woods.

*Below and Right*: Frames from the film shot by Roger Patterson on October 20, 1967.

*Above and Right*: Frames from the film shot by Roger Patterson on October 20, 1967.

*Left and Below*: Frames
from the film shot by
Roger Patterson on October
20, 1967.

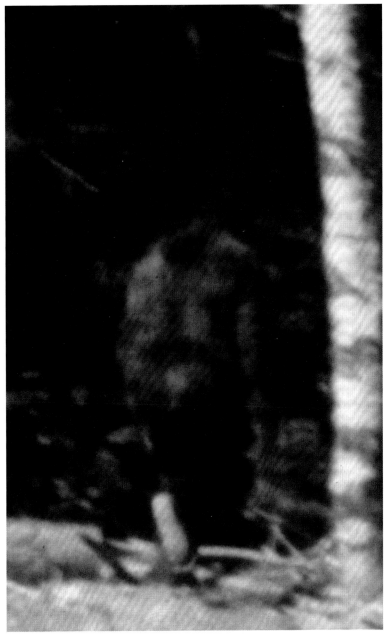

*Above*: A comparison of the 1967 Patterson footage of bigfoot walking with a man in a costume trying to walk in the same unusual manner. *Below*: Roger Patterson holds up footprint casts, circa 1968.

*Above*: A sasquatch coin that was minted by the Canadian Mint. *Right*: A poster for the never-made film, *The DuPont Monster*.

The DuPont Monster

Famous Canadian sasquatch researcher Bob Titmus holding up footprint casts in 1976.

sightings of what would seem to be older white-haired bigfoot that had perhaps been cast out from their tribe and were now dumpster diving. Near Richland, Washington a group of teenagers described a series of encounters they claimed happened with an 8-foot-tall bigfoot with whitish-gray hair and red eyes in the summer of 1966.

These teenagers claimed that they drove around at night all summer looking for the white-haired bigfoot. As in some sort of Hollywood movie these vigilante teenagers—armed with .270 caliber rifles and such—decided to spend their summer shooting at this elderly bigfoot.

The teenagers, Greg Pointer, Roger True, and Tom Thompson all testified, and took lie detector tests, that they had fired at the white-haired bigfoot on several occasions, often at an old gravel pit that they knew was a good place to find the creature. Roger True claimed that he hit the 8-foot-tall bigfoot with at least three bullets from a .270 caliber rifle but it did not knock him down; Tom Thompson claimed that he fired a shotgun 10 yards from the bigfoot but it hardly flinched. Other teenagers claimed that the bigfoot threw rocks at their car and as it came onto the road they tried to run it down, but it dodged to the side and left scratches on the top of the car.[3]

Standing with their bigfoot casts are Rene Dahinden and Roger Patterson in 1966.

**97**

It is always interesting to study cases where hunters—or in this case, excitable teenage boys with guns and little sense—are suddenly in a position to fire their weapons at bigfoot and unload two or three shots at the bulky, hairy animal. Bigfoot is a thick-skinned and thick-boned hominid that can take a great deal of abuse—including bullets fired into its body.

All large animals can take all sorts of metal bullets penetrating their skin and only bullets to vital organs like the heart, brain or lungs can really bring down a large animal. Similarly the force of a shotgun blast at 10 yards (30 feet) might bring down a duck or a pheasant, but it will not bring down—or even significantly slow—a bigfoot. In fact, no quantity of shotgun blasts, unless at pointblank range, would kill bigfoot. The only known (and essentially rumored) stories of bigfoot being killed say that he is shot in the head, and for those sharpshooters who know what they are doing, they have shot bigfoot in one of his eyes with a high-powered rifle. This is what happened in the case of the Minnesota Iceman, to be discussed later, a frozen bigfoot that had apparently been shot through its left eye. Otherwise bigfoot just has such thick, matted hair and skin, plus bulk, that it seems any bullet would barely penetrate the skin.

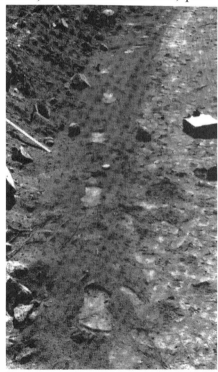

If it did penetrate the skin, it would have to hit a vital organ to cause any damage, and even then bigfoot is likely to stagger away into the forest with some life in him for a few hours. There are many reports of bigfoot that are missing toes, apparently lame or disfigured in the foot for some reason, or (and on top of) an arm that is broken and useless. These reports are possibly the result of the creature taking some bullets or shotgun blasts in these described encounters. Older bullets in past centuries were often homemade

Footprints at Blue Creek Mtn, CA in 1967.

or of older boxes of bullets that had also gotten damp. The firepower of these yesteryear bullets was much weaker than the modern bullets of the same caliber, and any high-powered rifle bullet would probably bring down bigfoot pretty quick. Most people know today that shooting at bigfoot would be a breach of the unofficial treaty with Bigfoot Nation.

Another incident involving firearms and bigfoot occurred in the fall of 1966 in Lower Bank, New Jersey. An unnamed couple living in the area saw a face peer in the window of their house—a window that was over 7-feet high. Outside they found five-toed tracks that were 17 inches long. Curious about the bigfoot, they started leaving scraps of vegetables outside and they were being eaten. The only thing that the bigfoot reportedly did not eat was a peanut butter and jelly sandwich that was left for him. This is interesting, because bigfoot apparently does like peanut butter, and an open jar of peanut butter hung at nine feet with a string from a tree branch is a common way of baiting bigfoot. A Snickers candy bar hung from a string is another common way to try to lure bigfoot to a clearing in order to get a photo.

In the case of the Lower Bank, New Jersey bigfoot, one night the couple did not leave any vegetable scraps out, and in the middle of the night they heard a loud banging outside of the house. The husband decided to arm himself and then go outside to see what was causing the noise. What he found was a gray-haired bigfoot throwing their garbage can against the wall of the house repeatedly. He fired a shot into the air to frighten the bigfoot, but the old bigfoot just stood there. The man then fired directly at the chest of the bigfoot and shot it. At this point the bigfoot turned and ran off. He certainly wasn't killed by the shot, but he did not return to the house again.[3] This bigfoot seems to be the classic white-haired bigfoot who is old and cast out of his tribe. He ventures close to civilization in order to find easy food. Sadly, this seems to be how Bigfoot Nation treats its older generation.

## 1967: Roger Patterson and the Bluff Creek Film

One of the most famous, if not the most famous, incidents in the history of Bigfoot Nation is the October 1967 filming of a female bigfoot at Bluff Creek, California by Roger Patterson. As I said earlier, as a youngster I had met Roger Patterson in 1967. It was later that year that Patterson was to film the most controversial of all sasquatch photos and movie footage.

Patterson was a former rodeo rider who took an interest

The 1967 photo of a female bigfoot walking along a river in Bluff Creek, CA.

in bigfoot after reading Ivan T. Sanderson's book *Abominable Snowmen: Legend Come to Life*.[9] Patterson was born in Wall, South Dakota (famous for Wall Drug and its billboards across the country) on February 14, 1926 and died on January 15, 1972. Starting

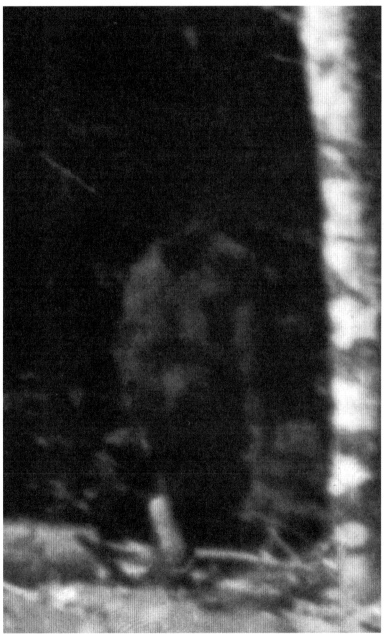

Another photo of a female bigfoot walking along a river in Bluff Creek, CA.

**101**

around 1958, Patterson and his friend, Bob Gimlin, began going into Washington State to gather follow-up reports on sasquatch sightings and explore remote areas of wilderness where the apemen were reported to live.

During late August and early September of 1967, Patterson and Gimlin were exploring the Mt. St. Helens area. While they were away, friends in Willow Creek, California, phoned Patterson's home to report footprints found in the Bluff Creek area. The tracks, which were said to be of three different sizes, had been found on new logging roads being built in the Bluff Creek region. This same area

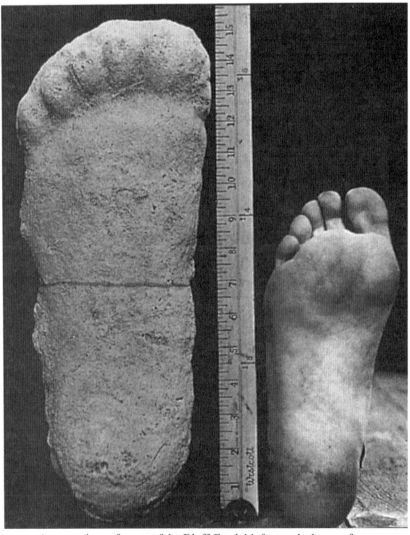

A comparison of a cast of the Bluff Creek bigfoot and a human foot.

was the scene of considerable bigfoot activity nine years earlier. It was here in 1958 that Jerry Crew found large human-like footprints. As mentioned above, newspaper stories of this event coined the term "bigfoot."

When he returned home to Yakima, Washington and got the news, Patterson contacted Gimlin and the two men made plans to investigate Bluff Creek, a wilderness area just north of the Hoopa Indian Reservation in the northwest corner of California. Patterson and Gimlin wished to find and film fresh footprints as evidence of the creature's existence in and around Willow Creek, a frontier town that sits near the Oregon border, right in the center of the Klamath and Six Rivers National Forests. Patterson wanted to make a documentary, and rented a Kodak 16mm handheld movie camera and purchased two 100-foot rolls of color movie film for the expedition. Patterson and Gimlin traveled to the Bluff Creek area in a truck, taking with them three horses.

Patterson and Gimlin set up camp near Bluff Creek and set out on horseback to explore the area. Patterson used 76 feet of the first film roll gathering footage of the scenery to be used as a backdrop, plus took shots of both himself and Gimlin.

Not much happened for the first seven days, Patterson claimed, but in the early afternoon of October 20, 1967 Patterson and Gimlin spotted a female sasquatch down on the creek's gravel sandbar. Patterson's horse reared in alarm at the sight of the creature, bringing both horse and rider to the ground, with Patterson pinned beneath the animal.

Since Patterson was an experienced horseman, he quickly disengaged himself and grabbed his camera. While running toward the creature, he took 24 feet of color film footage. During this time, bigfoot quickly but calmly walked away across the sandbar into the woods.

During all this, Gimlin watched Patterson and sasquatch, his rifle in hand, in case his friend was attacked by the creature. The two had previously agreed that under no circumstances would they shoot a sasquatch unless in self-protection. The female sasquatch was estimated to be seven feet three inches in height and weigh 700 pounds; she left footprints 14½ inches long by six inches wide.

Patterson and Gimlin decided not to pursue the sasquatch into the woods for fear of a possible confrontation with the creature and perhaps others of its kind.

The film gained instant fame. The very clear, daylight footage has been subjected to many attempts both to debunk and authenticate it. Some qualified scientists have judged the film a hoax featuring a man in a gorilla suit, while other scientists contend the film depicts an animal unknown to science,

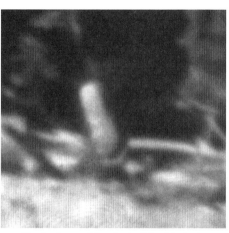

The bottom of the foot of the bigfoot.

claiming it would be virtually impossible for a human to replicate the subject's gait and muscle movement. Indeed, if it is a hoax, it is a very good one. In his book *The Making of Bigfoot*,[25] Greg Long claims that it is a man in a gorilla suit named Bob Hieronymus who lived near Patterson in Yakima, Washington. However, Long has difficulty in explaining why Patterson would want to fake a female bigfoot and suggests that black bags were sewn onto the gorilla suit to make the breasts.

Both men continually dismissed allegations that they had hoaxed the footage by filming a man wearing a fake sasquatch suit. Patterson swore on his deathbed that the footage was authentic and he had encountered and filmed a large bipedal animal unknown to science. Gimlin avoided appearing in public and discussing the subject until about the year 2000, when he began to make appearances at bigfoot conferences and give some interviews.

The documentary featuring the Bluff Creek footage of the female sasquatch was eventually released as a film entitled *Sasquatch, the Legend of Bigfoot*. Though there was little scientific interest in the film or the Bluff Creek footage, Patterson was still able to capitalize on it. Beyond the documentary, the film generated a fair amount of publicity. Patterson appeared on several popular television shows such as the Merv Griffin and Joey Bishop talk shows.

Today, still photos from the film are the most familiar of all sasquatch pictures. Entire books, skeptical and otherwise, have been written about this event. Hopefully, more film footage of bigfoot will emerge. In fact there are now a number of good photos of sasquatch as can be seen in the color section of this book. Although, unfortunately, some of it will probably be deliberate hoaxing, part of the fun will be sifting through the video footage as it comes to us—fast and furious.

An enhancement of Patterson's bigfoot.

## 1967: Bigfoot Eating Rodents in Oregon

Janet and Colin Bord tell an interesting tale which happened at the end of October 1967. A forest worker named Glenn Thomas had been operating a saw at nearly 6,000 feet on a mountainside near Estacada, Oregon. Thomas took a break from his work and walked down a trail into the woods. He came to a clearing where he saw three bigfoot digging among the rocks. Thomas took them to be a bigfoot family of mother, father and child who were busy foraging for food.

The group was sniffing at the various piles of rocks and suddenly the male began digging furiously and throwing up large rocks, some that would weigh 100 pounds or more. He then brought out some sort of nest of rodents, Thomas thought. The trio chomped the rodents down in several bites each and Thomas said he watched them for about 15 minutes. They then became aware of him and moved off into the forest. He described their faces as more cat-like than human.[3]

Two teenage girls reported that they came face to face with a bigfoot on September 28, 1967 on Vancouver Island, British Columbia. They were near Comox in the Comox Valley area when they heard the loud sound of the slapping of water. They walked

**105**

around a point and came upon a 7-foot sasquatch with long, dripping reddish-brown hair. The creature held four ducks in one hand and a four-foot-long stick in the other. The girls and the sasquatch stared at each other for several seconds and then both parties ran in different directions. The girls assumed that the stick had been used to slap the water and possibly to kill the ducks.[7]

## 1968: Flying over Bigfoot

On January 6, 1968, two men were piloting a light plane over Yosemite Park. The pilot was Robert James and his passenger was Leroy Larwick. As they flew over a remote area known as Confidence Ridge they both saw a brown fuzzy creature below the aircraft. The creature seemed to be 10 or 12 feet tall as it walked on the ridge on two legs.

James and Larwick wondered if it was bigfoot as it did not look like a bear. They took another pass at the creature and Larwick took a photograph of a huge bigfoot. They landed and returned to the spot where they had made the sighting, where they said they found 20-inch -ong footprints.[3] They took photographs of the prints but their photo taken from the airplane has never been released. We might think that it was just a bad, fuzzy photo that didn't show anything, or perhaps it is one of the great lost bigfoot photos of all time!

In November of 1968 a series of reports surfaced around Deltox Marsh, near Fremont, Wisconsin. A "powerfully built" bigfoot covered in dark-brown hair and with a hairless face and palms was seen around the marsh. Then on November 30, 1968, twelve men were on the marsh strung out in line on a deer drive. Each man was walking forward with a rifle in his hand when some of the men on the left noticed that they were being watched by the bigfoot. They passed the word down the line and all the men knew that a bigfoot was watching them. The bigfoot kept a distance but moved forward with the men, seemingly fascinated by what they were doing. He eventually became a shadow in the woods and the hunters continued their deer drive. While all of them were armed, none of them considered shooting at the creature as they thought it looked too man-like. Ivan T. Sanderson and Bernard Heuvelmans both took an interest in this bigfoot case and went to the site and interviewed witnesses.[3]

**106**

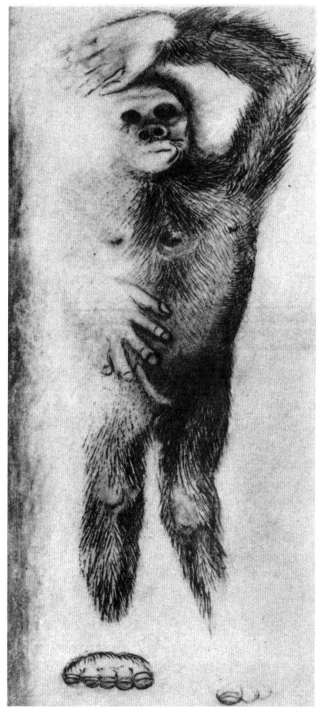

The Minnesota Iceman was examined in 1968 by Ivan T. Sanderson and Bernard Heuvelmans. It is now thought to be a fake made of latex and frozen in ice.

### 1969: Bigfoot Hits the Bigtime

On March 14, 1969, the *Skamania County Pioneer* newspaper published in the Mount St. Helens area ran a story about a man named Don Cox who spotted a large bigfoot while driving at 4 a.m. He drew some pictures of the bigfoot which were published.

Another report occurred in the same newspaper on March 28, 1969 about large footprints found in the snow south of Ape Caves and Mount St. Helens. A photo appeared in the newspaper that mentioned that the Skamania County Sheriff's Department made casts of the prints.

Janet and Colin Bord chronicle over 50 bigfoot incidents during 1969 including an April encounter near Oroville, California where Ed Saville and Eldon Butler reported to the local newspaper that they had seen an 8-foot-tall bigfoot with greenish eyes that came to investigate their rabbit call one night.

In the spring of 1969 a sailor with three friends said that after they were parked near Marietta, Washington, their headlights lit up a white-haired bigfoot with long arms. It jumped up and then ran into the woods. Probably another older bigfoot, now dumpster diving on the edges of civilization.[3]

The June 1969 issue of *Saga* featured an article on bigfoot that contained a number of reports including one of a student named Larry Hopkins who saw a bigfoot crouching on the roadside near Rochester, Minnesota in early 1969. Hopkins stopped the car to look at the creature and it ran off, leaving behind a dead rabbit.

On June 26, 1969, Mrs. Doris Newton saw two black-haired bigfoot walking upright across a field near Dalles, Oregon. Also in June, Bob Kelley along with his family and other people at the Wildwood Inn in the Shasta-Trinity National Forest of northern California say they witnessed a

Bigfoot in the news, March 28, 1969.

6-foot, dark-brown bigfoot fighting with dogs. The bigfoot was throwing the dogs four or five feet into the air and "one dog was covered in saliva but had no teeth marks on its body." When several people arrived on the scene, the bigfoot retreated by running up a steep embankment. Usually bigfoot and dogs show an extreme antipathy to one another, and in many cases dogs will cower and even refuse to track bigfoot. The Bords' comment: "If the dogs do not cower away in terror they attack the bigfoot wildly."[3]

Another curious encounter which included a mysterious dog also happened during the summer of 1969, wherein several bigfoot were seen around a sawmill situated about 20 miles north of Orofino, Idaho. The watchman was a Mr. Moore who had seen three different sizes of footprints in the sawdust, ranging from child-size to very large. He also claimed he heard jabbering and timber being thrown about. Moore said he watched a large, black-haired female bigfoot with large breasts and red eyes for five minutes. The nipple area, face and breasts were not covered with hair. An unpleasant odor was associated with the bigfoot, as is typically indicated, but Moore also said that he saw an enormous dog (black?) with the bigfoot at times.

Reports of bigfoot with pet dogs—or perhaps a pet wolf—are extremely rare but they have been filed occasionally, as well as a bigfoot with two large cats, like cougars.

The cats feature in the Cayton family sightings near Paris Township, near Minerva, Ohio on August 21, 1978. The family of nine witnesses were sitting on their porch at 10:30 in the evening when they heard noises near a demolished chicken coop. Several in the family shone flashlights in the direction, some distance away, and saw two pairs of large yellow eyes reflecting the light of their beams. Eighteen-year-old friend Scott Patterson then drove to the area in his car to see the animals more clearly. He was astonished to see that the two pairs of eyes belonged to two cougar-like animals. As he watched the cougars, suddenly a large bigfoot strode out of the darkness between the two cougars, as if protecting them.

The large bigfoot then lurched at Patterson in his car and the teenager drove back to the house where they phoned the police. The family all sat in the kitchen in a frightened commotion waiting for the police when the bigfoot looked in the kitchen window and then was clearly seen by outdoor lighting for ten minutes while it stood

**109**

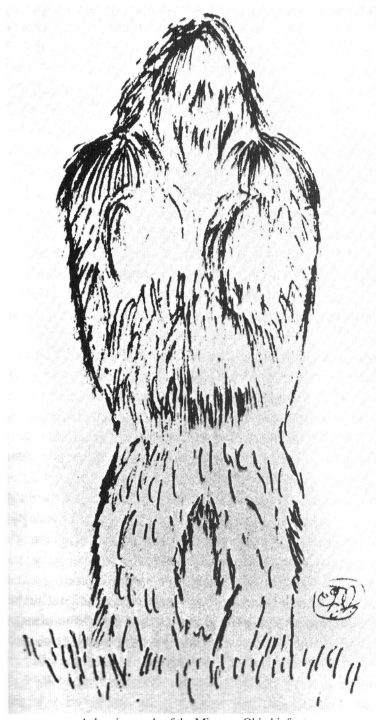

A drawing made of the Minerva, Ohio bigfoot.

there in the backyard. The bigfoot—and accompanying pumas—suddenly left and when the local sheriff arrived, deputy James Shannon, he could find nothing, except for the putrid smell which was lingering.

The next day Mrs. Cayton and a Mrs. Ackerman saw bigfoot around the house, and this time there were two of them. The authorities told them that they thought they had seen a mother bear with two bear cubs. Mrs. Cayton rejected that analysis.[3] In the summer of 2015 a film was released of the incident called *Minerva Monster*.

On July 12, 1969, a man named Charles Jackson was in his backyard with his six-year-old son, Kevin, in a forested area on Cherokee Road near Oroville, California, burning rabbit entrails in a pit. This activity attracted a female bigfoot with long grey hair and large breasts. She was about 8-feet tall with no hair on her face, breasts or palms. Jackson later said that the bigfoot seemed curious as to what he was doing, staring at him with a puzzled look. One might think that the smell of roasted rabbit entrails, rabbits being probably a standard food for bigfoot, had attracted her.

Jackson's immediate reaction was to grab his son and run inside the house. His three normally fierce dogs were all cowering beneath the furniture. This is the typical reaction to bigfoot by dogs. One wonders if dogs have an innate fear of bigfoot in their DNA or whether the smell puts them off or if previous contact with bigfoot (unknown to their owners) might have occurred. Most dogs will not attack bigfoot out of sheer fear, and as David Paulides says in his books, dogs will often refuse to track a bigfoot as well.

After they felt it was safe to leave the house, the Jackson family left their cowering dogs behind and drove to the police station in Oroville to tell the cops what was going on around their house. Yes, throughout the years police departments—and the FBI—have been called in on bigfoot reports and missing person reports that may involve bigfoot. Generally the police take these reports seriously and professionally, but there is often little they can do. The police went to the Jackson home, with the Jacksons, the next morning, as the Jackson's refused to return to their home that night. The police could not find any tracks on the hard ground around the Jackson home and some sort of vague report was filed. Later that same month a neighbor who lived on the same road also saw bigfoot and then heard strange screaming in the night.

It was a deputy policeman named Verlin Herrington who saw bigfoot in the headlights on July 26, 1969 in Gray's Harbor County, Washington. The 30-year-old deputy was driving alone in the middle of the night on Deekay Road in the direction of Copalis Beach when he rounded a curve at 2:35 A.M. to find a large creature standing in the middle of the road. He braked hard and coasted toward the figure; at first he thought that it was a bear, but noticed that it did not have the snout of a bear and he could see fingers and toes on the large critter.

Herrington took out his revolver, got out of the patrol car and put his spotlight on the creature. He later said he was prepared to shoot the bigfoot in the leg and come back in the morning to follow the trail. However, he had about two minutes to look at the bigfoot which he said was 7- to 8-feet-tall, covered in dark brown hair and had two large breasts covered with hair with nipples that were black, as was the face. Suddenly the bigfoot was gone and Herrington finished his patrol.

Herrington had not planned to publicize his sighting, as probably many policemen have decided over the decades. However, he made the mistake of telling two of his colleagues about the incident at a café, where the whole story was overheard by others. Suddenly the next day it was in the news and news agencies around the country were carrying the story. The chief of police originally wanted Herrington to change his story to that of seeing a bear, but Herrington stuck to his story and the police chief decided to be more helpful, encouraging the bigfoot story and allowing researchers such as John Green and Rene Dahinden to interview Herrington. Dahinden noted that the position of deputy sheriff was reviewed on an annual basis and Herrington lost his job the next year, but found one with the Parks Department.[3]

In September of 1969, at about three in the afternoon a worker was cutting poles with a power saw at Lost Trail Pass in Montana. He felt he was being watched and, switching off his saw, turned to see a 7-foot-tall "apeman" that must have weighed about 300 pounds watching him from about 25 feet away. Thinking that he might be attacked, he turned his saw on again. The bigfoot did not

**112**

move but the hair on its neck stood up. The man turned off his saw and the hair on the bigfoot fell flat. The bigfoot kept his eyes on the man and then gracefully moved into the trees.

Throughout the summer and fall of 1969 were the famous Fort Worth, Texas sightings in which a white-haired bigfoot cavorted through a local nature reserve, which was often packed with cars as the beast moved up and down a bluff during evening hours. At one point, the bigfoot apparently became annoyed at the onlookers and it picked up a spare tire and hurled it 500 feet towards the spectators. They all quickly got into their cars for protection.

The bigfoot was said to be 7-feet tall, was covered in white hair and weighed about 300 pounds. The local dress shop owner, Allen Plaster, took a photo of the back of the white-haired bigfoot and a local author named Sallie Ann Clarke said she saw it tearing down a barbed wire fence, rather than jumping over it.

In one frightening encounter, on November 7, 1969, a local named Charles Buchanan was sleeping in a sleeping bag in the back of his pickup truck along the lakeside in Fort Worth when he was awoken at 2 a.m. being pulled out of the pickup truck and onto the ground, while still in his sleeping bag. Buchanan said the smell of the beast was overpowering; he said he picked up a bag of leftover chicken and thrust it into the bigfoot's face. The bigfoot clenched the bag in its teeth and then shuffled into the water and "swam powerfully toward Greer Island."[3]

## 1969-1971: Ivan Marx and the Bossburg Cripple

The Bossburg Cripple footprints were first discovered in October 1969 by a local butcher named Joe Rhodes in Bossburg, Washington. The sighting was reported to Ivan Marx, whose interest in the sasquatch was well known, and who happened to live in the area. Marx made casts of the footprints. Subsequently, in the same area, Marx and the Canadian sasquatch researcher Rene Dahinden discovered a set of tracks and followed them for half a mile. Dahinden told researcher Dr. John Napier that he had counted 1,089 prints in all. The remarkable feature of the Bossburg tracks to Napier, Dahinden and Marx was that the sasquatch had a deformed

**113**

right foot.

Said Dr. Napier on examining the casts:

> The left foot appears normal, and in every respect is similar to a modern human foot—similar, that is, until one considers the matter of size. The Bossburg tracks, large even for a Sasquatch, measure 17-1/2 inches by 7 inches. Apart from satisfying the criteria established for modern human-type walking, the Bossburg prints have, to my way of thinking, an even greater claim to authenticity. The right foot of the Bossburg Sasquatch is a club-foot, a not uncommon abnormality that labors under the technical name of talipes-equino-varus. The forepart of the foot is twisted inwards, the third toe has been squeezed out of normal alignment, and possibly there has been a dislocation of the bones on the outer border (but this last feature may be due to an imperfection in the casting technique). Club-foot usually occurs as a congenital abnormality, but it may also develop as the result of severe injury, or of damage to the nerves controlling the muscles of the foot. To me, the deformity strongly suggests that injury during life was responsible. A true, untreated, congenital talipes-equino-varus usually results in a fixed flexion deformity of the ankle in which case only the forepart of the foot and toes touch the ground in normal standing. In these circumstances the heel impression would be absent or poorly defined; but in fact the heel indentation of the sasquatch is strongly defined. I conclude that the deformity was the result of a crushing injury to the foot in early childhood.

Marx had earlier accompanied Texas oil millionaire Tom Slick on some of his bigfoot expeditions, and was trusted by many of the early researchers in the field. In 1959, Slick financed the Pacific Northwest Expedition, a foray made by a group of "professional bigfoot hunters" including Bob Titmus, Rene Dahinden, John Green and Ivan Marx. This seems to be Ivan Marx's first foray into the world of professional sasquatch investigation.

Marx's early career does not seem to be marked with hoaxes.

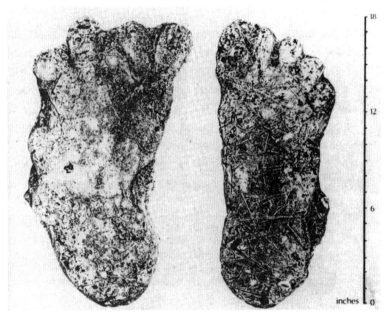

The Bossburg Cripple bigfoot casts made by Ivan Marx in 1969.

Nor were the Bossburg Cripple footprints thought at all to be a hoax—then or now. On the possibility of the Bossburg Cripple footprints being hoaxed by someone, Dr. Napier said, "It is very difficult to conceive of a hoaxer so subtle, so knowledgeable—and so sick—who would deliberately fake a footprint of this nature. I suppose it is possible, but it is so unlikely that I am prepared to discount it."

Marx, however, apparently decided to go into the bigfoot hoaxing business after this discovery. The reason for this seems to be money. Dahinden returned to Vancouver but was in regular telephone contact with Marx; it seemed that every time he called, Marx had found something—a handprint here, a footprint there, signs of an unusually heavy creature bedding down in the bush— always something to keep the trail warm. Marx was hot on the trail of sasquatch!

Marx phoned Dahinden one evening in October 1970 and proclaimed, "I've got a film of the cripple." The details of the filming were reported in the *Colville Statesman Examiner* under the byline of Denny Striker:

On the night of Oct. 6 an unidentified person called the

**115**

Marx home, leaving a vague message that either a car or a train had struck a large upright creature on the highway about seven miles north of Bossburg. Marx was away at the time but when he received the message… he left immediately for the area with a hunting dog he hoped would follow the spoor of the sasquatch, if indeed that was what it actually was.

Marx was armed with nothing more than a Bolex 16mm movie camera with a 17mm lens, a 35mm Nikon and a two-way radio with which he had contact with rancher Don Byington, who was in the area by the time Marx's dog had located the creature.

The day was heavily overcast with smoke… when Marx jumped the creature in the bottom of a dense draw and began filming. The initial footage shows a large black upright figure moving stealthily but rapidly through the dense growth, but only in silhouette.

Marx pressed the pursuit with his hound, forcing the sasquatch into a clearing where, with his movie camera set at f2.8 he took the remarkably clear footage of an impressive looking creature. On the screen the sasquatch is shown moving from right to left at an angle of about forty-five degrees away from the photographer. Distance from the subject according to Marx ranged from twenty-five feet to more than a hundred feet as it made its way into the heavy underbrush on the far side of the clearing.

Probably the most impressive part of the film, besides its extreme clarity, is the fact that the sasquatch is visibly injured, holding its right arm tightly to its chest and using its long muscular left arm for compensating balance. Also, both ankles of the creature seem badly skinned, the wounds showing plainly raw against the black hair of the legs and feet.

The story was released to the wire services and the second siege of Bossburg, Washington, was underway. Film producers made offers for the film and author Ivan T. Sanderson phoned on behalf of *Argosy Magazine*. He offered to buy the serial rights to the story, as he had done with Roger Patterson's famous 1968 film footage.

Then appeared on the scene Peter Byrne, who had been part of some Tom Slick-sponsored expeditions in the Himalayas and northern California. Tom Slick had died in a plane crash nearly a decade before, but Byrne still had a source of financing. He and Marx came to an arrangement: Marx would be paid a monthly retainer of $750 as a sasquatch hunter, and his film would be placed in Byrne's safe deposit box as security. This arrangement carried through to the spring of 1971, Marx being comfortably subsidized to pursue his hunting while at the same time having to make no commitments about the film. But Peter Byrne was considerably less gullible than he might have seemed. The young son of rancher Byington insisted that he knew exactly where the film had been shot, and Byrne listened to him. The child led him and a group of investigators to a spot at the back of the Byington property immediately recognizable as the film site. Ivan's footage was clearly a hoax.

Ivan Marx was a complicated man, as far as I can tell. He was a genuine outdoorsman, one who fought cougars bare handed and drank with the best of them. He had clearly learned to tell a tall tale around the campfire with the best of them, too. Given the bigfoot craze waxing in 1969, there was money to be made if some hunter could bag himself a real-life abominable snowman. Marx was determined to be that person (at least he said so in his movie)!

Though Marx may have genuinely believed in bigfoot, and occasionally gathered some slim evidence for the creature's existence, he decided he needed better evidence. Evidence that paid better—evidence that would make him rich and famous.

### 1972: Grover Krantz and the Ivan Marx Handprints

Longtime sasquatch researcher Grover Krantz began examining evidence from Ivan Marx starting in 1972 and found Marx to be a credible investigator. Though he had some doubts about Marx and his motives, Krantz was particularly impressed with handprints that Marx claimed to have discovered in the summer of 1972 in northern Washington.

Says Krantz:

> During the summer of 1972, handprints of two of these animals were photographed and plaster casts of them

were made by Ivan Marx, a game guide in northeastern Washington State. Marx loaned the original casts to the writer who then made latex molds from them in order to produce exact duplicates for further study.

The authenticity of these casts is impossible to demonstrate by any direct means. That they were not faked is strongly indicated by the fact that these are only the best two out of several prints that were cast, and that photographs of many more were taken. For a hoaxer to have made them all would have involved a considerable amount of difficulty.

The two good prints described here are both of left hands which were imprinted flat into soft ground showing all digits and outlines of the palms. The longer print shows all digits somewhat flexed and their tips were well indented into damp ground. It measures 292 mm. in actual length to the end of digit III, but the hand would be closer to 300 mm. long if fully extended.

The hands which supposedly made these imprints can be compared and contrasted with those of recent man in several particulars. Most obvious is their immense size—in linear dimensions they are more than half again greater than an average European's hand. My own hand, of average proportions but quite large, measures 205 mm. in length and 95 mm. in breadth. The Sasquatch hands are thus 46.4% and 29.3% longer than mine, and 83.2% and 94.6% broader, giving a mean of over 63% greater in these two dimensions. This is at least commensurate with claimed stature estimates.

Probably the most unexpected feature indicated for these hands is the apparent non-opposability of the thumb, which is clearly evident in both individuals. In the short hand the *palmar* surface of the thumb is quite flat and is in the same plane as all of the fingers. In the larger hand the thumb flexion parallels that of the other digits in digging into the ground. Still, these thumbs both separate from near the base of the palm and extend out to the side in a quite human direction.

There are many other irregularities in the casts' surfaces which cannot be identified in terms of human anatomy. Most

Two different left handprints taken by Ivan Marx in 1972 and examined by Krantz.

of these irregularities no doubt resulted from unevenness in the dirt into which the hands were pressed, and also from various particles which fell into the impressions before the casts were made.

The *thenar* pad, or eminence, at the base of the thumb is virtually non-existent. In this eminence would be found the major muscles (abductor pollicis brevis, opponens pollicis, and flexor pollicis brevis) which in man pull the opposable thumb in various ways across the palm. Since in this case the thumbs do not oppose, it is consistent that the *thenar* area is not thickened. It would require someone quite familiar with the anatomy of the human hand to make the connection between a non-opposable thumb and an absence of a *thenar* eminence. This tends to support the authenticity of these handprints. Ivan Marx has no known training in human anatomy, and no other person could have planted the many impressions without leaving his own track for Marx to observe.[45]

Ivan Marx was clearly a respected hunter and trapper, as far as Grover Krantz was concerned. In fact, Krantz considers the possibility that Marx may have hoaxed the handprints and decides that he did not. Some of the Bigfoot evidence that Marx is associated with seems quite authentic. But other "evidence" is clearly hoaxed

**119**

*The Heyday Years*
by him.

## 1971: Peter Byrne and The Bigfoot Project

The year 1971 was a big year for Bigfoot Nation. It was the year that the movie *Bigfoot* was released to theaters in northern California. A low-budget film, it nevertheless had some stars in it, plus some bikers and some decent special effects. Bigfoot was now on the big screen!

That year was also a time when Ivan Marx was promoting his discoveries of the last few years, including footprints from northern Washington State famously thought to belong to the "Bossburg Cripple." Peter Byrne, the British explorer and former head of The Bigfoot Project, had this to say about Marx and his discoveries at Bossburbg in 2003:

> Some bumbling statements have recently been made via Internet lists about the original Ivan Marx 1971 Bigfoot film footage and my association with it. The origin of the statements, the person who made them, is unimportant. But in them the footage is described as an actual film and it is suggested that at the time Marx produced it, I am guilty, with the end in view of commercial gain, of exhibiting it to local "dignitaries" in Bossburg, northern Washington, where Ivan Marx lived at that time and of making, as a result, "Lord knows how much money." The statements, like others that emanate from this same petulant source on a boringly regular basis are, as I can prove, blatantly untrue. Firstly, let's set the record straight. When I was associated with Ivan Marx, which was for the brief three months that he worked for me in early 1971, there was no film. There was a short piece of 16 mm film footage made by him, of what he said was a Bigfoot, that ran for about 30 seconds. That, truly, is all there ever was. Ivan Marx, an amateur cine photographer (and a mediocre woodsman), shot the footage in late 1970—or so he said—and when I came on the scene in early 1971 my job, as the primary focus of a new Bigfoot research program, was to examine the footage, determine its authenticity and then, like my work as designer and director

of the original northern California Bigfoot project, follow up with full time research.

When I first met Marx at the start of the 1971 Bigfoot Project—at which time I recruited him into my team as a salaried, full-time employee and provided him with camping gear, outdoor clothing, a snowmobile and a new International Scout—he told me that his BF encounter began with an early morning call from a railway train driver who said that his engine had hit a Bigfoot the night before; the man, Marx said, gave him the location of the accident and so the same day, without delay, he set out to track and find the Bigfoot. There was a blood trail, he stated, that led him up into some 4000/4500 high foothills, roughly six miles north and east of Bossburg, Washington. About midday, in bright sunshine and under a clear sky, close to the deep snowline of the upper hills, he caught up with the Bigfoot, which, he said, was limping and appeared to be injured. The creature, he stated, weighed at least 650 pounds, was covered with thick, dark brown hair and stood a minimum of eight feet in height.

Marx said that as soon as he saw the creature he turned his 16 mm movie camera on and shot about 30 seconds of footage, in three ten-second sequences, and then, dropping the camera, which he apparently carried on a shoulder strap, he quickly and with seconds to spare, pulled out his still camera and took half-a-dozen pictures. The bigfoot then disappeared and so he left the area and walked back down to a main road. There, coming out of the woods, he met several people, among them Norm Davis, the owner operator of the Colville Radio Station, Bill Harper, a Department of Immigration and Naturalization officer and Don Byington, a local rancher who later joined my research team; he told them that he had caught up with the Bigfoot and had been able to get footage and still pictures of it. Discussing the event with Marx, he told me that the place where he got the footage definitely had more Bigfoot living in it. He had, he said, seen several sets of fresh footprints while tracking the injured one and that as soon as it was spring and the snow drifts melted off, he would lead me in there and we could get more footage.

In the meantime, the area being too rugged for snowmobile access, he suggested we wait for the snow to clear; I agreed and in turn told him that in the interim he could work for me on full salary, with all expenses, on general research in the Bossburg and Colville area. As to the footage itself, which he wanted to sell to The Bigfoot Project's sponsors for $25,000, I guaranteed him this amount, to be paid after we had thoroughly examined it and were satisfied with its authenticity; in return, as a guarantee of good faith, he agreed to let us hold the master copy. He gave this to me in a sealed metal film container and I immediately sent it by registered mail to Washington DC, to the offices of my attorneys there, to be held in trust, unopened, until such time as we made a positive decision about the work. He also gave me, on request, a working copy of the footage, for study and analysis, allowing me to take selected 8x10 prints from this for the same purpose; in addition, he gave me enlargements of the still pictures he said he had taken of his film subject.

The first cracks in the authenticity of the footage appeared when I was about two and a half months into the project, in late March 1971 and they surfaced one evening during a study showing of the working copy of the footage at the home of Don Byington at his ranch about a mile to the east of Marx's Bossburg home. Present at the showing were Don, his young son Stephen—about eight at the time, Don's wife, Alta, Dennis Jensen, a veteran Bigfoot researcher who had worked with Roger Patterson and was now a member of my research team, Bill Harper and Norm Davis with his wife. (These, incidentally, were probably the local "dignitaries" referred to by the accusatory source mentioned at the beginning of this article; at the least, I feel sure, they would all have been delighted to be have been given this elevating title.) When the showing was over, I heard young Stephen whisper to his father that he recognized the place seen in the footage, the place that Marx said was the site of his Bigfoot encounter; the boy was puzzled, he said, because the place was not six miles north of Marx's house, in the hills, as Marx had stated, but actually at the edge of the forest that bordered the northern boundary of their ranch.

Stephen's remarks were heard by others but were discounted at the time as the imagination of an impressionable young boy. But later that night, lying in bed in my research base house at Evans, a scattering of small houses about halfway between Colville and Bossburg, and listening to the bitter winds of the end of winter howling in the frozen trees, I kept thinking about what the boy had said; and I found myself bothered by it. Next day I went to see Don and his wife and a little later that morning, accompanied by Don, Bill Harper, Dennis Jensen and Norm Davis, young Stephen led us on a search for the place he thought he recognized as the footage site. Sure enough, we soon found it and, using the two sets of 8x10 enlargements from the footage and the still pictures, were very quickly able to positively identify it via objects clearly seen in both the pictures and at the site itself. These latter included large rocks, stones, dead branches, frozen cow droppings, a rusting piece of metal from an old tractor and, most important, a small tree past which Marx's "creature" is seen moving in the footage, a tree with a horizontal branch under which it walks, without stooping, just before it disappears. The branch, it was noted by all, measured six feet from the ground; to walk under it, without stooping, the subject of the footage could only have been a maximum of five feet eleven inches in height.

We said nothing to Marx about our discovery, which was plainly that he had misled us about the site of the footage, but continued to employ him, his principal job being to search for footprints. (He reported finding several sets over the course of some weeks but for various reasons was never able to lead us back to them.) In the meantime we pondered on our discovery, and privately discussed it, and it worried us. In the last days of March I got a call from Norm Davis. He said that he had made an important discovery about the footage and that I should come quickly to his offices at the radio station in Colville. I did so and there found Don

Byington, Bill Harper and Dennis Jensen waiting. Norm sat us down around his desk, on which he had laid out the aforementioned two sets of enlargements. He brought us all coffee, waited while we examined the pictures and then said, "So, do you see it? Do you see what I've discovered?"

We could not see whatever it was he wanted us to see and so he leaned forward and pointed. The film subject, in both sets of pictures, photographed in bright sunshine, had a distinctive shadow. And the shadow angles of each set were different, clearly indicating that the two phases of photography—the movie photography, and the still shot—had been carried out at different times and not, as Marx had told us, seconds apart. We had a brief meeting and then decided that it was time to have a serious talk with Mr. Ivan Marx to ask him, among other things, how he could have been mistaken—to put it kindly—about the site of his filming and how it was that the movie footage and the still pictures appeared to have been taken at different intervals. And so next morning, at six am—to confront our enigmatic employee while he was still drinking coffee, so to speak, we all went to Marx's rented home, a dilapidated tar paper shack just off the highway at Bossburg, to find out what he had to say about the little discrepancies in his story.

Alas, we were too late. In the night—as was clearly indicated by the discarded personal belongings strewn across his front yard—our quarry had got wind of our plans and, as they say, had upped and run for cover. And in a hurry he left a veritable river of trash running from the open, flapping-in-the-wind front door of the shack to where he parked his Volkswagen Bug, one that included ancient and tattered magazines and newspapers, old patched and re-patched gum boots, torn cotton towels, plastic rain coats, ragged shirts, woolen hats, ripped up, oil and grease stained work shirts and trousers, empty motor oil containers, rusting baked bean and soup cans, stained and ragged blankets, mayonnaise and jam and pickle jars and dog food cartons and half filled trash bags. (In answer to the unspoken question, no, the abandoned garbage did not contain a fur

124

suit.) Marx headed, as we heard later, for Burney, a town in northern California where he lived before coming north to make his Bigfoot film and find fame and fortune in the Bigfoot world and, yes, as was to be expected, we never saw or heard from him again.

Meanwhile, back in Washington DC, Marx's original footage supposedly lay in the office safe of my attorneys and that posed a question… in the light of our discovery of the fact that the footage was obviously a total fabrication, were we justified in opening the sealed canister that he had left with us in good faith, pending its purchase by us for an agreed $25,000? I consulted with the members of my team and then made a call and told my attorneys to go ahead and open it. They did this, to find that the canister did indeed contain probably a hundred feet of neatly coiled film. Original Bigfoot footage of Marx's immortal achievement? Alas no, or if you like, laughingly no… for what the wily Mr. Ivan Marx had given us was about a hundred small cut pieces of old Disney, black and white Mickey Mouse footage from the fifties and sixties.

The Marx "film" from which we all made "Lord knows how much money?"—There never was a film. And there certainly was never any money made from it. How could there be, when it never existed? Later, I understand, Mr. Marx went on to make several full-length Bigfoot films, which he distributed commercially. Some of them, I have been told, are quite extraordinary—hilarious might be a better word—and show Bigfoots swimming, running and jumping, bathing in a river, playing kick-the-can, climbing trees and, in one case, actually waving at the photographer! But this was later, and not while we were associated with him. Nope. All we got for our honest efforts was Mickey Mouse and, darn it, not even in color.

There was a sequel to Marx's venture in cinematography in the fall of 1972. On Saturday Oct. 21 he appeared on "You Asked for It," a U.S. television show that pursues odd and interesting items at the request of its entranced audience. This time Marx appeared with the show's host, clutching a sealed container of movie film of a creature he said he had photographed during a snowstorm in northern California. Marx's never-ending search for the truth had once more culminated in his seeing a sasquatch, this time a white one.

He had followed it through the deepening snow until he realized he could predict its route and, as he quaintly put it, "head it off at the pass." This he did, having enough time to set up his camera, tripod and all, before the thing lurched into view. The TV host then explained that Marx had brought the film straight from the camera, undeveloped, and that the show's producer would process the film under the strictest of supervision and would then examine it. Following a commercial break we were flashed ahead in time to where the film had been processed, and then the film was shown.

It was marvelously clear footage. I remember seeing it myself on television. A primate expert whom the TV people had co-opted for an opinion said it best: "I think it's a man in a beast's suit." It certainly looked like someone in a beast's suit. Great folds of the suit swung around like an old army blanket amid the California snows as might happen if one were running through deep snow in an overcoat. The thing cavorted before the camera, now running comically toward it, now turning about and gallivanting off through the drifts, flipping its clumsy feet backwards and sideways as it went. Marx had clearly hoaxed the footage and most of the audience had little doubt that they were watching a snow job in a blizzard.

One of the things that makes Ivan Marx' hoaxed footage valuable is that it shows what is the best effort of the time (1971-72) to fake movie or video footage of a walking bigfoot. Here is Marx, doing his best to fool the inspectors with his gorilla suit. It doesn't work. Everyone can see that it is a tall man in a gorilla suit, folds of fur, zippers and all.

If we look at that most famous of

The film *Bigfoot* came out in 1971.

all bigfoot footage, the 1967 Patterson Bluff Creek film, does this look like someone's best effort at being a (female) bigfoot in a store-bought gorilla suit? I mean, wow, this is the best gorilla suit footage one could possibly hoax! The sad part is that rodeo riders need love—and money—too. These outdoorsmen know bigfoot exits, but cashing in on their years of searching for the elusive critter is pretty darn tough. You can fake some photos for a while, but sooner or later, you are going to actually film bigfoot. Why? Because he's out there! However, Bigfoot Nation does not seek publicity and therefore its citizens know better then to pose for the camera as they may have done in the past.

⚬ —ᨆ— ⚬

### 1971: The Creature of Sycamore Flat

One amusing incident, almost out of a B-horror movie, was the Sycamore Flat Campground incident that took place near Palmdale, California in the summer of 1971. During that summer, three local students (Brian Goldojarb, Richard Engels and Willie Roemerman) were driving along an area known as The Flat, which is really just a narrow strip of camping area with picnic tables on the edge of the road, on the western edge of the Antelope Valley in the Angeles National Forest, southwest of the town of Pearblossom.

The three boys were in Willie's pickup truck with Willie driving. Richie and Brian were riding in the truck's bed. As they drove past the campground late at night a huge creature suddenly bolted from the campground and followed the men in their pickup. After running (seemingly) after the truck for about 50 feet, the dark-colored creature suddenly veered off the road and plunged into a swamp. The whole episode lasted for about 20 seconds.[3]

As it veered, according to the witnesses, its head brushed an overhanging tree branch that was nearly 10 feet off the ground. The height of the cardboard cutout in their famous photograph was based on the tree branch. The Creature of Sycamore Flat was later dubbed "Big Ben" by locals and it made continual appearances in the area. It had a habit of standing straight-backed, arms akimbo, on high ridges at night as if surveying the action down below.

In July of 1971 two women in the backwoods of Missouri

encountered a bigfoot. Joan Mills and Mary Ryan had stopped their Volkswagen on Highway 79, a backwoods road near the town of Louisiana, Missouri. They were planning on having a picnic lunch and had just set out the food and began eating when a powerful and terrible smell assaulted them. Mary Ryan said, "I never smelled anything so bad in my life."

Joan Mills likened the smell to a "whole family of skunks." Then the women saw a figure standing behind them in the bushes and waist-high weeds. Mary described the figure as half human and half ape, "the face was definitely human… like a hairy human."

With a gurgling sound the bigfoot began to walk toward the women who ran to their car and locked the doors. The bigfoot, still making gurgling sounds, walked up to the car and rubbed it with his hands and tried to open one of the doors. The women could not start the car because the keys were in Joan's purse that was still on the picnic spread. Joan sounded the car horn and the bigfoot jumped backward and then kept his distance He eventually examined the food on the picnic spread before him and wolfed a peanut butter sandwich down in one gulp after sniffing it. It then picked up the purse holding the car keys and took a few steps before dropping it and continuing on into the forest. Once he was out of sight Joan sprinted to the purse and returned to the car with the keys and they drove out of the area at high speed.[3]

## 1972: Roachdale, Indiana Terrified by Bigfoot

During August of 1972 people in the rural areas around Roachdale, Indiana had a number of bigfoot encounters. Roachdale is in central-western Indiana, near the Illinois border, and is famous for its Fourth of July cockroach races, a gimmick started by the town mayor in 1981. During 1972, husband and wife Randy and Lou Rogers, were living in a farmhouse outside of the town when, for several nights in a row, a loud banging on the walls and windows of the house occurred. Randy ran out of the house one night with a shotgun in his hands to catch the culprit and saw a 6-foot-tall bigfoot running into a nearby cornfield.

The nighttime visits continued for nearly three weeks, with the smelly creature arriving between 10 and 11:30 every night to pound on the walls of the farmhouse. Lou Rogers became curious about the bigfoot and reasoned that if it had meant to harm them it would have already done so, therefore she began leaving scraps of food out in the evening. The bigfoot began taking the food and would occasionally pop his head up to a window and look inside at Mrs. Rogers. Both Randy and Lou said that the bigfoot would stand on two legs but it ran on all four limbs. A curious illuminated object, like a UFO, was seen hovering above the cornfield where the bigfoot would often disappear.

Then on August 22 at least 60 chickens were found dead on the Roachdale farm owned by Carter Burdine and his uncle Bill Burdine. The chickens had been dismembered and drained of blood, but their bodies not eaten. They were strewn for 200 feet around the chicken house; when they brought the local marshal out to survey the scene, he, together with the Burdines, saw a large animal dash across a nearby road and smash part of a fence down. It left a deep trail through the weeds.

The next day the two men took Carter Burdine's wife into town to stay with relatives until the strange episode was over, and when they returned to the farm they saw a massive bigfoot standing in the 8-foot-high doorway to the chicken house. It completely filled the doorway with its head about a foot higher than the opening, giving the bigfoot a massive appearance. The two men were joined by Carter's father, Herman, and the three of them grabbed their shotguns and cornered the bigfoot in the nearby hay barn. It broke out and ran into the night with the men firing their shotguns at the creature. The men then discovered that another 110 chickens, out of an original flock of 200, had been dismembered and drained of blood. It appears the bigfoot had so much available food in the chicken house that he gorged himself on chicken blood. He did not return to the farm and things quieted down in rural Roachdale.[3]

### 1973: Bigfoot in the Rear Window

A curious incident occurred in early June 1973 in the northwestern part of rural Jefferson County, Arkansas when four teenagers— Sandra, Gail, Ricky and Jessie—were in Ricky's car taking some trash to a dump off Gravel Pit Road. Caught in a downpour from a sudden thunderstorm, the group was waiting in the car for the rain to stop when they heard the crunching of gravel on the road behind them followed by a sudden scream followed by a growl.

They turned and looked out the rear window and saw—lit up by the taillights of the car—a bigfoot that was 7 to 8 feet tall with glowing red eyes. They could smell a foul odor, "like rotting flesh;" Ricky started the car and they moved out of the area. They saw the bigfoot (or an identical one) three more times that night, as it darted out and crossed the track in front of them as they drove down the hilly road, and then they saw it behind them a while later. The bigfoot seemed to be following them, and after they got home, some 7 miles from the dump, they later heard a noise outside and discovered the bigfoot standing next to some rabbit cages on the property. The creature ambled off into the woods and continued to be seen in the area throughout the summer.[3]

On the evening of September 27, 1973 two girls were waiting for a lift in rural Westmoreland County, Pennsylvania when they saw a white, hairy bigfoot with red eyes standing in the nearby woods, apparently watching them. The girls were also surprised to see that it was carrying a luminous sphere in its hand. The girls rushed to their nearby home and told their father who went into the woods for an hour and later told the girls to stay out of the woods. Later it was reported that some sort of UFO was seen in the area, hovering over the forest with a powerful searchlight coming to the ground from the object.

Strange things started happening around Greensburg in western Pennsylvania in October, where approximately 15 people saw a dome-shaped luminous object near the ground and then later two bigfoot were seen in the area, one about 7 feet tall and the other about 8 feet tall. Then in Uniontown, Pennsylvania in November of 1973 a man was walking his dog one night when he saw a trespasser on his land and called out to him. The figure came toward him and he saw that it was a tall bigfoot with red glowing eyes. Because of wild dogs in woods, the man always carried a revolver and he promptly emptied all six rounds from the pistol into the bigfoot. The creature suddenly vanished but a screaming could be heard. The wife also heard the bigfoot making a sound like "a human that was in deep pain."[3]

## 1974: Bigfoot Continues to Terrorize Pennsylvania

130

The sightings around Uniontown, Pennsylvania continued in February of 1974. On the night of February 6, a woman, identified as "Mrs. A," was sitting in her house watching television. Around 10 p.m. she heard a noise on her front porch where she kept two large tins of food. Her house was in a wooded area and there were wild dogs that she suspected of rummaging around the porch. She picked up a shotgun and stepped onto the porch expecting to scare off some dogs. Instead she was facing a 7-foot-tall bigfoot that was standing about six feet from her. The bigfoot raised both of its arms above his head and the woman took it to be a sign that he was about to jump at her. She pulled the trigger on her shotgun and with a huge flash the bigfoot was completely gone.

Her phone suddenly rang and it was her daughter's husband who lived in the next house, about 100 feet away, who had heard the shotgun blast. Mrs. A told the man her story and he grabbed his revolver and began walking to her house. Along the way he supposedly encountered four or even five hairy creatures, all seven feet high with glowing red eyes, emerged from the woods and headed towards him. He fired at them and ran to the house of Mrs. A. Together they decided to phone the police, and while waiting for the sheriff to arrive, noticed what seemed to be a glowing red UFO hovering over the woods near the house. The state police quickly arrived and could find no footprints on the frozen ground but noted that the animals on the property, including a horse, seemed to be acting in a frightened and atypical manner.

Beginning in July of 1974 a woman from Watova settlement near Nowata, in northeast Oklahoma, began seeing a brown-haired bigfoot around the house she shared with her husband. Nowata was originally part of the Cherokee Nation reservation. Mrs. Margie Lee would spot the 6-foot-tall bigfoot, which she considered a young male, around the settlement and she noted that the bigfoot was interested in homes where women lived and completely ignored houses where single men lived. She and her husband, John Lee, theorized that the young male was seeking a mate. Indeed, it has been shown that bigfoot takes more interest in homes with women in them and seems to have a desire to mate with these women. One can surmise that it can get lonely for the young bucks out on the weekend in Bigfoot Nation.

Margie and John became rather fond of their neighborhood bigfoot and even played a little game with him. They discovered that the bigfoot would put a feed pail in the doorway of the barn, blocking the door. So they began hiding the feed pail every day somewhere around barn and the bigfoot would sniff it out every night and place it in the barn doorway. The only time Margie ever heard the bigfoot make a sound was once when it seemed to be laughing. Eventually it became a nuisance, breaking chicken wire windows in the barn and stealing chickens from their neighbor.

Two sheriff's deputies, Gilbert Gilmore and Buck Field, encountered the bigfoot one night late in the summer of 1974 and opened fire on it. It was in the headlights of their patrol car and they both opened up on the bigfoot which ran off into the woods, seemingly unhurt. The next morning Margie said she was taking a shower when she heard a big thump on the wall outside the shower. She dashed to the window to see if she would see bigfoot but he was already gone and that was his last farewell to Margie. He was not seen in the area again.[3]

The next year in Noxie, Oklahoma, only a few miles north of Nowata, a farmer named Kenneth Tosh heard a scratching sound coming from a derelict house near his own home. He called a friend and they approached the empty residence around 8 p.m. where they came within 10 feet of a 7- to 8-foot-tall bigfoot. It was completely covered in long hair except for the nose and eyes. The men fired pistols at the bigfoot which ran off, apparently unharmed. During that year over 20 people reported seeing or hearing the Noxie bigfoot.[3] Was it the same lonely bigfoot seen at Nowata the year before?

## 1975: The Legend of Bigfoot Film Hoax

During the summer of 1975 a number of bigfoot were reported around the Lummi Indian Reserve near Bellingham, Washington. There were over 100 reports including some by Reserve policemen. One of these, Sergeant Ken Cooper, was called out on October 24 at 2:20 in morning to investigate a report of a prowler who had ripped a plastic storm door off its hinges. He was with several other people when his patrol car spotlight illuminated a black, hairy bigfoot that was seven-and-a-half-feet tall standing in the backyard of the house.

It had a flat nose, and two upper and two lower teeth were longer than the others, essentially fangs. Sgt. Cooper approached the bigfoot with a pistol but did not fire. There was a sudden movement when another of the witnesses (eight in all) shouted that there "was another one over there," and the officer retreated. Later they found large footprints.[3]

Also in 1975 the famous hunter and trapper Ivan Marx was at it again when an oddball documentary was released: *The Legend of Bigfoot. The Legend of Bigfoot* is a unique film by all standards. It is the true story of Ivan Marx, a professional tracker, who becomes obsessed by bigfoot and sets out to film, capture and/or kill a bigfoot.

The film starts with a shot of Marx in his signature red flannel shirt, introducing himself and his topic. Apparently shot in a combination of 16 mm and 35 mm film, the documentary is like an extended episode of the 1960s television show *Wild Kingdom,* or some Lion's Club presentation on big game hunting—except the quarry this time is the elusive bigfoot. But, for Ivan Marx, bigfoot is not so elusive. With his amazing tracking ability, Marx is able to find bigfoot just about everywhere he goes!

In fact, as the movie goes on, it is astonishing how Marx is able to find—and film—bigfoot from the Arctic Circle to the American Southwest. The bizarre mix of seemingly real bigfoot footage with Marx's authentic backwoodsman style (and the gnawing sense that it just isn't quite real), makes the film a genuine curiosity that is quite amusing. If the various shots of bigfoot in this movie were genuine, then Marx would be the most prolific photographer of bigfoot ever to live—or conversely, the biggest hoaxer of bigfoot who ever lived. Indeed, the latter is more probable. But is everything hoaxed in the film? Definitely not. Was Marx a believer in bigfoot? Well, it would seem that he did believe in bigfoot, but hoaxed film footage of the beast anyway. Either way, the saga of Ivan Marx is a fascinating story.

Marx tells us at the beginning of the film that he is a professional tracker who, working occasionally for the government, "removed" rogue animals from areas where they were presumably killing livestock and such. Marx first

Ivan Marx in his movie.

**133**

heard of bigfoot in Kodiak, Alaska where ranchers claimed it was killing their cows. Interested by the stories he heard, Marx began a quest to track down the mysterious beast and bring back proof of its existence.

Marx first travels to the Petrified Forest of Arizona where 700-year-old petroglyphs reveal mysterious man-like creatures with mighty big hands. Marx then finds footprints 18 inches long in 52-inch strides that could only have been made by a critter in excess of 500 pounds. The hair samples he finds nearby were tested and "couldn't be matched with any known animal."

He heads up to the Yukon in his VW bug where lumberjacks show him some rock cairns that could only have been made by bigfoot because they are in an inaccessible area. After this there is a segment about the gold rush and Marx muses how the influx of gold miners must have had quite an impact on the local bigfoot population, but concludes that bigfoot must hide himself to survive.

Farther north, Marx expounds upon a theory that a local has told him that the reason no one has found any bigfoot remains is because the creatures carry their dead thousands of miles north to bury them in crevasses that open up in glaciers in the summer. He is told by the local Eskimos that bigfoot breeds in the mating grounds of the Alaskan moose. We are treated here to scenes of Glacier Bay and a glacier falling into the ocean, followed by Marx's obligatory moose mating shots and an extended interlude of the Northern Lights.

It's time for some more (faked?) bigfoot shots,

One of Marx's presumed fake bigfoot photos.

though. Marx sets up some walkie-talkies on the tundra and waits. Then things get kind of kooky. We're shown footage of something in the early light of dawn that Marx says is the glowing eyes of a bigfoot. It's odd footage, that's for sure, though it seems like a puppet with flashlights for eyes more than anything else. Marx later confesses that it must have been swamp gas. One begins to guess that Ivan Marx is a heavy drinker, among other things.

Winter is coming up in the Arctic, so Marx knows he has to find bigfoot fast. He charters a plane and finds a young Bigfoot standing on a sandbar in a river and gets crystal clear, daylight shots of the dark biped. After footage of some hunters shooting caribou, Marx beds down in Beaver Swamp where he finds more of the giant hairy critters. This time there are two of them splashing around in the water and getting some of that famous stink off of themselves.

With that, the film winds up as best it can, and Marx seems satisfied at last with the evidence for bigfoot that he has presented. Thank God he never shot one of the beasts, though the film has plenty of animal gore and death in it. What is particularly captivating about the movie is that Marx seems so genuine in his demeanor and in his earnestness to capture bigfoot, yet the hoax is so blatantly apparent. It's like Marlin Perkins in the aforementioned *Wild Kingdom* drinking a bottle of Yukon Jack and filming a sasquatch around practically every corner of the woods he stumbles upon.

If Bigfoot Nation had ever hired a publicity department, it was probably headed by Ivan Marx in the early seventies. He did the best he could, portraying the denizens of Bigfoot Nation as going about their daily chores such as bathing and hunting with a certain zest for life. In the evening they create mysterious lights that amuse both bigfoot and humans. Ivan Marx may not have been the most sophisticated pitchman for Bigfoot Nation, but he was basically all they had.

## 1976: Bigfoot tries to Grab Child

A frightening incident happened in Flintsville, Tennessee on April 26, 1976 after a number of bigfoot reports had been made around the town in the preceding days, including a report of a bigfoot grabbing the aerial of a woman's car and jumping onto its roof. On April 26, Mrs. Jennie Robertson was in her house while her 4-year-old son Gary was playing outside in the evening when she heard her son cry out. She rushed out and said she saw:

> …this huge figure coming around the corner of the house. It was 7 or 8 feet tall and seemed to be all covered with hair. It reached out its long, hairy arm toward Gary and came within a few inches of him before I could grab him and pull him back inside.

Mr. Robertson ran to the door when he realized something was happening and glimpsed a big black shape disappearing into the woods. Six men then tracked the bigfoot and got near enough to fire guns at it. It threw big rocks at them and ran into the bush. The next day they returned to the scene and found 16-inch-long footprints as well as hair and blood.[3]

In August of 1976 there were a number of bigfoot sightings in the Whitehall area of New York state. The 7- to 8-foot hairy creature, described as having red eyes, was seen on August 24 by Marty Paddock and Paul Gosselin several times and they telephoned Gosselin's brother who was a state trooper. The trooper also witnessed the bigfoot, flashing his spotlight at the hairy creature, who covered his eyes and ran off screaming.[3]

On the evening of September 3, 1976 Barbara Pretula claimed that she saw a bigfoot behind her store in Wycliff, British Columbia (a small ski town near Kimberley in southern British Columbia, near the U.S. border). She said it was black with a light haired stomach and was 6 or 7 feet tall. She managed to take a Polaroid photo of the creature and the flash of the camera frightened it and it ran into the bush. Said Pretula: "I was about 15 feet from it when I took the picture. It didn't seem me come up, I snuck around beside the building. It was just looking down on its hind legs." The fuzzy photo purportedly shows the size and shape of the sasquatch. Apparently the photo has never been published.[7]

Earlier that day in Wycliff a fireman named Mickey McLelland reported that he and a friend plus several other witnesses saw a sasquatch in a field north of Kimberley, British Columbia.

**136**

McLelland described the bigfoot as 7 feet tall with black hair and a tan-colored chest and long arms. McLelland and his friend got out of their car and chased the bigfoot who ran down the road at a quick pace. The two returned to their car and began to chase the bigfoot down the road, clocking it at 50 miles per hour when the bigfoot suddenly veered into the forest. There were two other cars that were parked in the area with 6 to 8 witnesses who all saw the whole event which took nearly four minutes. This may have been the same sasquatch that was apparently lurking behind Barbara Pretula's store in Wycliff about half an hour later.[7]

## 1977: Bigfoot Lifts Truck in Maryland

On May 11 at a remote farm near the town of Wantage in northern New Jersey, the Sites family noticed that seven of their pet rabbits had been killed inside the barn where they were kept. They then noticed a 7-foot-tall bigfoot standing beneath the farmyard lamp. Mrs. Sites described the bigfoot:

> It was big and hairy; it was brown; it looked like a human with a beard and moustache; it had no neck; it looked like its head was just sitting on its shoulders; it had big red glowing eyes.

The bigfoot was seen again the next day and on May 13 the children were taken to stay with relatives while armed men staked out the farm. When the bigfoot suddenly showed up beneath the farm lamp two men opened fire with a rifle and a shotgun. The bigfoot ran into the woods and Mr. Sites attempted to follow in his truck.

Ronald Jones of Anne Arundel County, Maryland was driving a pickup truck down Route 258 on the night of August 30, 1977 when he saw what he thought was a human body lying near the road and stopped to investigate. The body was in fact an 8-foot-tall bigfoot exuding a strong odor and it stood up as Jones approached it. The frightened motorist threw a tire iron at the approaching bigfoot and ran back to his truck. The bigfoot allegedly hit Jones on the back of his head as he got into the truck. The bigfoot then prevented Jones from driving away by holding the back of the truck up. Jones was able to reverse the truck and back into the bigfoot before speeding away. The bigfoot screamed "like a woman" and left claw marks on the driver's door.[3]

The remote town of Little Eagle in South Dakota had a series of bigfoot encounters in September and October of 1977. Hanna Shooting Bear, a 70-year-old grandmother spotted a smelly bigfoot in her trailer park and tried to get her dogs to attack it but they hid beneath a car instead. Then on October 29 Lieutenant Verdell Veo of the Bureau of Indian Affairs, together with his sons and two other police officers, spotted a bigfoot in the moonlight near Elkhorn Buttes outside of Little Eagle. One of Veo's sons reported seeing a second bigfoot at the scene and they watched one of the creatures through a night scope on one of their rifles. Then on November 5, officer Veo and his men were joined by a rancher who helped them chase down a bigfoot in their pickup trucks but the creature escaped.[3]

## 1979: Knobby, the South Carolina Bigfoot Appears

Knobby, the South Carolina bigfoot was seen in the last months of 1978 and then appeared again on January 15, 1979. The creature had been seen from time to time around Carpenter's Knob in Cleveland County, South Carolina and as such got the name "Knobby." On that January day, 18-year-old Gaye Smith was driving with her two sisters on Highway 10 in broad daylight when her sister saw the creature and screamed. It took them a few minutes to turn the car around and they then saw Knobby standing in some woods near a farm pond. Gaye ran from the car and approached the bigfoot which was crouching on a dam next to the pond. Knobby stood up and spread his arms out. Said Gaye:

> It was awful! Just terrible! He was great big—maybe bigger than Dale [a 6-foot-2-inch friend] and terribly strange looking …he had wide shoulders and a shining black chest. …he looked more like a gorilla than anything else I can think of. And there was something white beside him on the dam. I don't know if it was a bird he killed or just an empty sack or paper bag. Whatever it was it didn't move, and I couldn't tell if it was some kind of animal or not.[3]

**138**

In March of 1979 Tom Goff and his wife were in their home at Flower Lake near Tunica, Mississippi, when they heard a ruckus outside. Investigating, they smelled a strong, foul odor and the next evening they spotted a 7- or 8-foot bigfoot in the woods near the house. The next evening, March 9, Tom and his son Rodney armed themselves and waited for bigfoot. When he showed up again they fired a volley of .22 bullets from their rifles and the bigfoot ran away. He came back later that night, however, and pushed on the front door, breaking the frame. The next day the terrified family found blood spots on the door and footprints 16 to 18 inches long.[3] Yes, bigfoot does bleed, but the medical facilities in Bigfoot Nation are scant.

Bullets were flying again in late April of 1979 at Dunn Lake outside of Barriére, British Columbia. On April 28 Tim Meissner (16) with three of his friends saw a sasquatch at the lake. After the bigfoot disappeared the boys went to investigate and discovered a dead deer that was concealed under branches and moss. Its neck had been broken and the hind legs were missing.

Then on April 30 the boys returned to the site at Dunn Lake and separated in their search for the bigfoot. Meissner, now alone, suddenly encountered the bigfoot and shot at him. Said Meissner:

> He was about 9 feet tall, black and hairy. He had a human-like face with great big glaring bright eyes and shoulders 4 feet wide. He stood there glaring at me for at least three seconds. He was 50 feet away—so close I could smell him. I don't even know why I shot. I was just scared, really scared. I was aiming for right between the eyes and he went down on one knee and one hand. At first I thought he was dead, but I guess I only grazed him, because he got up and ran away at about 30 miles an hour. It couldn't have been any other animal, and it wasn't a human because no human can run that fast, especially straight up an embankment.

Meissner ran back to get his friends, one of whom had a camera, and they searched for evidence of the creature. They found a five-toed footprint with no evidence of claws that was 16 inches long and

9 inches wide at the ball of the foot.[7]

### 1980: Kentucky White-Haired Bigfoot

According to the Bigfoot Research Organization (Bfro.net) there were several sightings in Kentucky in 1980, including the reporting of a tall, white-haired apelike creature on October 7 near the town of Mayslick in Mason County.

According to the BFRO report, the witness, known as "C.F.," was watching television with his family when they heard a loud noise on the front porch. C.F. said that he heard his son's pet rooster squawking so he peered out the front door, where he saw a white, hairy creature with pink eyes. He said that the creature must have weighed about 400 pounds and was about seven feet tall. It was holding the rooster by the neck and then threw it against the side of the house. The white-haired bigfoot then proceeded around the back of the house to a vacant lot. C.F. says he grabbed his .22 pistol and followed the apeman. He fired at the creature twice, as it ran out of sight. BFRO says that there was a small article concerning the incident in the *Cincinnati Enquirer*.

The same white-haired bigfoot (or could it have been a different one?) was seen the next month, November 5, 1980, also in Mason County. According to the BFRO report, which was taken from a police report and information given by a reporter named Doug McGill from the local radio station WFTM, an Alabama truck driver identified as "N.C." said that he was hauling steel west on U.S. Route 68 when he saw a figure on the opposite side of the highway. He slowed his vehicle and turned on his high beams thinking that it was a hitchhiker.

When he approached the figure, he was shocked to see a six- to seven-foot-tall "apelike" creature with white hair. After his encounter, he contacted some locals on C.B. channel 22 to see if there was a circus or zoo in the area. He thought that possibly an ape had escaped. When police were called to investigate, they took N.C.'s statement and filed a report. He stated to police that he had never been to this area before and knew nothing about alleged bigfoot reports in the area.

The white-haired bigfoot that was seen at this time seems quite kingly as he stands by the highway watching the cars and trucks go

**140**

by. "What's it all about?" he may wonder as he stares at the big rigs with their lights and honking horns. These are the real monsters that we have to worry about, I suppose, on the lost highways of Bigfoot Nation.

## 1980: Bigfoot Sightings in Ohio

Bigfoot showed up in Ohio and surrounding areas during the 1980s with great regularity. A typical account from the time is the one that ran in Dayton's *Ohio Daily News* on June 24, 1980 with the headline, "'Bigfoot' Sightings Scare Socks Off Pair":

> Bellefontaine, Ohio—Does Logan County have a "Big Foot" stalking its wooded hills between West Mansfield and the Union County line? Sheriff's deputies are investigating a sighting by an off-duty Russell's Point police officer who said he saw a "seven-feet-tall, hairy animal" in his barn yard Sunday night and a similar report from Union County last Tuesday. Ray Quay, a Russell's Point police officer who owns a small farm on Twp. Road 132 near West Mansfield, said he was "surprised and dumbfounded" about what he saw Sunday night.
>
> "I was unloading eight pigs I had bought about 11 p.m. I shut off the light in the barn and went around the corner to see what my two dogs were raising Cain about. They never bark when I'm around. I stepped around the corner of the barn and saw this hairy animal. I thought it was a man so I hollered at him. It took off and I've got some weeds out back I haven't mowed and they are waist high or higher and the creature went through them with no problem," Quay said.
>
> Four deputies searched the area but found nothing. Deputies said that last Tuesday Patrick Poling, who lives on County Rd. 142 in Union County east of West Mansfield, was cultivating a field when he said he spotted a creature walking out of some woods and stride along a road near where the farmer was working.
>
> Poling said he walked over to try to get a better look at the creature, but it ran back into the woods. Poling's description was similar to that of the creature Quay said he

saw. Poling said the creature walked up-right all the time. The Lima [bigfoot] research team, a non-profit organization, took measurements and a cast of three claw marks found on the Union County farm. The claw prints are about 40 inches apart. The claw mark has four toes and measures 16 inches by 4 inches, deputies said.

Bigfoot has shown up along rivers, sleeping on roads (such as the one seen by Donna Riegler of Marysville, Ohio on June 24, 1980—a hairy creature that hobbled away after she put the car in reverse) and in cornfields in rural areas. He even showed up on the Jack Nicklaus-designed golf course near Dublin, Ohio several times in 1973.

Nicklaus designed the Muirfield Village Golf Club in 1966, and it was apparently named after him for some years. In October of 1973 two security guards, plus other witnesses, said they saw an eight-foot "hairy monster" near the course. Later they saw the creature actually on the golf course. The spokesman for the Franklin County Sheriff's Department said that the monster was spotted three times by the guards around the facility. A footprint about 12 inches long and seven inches wide was discovered alongside a creek, and the supervisor of the security firm for the course doubled the number of guards on duty.[66]

On May 1, 1980, newspapers in Indiana carried the strange story of a young couple, Tom and Connie Courter, who, with a six-week-old baby in the back seat, had a bigfoot encounter in rural Ohio County, Indiana.

The Courters had left their mother's house and were driving back up Henschen Road between the towns of Aurora and Rising Sun to their trailer. Once home, Tom got out of the car first so that he could get the diaper bag out of the back seat. As he turned around, he heard a strong noise which sounded like an "UGH." As he looked up, he saw a large hairy animal about "18 inches" away.

Tom said in an interview that the creature was about 12 feet tall, black and hairy, with large red eyes. He further stated that its head was shaped like a human's and that its arms were hanging to the ground. Tom quickly jumped into his car, and spun his tires as the creature took a swing at him. Tom said that the creature hit his car.

**142**

Both Tom and Connie were obviously very scared and they went directly back to their mother's house.

On the next night, they stayed at their mother's house until 11:45 before heading home. This time, Tom was prepared with his 16-shot .22. They had been parked in front of their trailer for a while when they saw the same animal standing next to a tree on the other side of the road. Tom fired one shot at the creature, but missed. He fired several more shots. He said that the animal seemed to dive to the ground and then vanish.

The Courters filed a police report, but the Ohio County Sheriff's department were very skeptical, and said they could find no evidence of the creature. (This incident was reported by the Bigfoot Research Organization)

### 1981: Something Big and Hairy in Indiana

The next year the Vincennes, Indiana newspaper *The Valley Advance* (Vol. 18, No. 6, October 6, 1981) reported that several people had encountered a hairy apeman in the White River area of southwest Indiana.

Said the article with the headline, "White River Encounters: Area Residents See 'Something Big and Hairy'":

> Jack Lankford is an avid fisherman and hunter who says he never left a fire unattended until the night of Aug. 22. That's the night he saw a "creature" while fishing in the White River bottom land about six miles south of Highway 50. Roger and Barbara Crabtree say they live in fear of a "hairy creature" they have seen twice near their Decker Chapel home in southern Knox County close to the White River.
>
> Terry and Mary Harper haven't seen anything, but something attacked their house at 2002 South 15th Street, Vincennes. The unknown assailant ripped and apparently chewed on aluminum siding and tore away part of the metal trim around the backdoor of the house. It left behind teeth marks, blood and tufts of white hair about two inches long.
>
> So far the incidents are unrelated. No evidence of a creature has been found in the areas where the sightings

took place. However, Lankford says what he saw was no bear, and the Crabtrees know that people may not believe, but their fear is "very real."

Lankford anticipated a "good bit of fishing" last Aug. 22 when he went to his favorite spot on the lower part of what is called Beaver Dam in eastern Knox County. The fisherman had built a campfire a few yards from the bank and was using a lantern to watch his lines.

The Washington, Ind., resident had been there a couple of hours when he started having an "eerie feeling" that someone was watching. About 20 minutes later Lankford looked up and saw two eyes, each about one-inch in diameter, glowing red from the lantern and nearby campfire glow and staring at him from about 50 yards away.

Lankford could see a hairy body sticking about four feet out of the water, but the light was too dim to reveal the face, he said. Lankford said the creature looked like a well-built, big-boned man with "extra" long forearms and covered with brown, matted hair. It apparently was standing in about four feet of water. "It just stared at me and me at it. It was trying to figure out if I was looking at what I was seeing," he said.

The "booger," as Lankford's grandmother called it, appeared to study Lankford, tilting its head from side to side and making no noise, he said. After a short time, the creature turned away, reached to grab a tree limb, and pulled itself from the water.

As it walked away Lankford noticed that the arms extended to around the knees and that it had to weigh "well over 200 pounds."

"It made a loud squeal or high-pitch shriek when it left, something like a young pig would make when you try to hold on to it."

Lankford heard the sound again while he was hurriedly packing his fishing gear. He says he has heard the noise in that area three or four times since early spring, but didn't think much of it.

Since seeing the creature, Lankford has not heard the noise. He said he would like to meet it again.

**144**

"The last time I didn't think to follow it because it didn't show any sign of wanting to harm me. I'm one person who respects other persons and beings, and I would like to see the creature captured unharmed and studied," Lankford commented.

Lankford told only his family immediately after seeing the creature. He decided to report the incident to the Daviess County Sheriff's Department after reading a newspaper article about the attack on the Harper house.

"I've talked to people who live in the area, and they said if it is someone trying to pull a hoax they are taking a big risk of getting shot. The sheriff's deputy told me the same thing," Lankford noted.

Terry and Mary Harper, their children and neighbors did not hear anything out of the ordinary between midnight and 6:30 a.m. on Aug. 26, but during that time about four or five feet of siding some three feet high was ripped and chewed, along with metal trim around the backdoor. One piece shows what looks like a claw mark.

"We had the house fans on all night and they can be noisy. We really didn't hear anything," she said.

Terry Harper was leaving for work when he saw the damaged siding. The damage amounted to about $500, Harper said, and included blood, large teeth marks and white hair. Blood was also found near the back light about six to seven feet above the ground, Mrs. Harper said.

The dog refused to come out of its house and had its paws over its eyes and whined when it was checked.

Officials from the Knox County Sheriff's Department have told the Harpers that tests on the blood reveal that it is not human, and that a wolf or some other wild animal may have done the damage. Investigating officers told Mrs. Harper that hair taken from the scene has been lost.

"We don't know what to be frightened of, and I can't say that it is a 'bigfoot' or not," Mrs. Harper said.

Harold Allison, an area naturalist and writer of a weekly nature column in *The Valley Advance,* studied pictures of the damage and believes no animal native to the area could have caused the damage.

"The only animal I can think of from my experience capable of that kind of damage would be a wolverine. But there are no wolverines within 500 miles of this part of Indiana," Allison commented.

The incident has kept the Harpers busy on the telephone, talking with newspaper, television and radio reporters about the "house attack." Mrs. Harper has been interviewed by radio stations from as far as Boston, Chicago, Dallas and Los Angeles. The incident received a brief mention on the ABC-TV World News program.

Through a United Press International news story, an investigator from S.I.T.U. Research Services, a private company in Little Silver, N.J., has contacted the Harpers and currently is looking into the incident.

"The investigator thinks it's a bigfoot, but he can't be sure because we didn't have any blood stains left to send him. He said if we could get him a blood sample, he could tell us exactly what it was," Mrs. Harper related. S.I.T.U., which reportedly specializes in unexplained phenomena investigations, sent the family a report of a 1977 attack in New Jersey.

The New Jersey incident involved a creature like the one described by Lankford, but with a human face covered by a beard and mustache. Wood panels on a barn were ripped up and chewed at about the same height as the Harpers' house.

The most recent sighting of what one area newspaper has called the "Knox-ness monster," occurred Sept. 26 at about 2:30 a.m., along the Decker Chapel Road, west of Highway 41.

Crabtree was returning with his family from Princeton and was less than two miles from home when he saw "something big" walking in the road.

As Crabtree came closer he noticed fur, long arms and a "skipping walk like an ape." The headlights appeared to startle it, Crabtree recalls, and the creature swung its arm at the car. Crabtree swerved off and back onto the road to miss the creature and stopped to watch as it continued its walk down the road.

Crabtree's wife, Barbara, who was awakened by the quick turn, persuaded her husband not to follow and to call the Knox County Sheriff's Department. Mrs. Crabtree said she had seen it the day before in a cornfield near the family's backyard, a "dirty, white-haired creature" not more than 50 feet away.

Mrs. Crabtree grabbed her two pre-school daughters and backed to the front porch, she said. The creature "took a couple of steps" toward her but stepped back when the family dog started barking and ran toward it.

She got her daughters and nine-year-old son, who was throwing rocks at it, into the house and locked all doors and windows. She tried to call the sheriff but was unable to get through because of a busy party telephone line, she said.

In her view the creature was about seven to eight feet tall and weighed around 500 pounds. It was covered with "fuzzy" dirty white hair except for its head, which was brown hair.

"It had a pinkish face and big, glassy eyes. The thing had an awful, sour smell, something like dead meat that had set out for three or four days," she said.

The creature also made a growling noise, which the family has heard at least two times since the second sighting, Crabtree said.

The sheriff's deputies have been unable to find any evidence of the creature and consider the case closed, officer Jim Wilson said.

"The department is treating it as an unconfirmed sighting because the Crabtrees were the only ones to report it," Wilson explained.

The family is now looking for another house and has purchased a shotgun.

"I don't care what anyone thinks. I saw what I saw and no one has to believe me," Roger began. "When nightfall comes around here, my family is plenty scared. I don't even go out after dark."

Well, something going bump in the night in southern Indiana was definitely scaring the Crabtrees. It probably wasn't a bear as is often postulated as a solution to such events. This bigfoot also had white or gray hair, which has been described on numerous bigfoot, thought to be older bigfoot. As they get older does their hair turn from reddish-brown to white? As with humans, this would seem to be the case.

In September of 1981 "Knobby" made another appearance in Cleveland County. *The Daily Star* of Shelby, North Carolina, ran a story by reporter Mark Hames that said that Mrs. Gene Hunt and her son, Robert, reported seeing the creature. Robert was walking along Webb Road from a trailer park back to their house when he saw "something about 8-feet tall walking on two legs…" He told his mother as he came to the house and Mrs. Hunt also saw the bigfoot, "dragging one leg like it was hurt." Knobby had first been seen two years earlier near a hill called Carpenter's Knob.

In October of 1981, *The Enquirer News* of Custer, Michigan ran a story about Kevin Barthel, an Augusta, Michigan police officer who, along with a fisherman and three others, saw a tall and hairy bigfoot near a river. Also in Michigan, in November of 1981 the Barone family of Yale had their barn doors ripped off their hinges and heard strange screaming in the night. When Tina Barone (13) went to the barn one night with her sister Roxanne (12) she encountered a 7-foot bigfoot with bright red eyes.[1]

### 1982: Why Did the Bigfoot Cross the Road?

In the spring of 1982 a number of good footprints were found near Aberdeen, Washington and others near Satsop River, Washington. Then in August of that year the San Jose *Mercury* reported that two boys and a girl were driving home in the Del Monte Forest near Pacific Grove, Califonia at 1:35 in the morning when a 7-foot-tall "gorilla-type" creature crossed the 20-foot-wide road known as Buena Vista Street "in three steps."[1]

They described the creature as bald and covered with long white hair that reached to its waist. It moved "bent over with a shamble." Perhaps another old bigfoot with a bad leg, like Knobby. One has to wonder if the creatures might have been hit by a truck or something? These white-haired dumpster divers might be living too close to the highways of a completely different country from Bigfoot Nation. We should also note here how the bigfoot was described as bald on the top of its head. Like humans, it seems, some older male bigfoot go bald.

## 1983: A Bigfoot in the Headlights

In May of 1983 the *Saginaw News* reported that witnesses had seen an "enormous" bigfoot walk in front of their car near the Cass River at Vassar, Michigan. Other residents in the area heard mournful, shrill screaming in the night.

In July of 1983 four children were playing in the yard of a farmhouse near Hazelton, British Columbia (on the Kitwanga First Nations Reservation) and noticed a 7-foot-tall bigfoot was watching them. One of the children ran into the house to get her father and grandmother and the father was shocked to see the creature when he stepped onto the porch. He ordered all the children inside the house.

When one of the children asked what the creature was the grandmother reportedly said, "Oh, it's probably bigfoot," and went back into the house with the children without giving a second look back.[7]

Then in October of 1983 the Eugene, Oregon newspaper *The Register-Guard*, reported that a Las Vegas, Nevada resident named Paul Claywell had told the police at Grants Pass, Oregon that he had seen a large hair-covered creature on Interstate 5 in his headlights. Captured in the glare of the headlights the bigfoot turned and looked at the car, and then turned again and ran off the road "hunched over" but still on two legs. Claywell said it was about 7 feet tall with long straight hair allover its body and face. Police said the witness "was clearly shaken but seemed quite sane at the time."[1]

During that same summer in British Columbia, a YMCA camp leader and 9 boys hiking near Gibsons in the Tetrahydren Ridge area noticed that a tall and dark figure (hairy?) was following the group on an overnight hike. It would appear and disappear in the distance. The bigfoot was huge and did not seem to have a neck. As they reached the area where they had seen the tall figure they found large footprints and broken tree limbs at the 9-foot level. They wanted to retreat but it was getting late and they decided to camp for the night at the summit of Tetrahydren Ridge. During the night they heard continual screaming and roaring. The camp leader later described it as "the longest night I have ever experienced."[7]

## 1984: Bigfoot Circles a Trailer

In June of 1984 *The Seattle Post Intelligencer* reported that an unnamed man living near the Lincoln Tree Farm saw a 5-foot-tall hairy creature with "a masculine face" come out of the woods and circle his trailer. Sheriff's deputies arrived within 15 minutes of the call and said the man "seemed perfectly legit… he wasn't a weirdo or anything."

The newspaper report also said that a neighbor had reported to the police that something terrified his dog and that his turkeys "went bananas." The sheriff's deputy was reported to say, "Obviously something went through that area, but we don't know what."

No one wants bigfoot circling their trailer. What was bigfoot looking for: teenage girls?

In June of 1984 huge footprints between 16 and 18 inches long were found in a river gorge north of Sacramento, California at the sight of a hydraulic rig being used to find gold on the river bottom. Then in August near Agassiz, B.C., Canada, the local newspaper *The Sun*, reported that two men, Bill Bedry and Gordon Flanders, were driving beside a gravel pit at 8:30 in the evening when they saw what they thought was a bear.[1]

The men got within 90 feet of the creature and took three Polaroid photos and said the creature was trying to climb out of the walls of the pit. It was well over 6 feet tall and walked on two legs. Said Bedry, "I know bears, and I know cougars, and I know every other animal. I am a hunter. What else could it have been unless some circus was around and an ape got loose? What else is it? It had to be a sasquatch… this thing just walked like a human being."

## 1985: Bigfoot Runs at Forest Service Employee

In September of 1985 *The Daily Herald* of Rutland, Vermont ran a story about Bob Davis and his family. The Davis family heard a loud thrashing noise in the woods near their property and called the police. It was about 8:30 in the evening and Ed Davis saw a creature "grunting and screeching" that was "taller than me." His brother went into the woods to investigate and could smell a distinct "swampy smell."

Later in September, a Forest Service employee named "Mr. P." who was a resident of the northern California town of Orleans was alone hunting deer in an area called Black Mountain, where he encountered bigfoot. Mr. P. heard brush breaking on a slope above him and when he looked up toward the sound he saw a "big, upright, two-legged, dark hairy creature coming down-hill right at me."

The startled Mr. P. said he hardly had time to react when the bigfoot made a quick turn and "just ran nonstop straight up the mountain." The creature got "as close as 70 or 80 feet." He said that the bigfoot didn't stop for "a breather" on its way up the mountainside but "kept on going at full run." Although he lived and worked in the area, Mr. P. said that he would not be returning to the Black Mountain region.[1]

## 1986: Ginseng Hunter in Georgia Meets Old Bigfoot

As mentioned in the swamp ape chapter, a startling encounter happened in August of 1986 along the Georgia-Alabama border. Reported in *The News* of Summerville, Georgia, the story was about a ginseng hunter named David Brown who turned and was shocked to see a heavy-looking creature with large eyes, a flat nose, a pointed head, and long arms that dangled to its knees. Brown was terrified and unable to move. The creature's left "hand" had long fingernails that curved "like corkscrews in a knot." Its left arm seemed to be useless and its left leg injured. The right hand looked normal and had short fingernails. Its body was covered with thick, long black hair and the creature had a monkey-like face.[1]

## 1987: Bigfoot Making a Lot of Noise

In March of 1987 *The Vancouver Sun* reported that a bigfoot had been spotted at Tumbler Ridge near Calgary, Canada. A group of men including Danny Crowe, Miles Jack and others encountered a bigfoot in the forest late at night while they were having a tailgate party. Said Jack:

> We were making so much noise out in the middle of nowhere that the thing was very curious to check us out. ... it was much larger than an ordinary man. Every time it saw

us looking at it, it ran off. This thing could motor real good; he could move as quick as a deer.

Jack and Crowe described the bigfoot as about 100 feet from the group and about 7 feet tall. Crowe said he first glimpsed the bigfoot in the truck's headlights. "I just couldn't believe what I'd seen," he said. There was snow on the ground and large tracks were found at different places.

Bigfoot was reported in November of 1987 in St. Clairsville, Ohio by a man named Frank Reynolds. Reynolds claimed that while walking to his car at eight in the morning he saw a tall creature "standing near the woodline" with its back to him. It was covered in long dark-brown hair and "its arms hung down near the knees." The creature turned and looked at Reynolds once before walking away into the woods. Reynolds had seen the bigfoot in the two months before.[1]

## 1988: Extra Large Gorilla in Pennsylvania

The Ligonier, Pennsylvania newspaper *The Echo* reported in May, 1988 about an unnamed man's night encounter in the area:

> At 11 p.m. while preparing to do some "lantern fishing" at a place called Sleepy Hollow "where the bridge goes across the Loyalhanna Creek," a man saw "a large, strange foul-smelling creature" that he said would make an extra large gorilla "look like a chimpanzee." The witness said he was about to light his lantern when he "heard a scuffling racket on the hillside in the woods about 25 feet away." In the beam of his "three-cell spotlight," the creature appeared to have red-brown "fur." And "large fiery eyes that glowed orange like [the eyes of] a bear." Convinced the creature was approaching him in an "unfriendly manner," the man ran to his car and left, but not before seeing the creature in the headlights. The witness was a hunter, tracker, and "live trapper with 50 years experience." He said it definitely wasn't a bear or a gorilla.[1]

## 1989: Strange Encounters with Bigfoot

In July of 1989 the *Times-News* of Thunder Bay, Ontario reported on an encounter in Webequie, Ontario:

> Caroline Yesno of Webequie was frightened while swimming in Winisk Lake by "something approaching in the bushes." Footprints measuring 14 inches long with a 40-inch stride were found in the area by a local constable. Harvey McKay of Big Trout Lake said he saw an upright, 7- or 8-foot-tall creature covered in "…long brown hair that shone in the evening sunlight." It ran off with long strides.[1]

Then, in September of 1989 an incident was reported by in *MUFON Journal #262* of an unusual encounter near Tillamook, Oregon. According to the journal, it involved two unidentified witnesses, a woman and her granddaughter who alerted her to something going on outside the house:

> She stepped out and was confronted by an object resembling an inverted toy top hovering just above the ground. It was 20 to 30 feet in diameter and had a flat bottom and a bright yellow-white light shining at both ends. The woman approached to within 30 feet of the craft and a door opened revealing a blond human-like entity of average height with fair skin and blue eyes, wearing a silvery coverall. The woman then noticed from a window next to the door a large hairy, Bigfoot type creature apparently seated and only visible from the chest up. The astonished woman stared at the object and beings for a few minutes until the object suddenly vanished.

Peter Gutilla reports in *The Bigfoot Files* that in the summer of 1989 he received this report from Sedona, Arizona:

> While "touring some property under construction" in the vicinity of Red Canyon/Loy Butte, an unidentified man encountered "something that looked like a window suspended in mid-air." Standing near the "window" were

"several 9-foot-tall bigfoot-type creatures that appeared to be guarding the site." The witness left in a hurry.[1]

Yow, windows in the sky with bigfoot guardians! A space port for Bigfoot Nation? A flying saucer-type craft with a bigfoot sitting in it? Perhaps there really are wookies with ray guns flying around in spacecraft as in the *Star Wars* movies. Though there is an occasional bigfoot-and-flying-saucer story, there are none that I know of where a bigfoot was actually armed with a ray gun. Bigfoot has been seen carrying clubs or a large branch torn from a nearby tree. A few reports have even had bigfoot wearing a belt of some kind with objects attached to the belt. Were these objects weapons?

### 1991: Bigfoot Encounter in Minnesota

The *News Herald* of Grand Marais, Minnesota reported this story about an encounter with a bigfoot near Hoveland, Minnesota in March of 1991:

> A department of Natural Resources forester, Orvis Lunke, brought his car to a stop behind an upright, two-legged creature that was walking away from him. "It wasn't a bear, but it was covered with shaggy red-brown hair." …"fur" was found on an overhanging branch. They retrieved, photographed, and later sent the "fur" to the University of Minnesota for analysis. The creature was estimated to be "nine-feet tall," based on saplings which Lunke thought were the same height. After following the tracks a while, "a commotion in some brush" caught their attention, and the two men watched the creature emerge and lunge toward the river. "It was mostly going on two legs, but occasionally dropped down to all four. I was so surprised that I forgot to get a picture," said Lunke. The creature broke through the river ice as it departed. …the men tracked the creature for three miles until the approach of nightfall ended their trek. A severe storm that night prevented plans to resume the search the next day.[1]

### 1992: Encounter with a Fanged Bigfoot

**154**

In January of 1992 the *Dallas Morning News* reported an encounter near Hamilton, Texas which indicates that some bigfoot have fangs:

In a letter Daniel Fisker said he and his family saw a large hairy creature while driving home one night from Stephenville. The creature was described as 7 or 8 feet tall, covered with hair, and having "long arms that extended down to its knees... a human face, showing four fang-like teeth, two on the top, two on the bottom, and the rest flat like humans. It hurdled the guard-rail and ran off into the night toward the brush along the river banks..."[1]

In June of 1992 the Somerset, Pennsylvania newspaper *The American* ran a story of an unnamed witness to a bigfoot encounter near the town of Somerset:

Near the "village of Scullton," south of Somerset, the "owner of a home in that area saw something his children had told him about the year before." The homeowner was awakened at 3 a.m. by barking dogs and saw a man-like "shape" looking in through his living room window. "Whatever it was, it was almost 9-feet tall and over 3-feet wide... it was completely covered with dark-colored hair and stood on its hind legs just like a human." The man turned on the front light and the creature was gone.[1]

**1993: The Mogollon Monster Gets Headlines**

A group called the Bigfoot Co-Op reported in January 1993 that a snowplow operator at 6:30 a.m. saw "a gorilla-like thing" standing in the light of his headlights. It had light hair, was 9 feet tall, weighed possibly 500 pounds, and had a pointed, elongated head and no facial hair. The man was scared and quit work for the day. An investigation turned up 19-inch-long footprints, and hair, which was submitted for analysis, was found 7 feet off the ground. A previously found hair sample was analyzed and identified as "hominid, human-like, but not human. DNA unknown."[1]

The same Bigfoot Co-Op quoted an article from *The Payson*

*Roundup* (Payson, Arizona) reporting that in September of 1993 a bigfoot had been seen near Woods Canyon Lake. According to a summary of *The Payson Roundup* story, Greg and Charlene Eairheart were hosts at Cook Campground near Woods Canyon Lake. A visitor from England was hiking along the Mogollon Rim, a long series of cliffs north of Payson, when he encountered a creature that he believed to be bigfoot. The man returned to the campground, terrified, and immediately left in his vehicle.

A short time later the Eairhearts and another man went target shooting and while Charlene was "answering a call to nature," she "had a feeling someone was watching… I looked up and that's when I saw it."

"It" was very large, human in appearance with extremely long hair of a "burnt orange color" that fell well below the waist. It was obviously a bigfoot. The men searched the area and found footprints and pods of chewed, bark-type food. They found tracks that were described as 19 and 22 inches long and 8 inches wide, and they were human-like in shape with webbed toes. One footprint seemed to show a disfigured foot. The Eairhearts drove to Payson and bought plaster to use for casting the prints.

It is interesting that a fairly high percentage of bigfoot that are encountered seem to have some sort of injury, often a foot that is mangled or crushed, or in some cases with one arm that is mangled and paralyzed, possibly from fighting with other bigfoot or from a fall. Are these crippled, older bigfoot—sometimes with white hair—venturing closer to civilization because they are having difficulty feeding themselves because of their disabilities? Have these older, disabled bigfoot been cast out of the tribe they were once part of and now they venture to campgrounds lured by the smell of barbeques and such? Are they castaways from Bigfoot Nation?

**1994: Bigfoot in Northern California**

The year 1994 saw a number of sightings in northern California starting in February in the small towns around Mount Lassen and the Caribou Wilderness area east of Redding. This area has the Stover Mountain Ski Area and small towns like Quincy, Paxton and Taylorsville. In a story by Dave Moller in the *Feather River Bulletin* in February 1995, Pat Farley and Jerry Paradiso were

**156**

moving Paradiso's belongings to his new home in Taylorsville slightly after midnight when they saw something at the side of the road a few miles east of Quincy. "It had a long gait," said Paradiso, "and its arms were swinging way up and down." Both men said the creature was covered in hair with a rounded human-like head and no snout. They reported their sighting to local police when they reached Quincy.

On the same night, also around midnight, two PG&E employees, Nate Soileau and Dan Fields, saw an upright creature nine to ten feet tall by the side of the road. Said Soileau: "It didn't have a snout like a bear. It had a blunt face like a human or an ape. It walked across the road and went up the steep bank in nothing flat. It made the hair stand up on the back of my neck."

Fields added, "I don't know what it was, but it had a lot of black hair. It was a clear night, and it was just unreal. If it wasn't bigfoot, it was somebody on drugs in a gorilla suit messing with traffic."

Later in July the Bigfoot Co-Op reported that they had been contacted by three witnesses about an encounter near Orleans in northern California, just north of the Hoopa Indian Reservation and very close to Bluff Creek where Roger Patterson claimed he filmed bigfoot in 1967. The three unnamed witnesses, who were part of a larger group, were sitting by a campfire late at night at the Notice Creek confluence with Bluff Creek, when they heard a "loud, very deep whistle from across the creek."

The trio also said that at an earlier camp in the same area two members of the group were awakened at 3 a.m. by the "heavy footfalls" of a large creature moving past their tent. Though they looked for footprints the next morning, they found none.

## 1995: Bigfoot Central and the Cliff Crook Photograph

One of the better photographs of a sasquatch was apparently taken in 1995. According to an article in *Fortean Times* (No. 93, Dec. 1996), a forest patrol officer from Tacoma, who wishes to remain anonymous for fear of losing his job, had an encounter with a giant apelike creature and was able to take a series of 35 mm photos. The ranger then called Cliff Crook at the sasquatch-monitoring group named Bigfoot Central.

Bigfoot Central is located in Cliff Crook's living room in Bothell, Washington. Crook held a news conference on December 9, 1995 to satisfy the mounting interest over the photos. Crook told the conference that the ranger had taken 14 photographs of the sasquatch but eight of them were dark because fleeting clouds blocked the sun on his 50 mm telephoto lens. The ranger said that he heard a splashing noise to his left while hiking along a ridge

One of two photos of a bigfoot released in 1995 by Cliff Crook.

in Washington state's Snoqualmie National Forest. He went to investigate the noise. Then, from a high bank, he observed the eight-foot creature just 30 yards away in a swampy lagoon. He used up what remained of his roll of film.

The photos are sensational, clearly depicting a hairy bigfoot creature with its head low on a pair of massive shoulders. One photography analyst declared that he had found tiny diamond shapes in the image indicating that it was a digitally created image. Cliff Crook countered that the analyst was examining a laser print and not an original.

One of two photos of a bigfoot released in 1995 by Cliff Crook.

Skeptics believe that the photo was digitally created, probably in Photoshop, while some think that it is genuine. Genuine bigfoot photos would be welcome by all cryptozoologists, but fakes occur from time to time. The Cliff Crook photo continues to fascinate researchers over 20 years later, and as time has passed the opinion is that the Cliff Crook photo may well be genuine.

Another encounter of note occurred in the summer of 1995 when several ex-Forest Service employees claimed that they had had an encounter with a bigfoot in the Pacific Northwest. An Associated Press story released from Walla Walla, Washington on Aug. 10, 1995 carried the headline "3 Men Claim Bigfoot Sighting." The story went on to say:

> A man who has frequently claimed to have encounters with a legendary creature dubbed Bigfoot says this time he's got witnesses.
>
> Paul Freeman, a former U.S. Forest Service employee, said he and two other men saw a tall, hairy creature on Saturday in the Blue Mountains, about 25 miles east of Walla Walla in the Mill Creek watershed.
>
> Freeman, who claims to have spotted a similar creature four other times, brought back part of a tree he says Bigfoot twisted, some hair samples and two plaster footprint molds.
>
> Freeman went on the expedition with Walla Walla resident Wes Sumerlin and former state game department employee Bill Laughery. The trio said they first saw signs of the creature's presence: a strong odor, small, twisted trees with clumps of long, black hair, and large footprints, 15 inches and 7 inches wide.
>
> Then on Saturday, through the dense timber, they saw bigfoot, nearly 8 feet tall and a hairy tan-brown, Laughery said.

1995 was a pretty good year for bigfoot, it seems. The Cliff Crook photo (reproduced in the color section) is one of the classic bigfoot photos that we have, if it is authentic. Sometimes photos and film seem too good to be true with bigfoot, but more and more photos and videos are coming out all the time, thanks to digital

**160**

cameras and smart phones.

## 1995: Bigfoot Eating Cattails in Upstate New York

In July of 1995 it was reported that a youngster in Indiana on a group hiking trip had seen a bigfoot. On the hike near Princeton, Indiana, the young boy (name withheld) was with other children and a counselor when he lagged behind the group and stopped to tie his shoe. He saw the creature standing with his back to him, apparently "watching something in the surrounding trees." The boy was terrified and ran down the trail screaming. The counselor did not believe the boy, but the youth refused to go hiking anymore and his mother believed the boy told the truth.

This boy may have been lucky in the sense that there are a number of puzzling cases where a younger child has disappeared on a hiking trip when they are the last one in line and lagging behind the group. David Paulides in his books[37] has chronicled a number of disturbing cases where children were hiking with adults and, lagging behind, suddenly vanished. Searches with forest workers, police and dogs could not find the youngsters who simply vanished in a moment. Sometimes these children are found dead, and missing some clothing, particularly shoes, at quite a distance away from where they were seemingly abducted—by bigfoot!

The Rathbone, New York newspaper *The Leader* reported in August of 1995 on incidents reported by Nellie Ferry around a neighbor's pond that month. Ferry said she had found footprints 15 inches long and 5 inches wide that were embedded in mud that was an inch deep in an area where she and her husband had been fishing. The prints were spaced about 40 inches apart and plaster casts were made of them. Other prints showed up the next week and locals heard loud noises in the woods and smelled a strong odor near the pond. Ferry said that a number of cattails on the edge of the pond had been pulled up and their roots eaten. It seems that there is a lot to eat for bigfoot around a typical pond. Cattails may be a major source of food for bigfoot in certain areas, especially in the East and Midwest.[1]

In August of 1995 the famous sasquatch researcher Jeff

Meldrum[32] investigated the sighting made by a television crew near Crescent City in northern California. The crew said they were parked at night in a 54-foot RV at the end of a dirt road when the witnesses spotted a 7-foot-tall, two-legged hairy creature that was swinging its arms as it crossed the road in front of the RV. The headlights were on and they could plainly see the bigfoot as it crossed the road. One of the crew attempted to video tape the creature as it walked into the forest. Meldrum said that he could find no evidence of a hoax.

### 1996: Bigfoot at Lost Lake, Colorado

Peter Gutilla relates that an encounter was reported at Lost Lake, near Rabbit Ears Pass in Jackson County, Colorado in July. A lone fisherman (name withheld) at Lost Lake spotted a tall, two-legged creature covered in "shinny dark hair" as it stood near a boulder overlooking the lake. The witness described the creature as having massive shoulders and very long arms. He said the creature had a wide, flat nose, dark eyes and a dome-shaped head. When the bigfoot noticed the fisherman it turned and walked away at a fast pace into the woods.[1]

In August an unidentified policeman in Coeur d'Alene, Idaho was driving near the city just before dawn on a night patrol when he glanced in his rearview mirror and saw a "large, hairy man-like creature walking across the highway just behind the vehicle." The officer made a quick U-turn and drove back to the spot where the bigfoot had crossed the road. There was nothing to see except the heavy timber of the surrounding forest.

Another occurrence in August of 1996 is the astonishing tale of skydivers, sitting in their plane waiting to jump, who saw a bigfoot from the air near Kapowsin, Pierce County, Washington. The skydiving plane was flying low near Mount Rainier when the group saw a "sasquatch running down a road with huge strides." As the plane flew over the creature to get a better look it "leaped off the road, running uphill [and] jumping stumps like nothing." Once the bigfoot entered into the thick timber of the forest he was lost from sight and the astonished skydivers flew on to their dive.[1]

### 1997: Why Did the Bigfoot Cross the Road? Part II

The famous bigfoot hunter John Green[29] investigated several sightings in 1997. The first was in June near Athol, Idaho. A retired California Highway Patrol officer was driving north on Highway 95 at 7:15 a.m. when he saw an upright, two-legged creature covered in dark brown hair walking across the road from right to left near Old House Road intersection. The retired officer described the bigfoot as "at least 7 feet tall and more than 300 pounds."

In August Green investigated an incident in Conejos County, Colorado. Near the town of Platoro an unidentified man and his wife were looking for elk along a logging road; they looked down the ridge they were on to a meadow a thousand feet down below. There they saw three hikers crossing the meadow toward a large two-legged creature covered in black fur on the edge of the meadow. The bigfoot was spooked by the hikers, who could not see him, and jumped a large creek and ran into the forest.

Peter Gutilla records a curious incident in September of 1997 in Windham County, Connecticut of an unidentified woman who was riding her horse down an old railway line that had been converted into an equestrian trail. The woman said that she smelled a strong odor that was "skunk-like with an overtone of wet dog and burning garlic." Her horse suddenly bolted out of fear and she then saw a "tall, dark, incredibly fast" two-legged creature that looked like "a cross between a man and a gorilla." It came crashing down a hill toward the woman and her horse. She said that the bigfoot's screams "reverberated in my chest and hurt my ears." As she road away from the area she saw the creature returning to the top of the hill where it had come from.[1]

### 1998: Bigfoot Smells Marshmallows in Northern California

In a letter to bigfoot researcher Bobby Short, a woman from Revilla Island in very southern Alaska named "R.A." said:

> Imagine my surprise at a personal sighting up here on Revilla Island, driving kids home from a school clam dig. 50 mph southbound, a 7-foot-tall black, hair-covered biped walks, then runs, across a forested highway 100 yards in front of my car, 12 miles north of Ketchikan. It covered the centerline to the forest (20 feet) in three bounds.

*The Heyday Years*

In October of 1998 local newspapers in northern California told about an encounter near Hayfork involving a young man named Tim Ford. Ford told several California Department of Fish and Game officials that he and six of his friends saw a 9-foot-tall, yellow-eyed, man-like creature close to their campsite during a hunting trip near Mud Springs, south of Hayfork, a small mountain town west of Redding and south of the Hoopa Indian Reservation and the Trinity Alps Wilderness Area.

While roasting marshmallows, they heard the loud sound of rustling in some nearby bushes. Ford said that he shined his flashlight in the direction of the bushes and was startled to see an enormous, furry, man-like figure standing next to the bushes on the other side of the creek, approximately 50 yards away from their camp.

"You could see his arms hanging way past his knees," said Ford's companion, James Harmon. They said the creature moved away from the campsite but left behind tracks that were 20 inches long and 6 inches wide. During that night they heard blood-curdling screams coming from the other side of the creek.

Bigfoot researcher Bobby Short filed a report from Massachusetts that took place in late October near Windsor. His report said that a hunter (name withheld) claimed to have seen a 6- to 7-foot-tall bigfoot with black hair covering its body. It had reddish-brown eyes. The next day the hunter went to the area with his dogs, which refused to track the scent of the creature.[1]

The millennium went out with a quiet note in Bigfoot Nation. The bad boy had made his mark across Canada and the U.S. and now

Bigfoot was constantly in the news.

sasquatch and bigfoot were household names. Towns in Canada were named "The Sasquatch Capital of [your region's name here]" and now there are bigfoot and sasquatch (need we mention yeti?) businesses all over North America and the world. Bigfoot Nation has come on full force as a marketing giant that shows no sign of stopping. Did some Bigfoot Yuga suddenly turn the page at the millennium? Or maybe something special happened in 2012? Bigfoot doesn't wear a watch or look at calendars—he is caught in his own timeless world. Where do the smelly fellow and the hairy hotties he chases in the woods go from here? Well as we will see, Bigfoot Nation seems to be forging ahead at full speed.

A bigfoot from Lane County, Oregon, drawn in
2002 by Autumn Williams.

A bigfoot bigfoot drawn by witness Alexa Evans.

# CHAPTER 6

# The Swamp Apes of Swamp Nation

"Did you ever see so many Wooly Boogers
in your whole life?"
—Clem Carruthers, *Farewell to Boogerville*

Down South they have their own names for bigfoot and his kin. They call them "skunk apes," "swamp boogers," "wooly boogers," and such. Famed skunk ape hunter David Shealy says that the term "Skunk Ape" originated in the southern states but gained in popularity in Florida in the late 1970s. Stories of this creature started when the early settlers came to Florida and reported a strange primate-like creature with a nauseous smell prowling the forests and swamps. Newspapers referred to it as the "Wild Man." The Seminoles refer to it as Esti Capcaki (Cannibal Giant) and one town in Florida calls it the Bardin Booger. We can trace the name of booger or wooly booger to these early days.

## 1818: Baboon Seen in Florida

Florida cryptozoologist Robert Robinson says the first recorded sighting of a skunk ape was in 1818 at Apalachicola, Florida. Apalachicola is the county seat of Franklin County on the Gulf of Mexico in the Florida panhandle. The creature was described as a five-foot-tall baboon.[67]

## 1829: Wildman Kills Hunters

An incident occurred in 1829 in which a wild man killed a number of hunters. Robinson says that the winter of 1828-1829 was extremely dry, and two men living on the edges of the Okefenokee

**167**

Swamp decided to delve as deep into it as they could. For two weeks, they journeyed from Georgia into Florida exploring the area known as the Okefenokee.

Upon reaching the heart of the swamp, they made a startling discovery. They found giant eighteen-inch footprints, with a stride of over six feet. The men had heard stories from the local Indians of giants living in the swamps. While camping right near where the tracks were located, their sleep was suddenly interrupted by strange screams. Then the men heard something large moving around the swamps surrounding their camp, which caused them to remain awake the rest of the night waiting for the sun to come up. The next morning the men beat a hasty retreat back to civilization.

Returning to their settlement in Ware County, the men related their tale to the rest of the settlers. Fearing for the safety of the settlement, one of these men put together a team of nine hunters and went back into the swamp to the source of the giant footprints. As they journeyed across the border into Florida, the hunting party encountered numerous bears, panthers and alligators; there was not a single sign of the monster.

Two weeks later, when the team was getting ready to return to the settlement, they stumbled upon more giant tracks. With the sun going down, they decided to set up camp nearby and pursue the creature at first light.

According to the newspaper account, that evening the hunters were attacked by a "horrible monster covered with hair." The hunters quickly opened fire, but the creature seemed unstoppable. The hunters continued to fire volley after volley at the huge being. The creature, shrieking and roaring, leaped at them, killing five of the hunters by ripping their heads off. The terrified survivors continued to shoot the large beast until it finally fell. "Wallowing and roaring," the enraged creature continued to lash out at the hunters, until it finally died of numerous gunshot wounds.

Once they were sure it was truly dead, the dazed hunters approached the monster carefully. They measured the beast and found it be 13 feet in length.

More screams echoed through the night and, fearing further attacks from more of these giant creatures, the surviving hunters gathered up their headless comrades' rifles and fled from the swamp.[67]

## 1884: Bigfoot at Ocheesee Pond

The next known report is from 1884 when a creature, which was reported as a wild man, appeared at Ocheesee Pond, a large wetland covering nearly nine square miles in southeastern Jackson County, Florida. Located below Grand Ridge and Sneads in the southeast corner of Jackson County, Ocheesee Pond was a focal point for early settlers. The pond is covered by a vast cypress swamp, although there are some stretches of open water, most notably its southern arm. The strange human-like creature was often spotted roaming the swamps or swimming from place to place.

As more sightings occurred in the remote area, the local residents—many of them former Confederate soldiers—met and launched an expedition to capture the Wild Man of Ocheesee Pond. In August of 1884, they succeeded! It was reported his body was covered in thick hair, but the captors believed he was a human who had probably escaped from an asylum. No asylum reported such an odd escapee, however, and his captors became even more baffled by the Wild Man. Newspapers at the time were silent on the eventual fate of the Ocheesee Pond Wild Man. The last account says the strange beast was sent to Tallahassee and then back to Chattahoochee after scientists could not identify it.[60] A case of a missing captured bigfoot?

## 1938: Bigfoot Family Chases Dogs

Chad Arment reports a strange story from Anniston, Alabama that ran on April 15, 1938 about a wild man being sought in a swamp in the Choccolocco valley. Reported in the *Oshkosh Northwestern* and other newspapers, the story was entitled "Hairy Wild Man Sought in Swamp." Said the newspaper story:

> A wild man who runs on all fours, chases dogs and frightens farmers is being sought in a dense swamp in the Choccolocco valley.
> Sheriff W. P. Cotton led a posse in search of the strange beast which, farmers insisted, was accompanied by a woman and a child—both as savage in appearance and actions as

the man.

Rex Biddle, a farmer, told Sheriff Cotton that the man approached his home walking on all fours in the manner of an ape.

"He was about five feet tall, and had hair all over his body," Biddle said. "He was unclothed. Despite his beastlike appearance, his nose and other features indicated he was human."

Biddle said he reached for his gun but didn't shoot because "I didn't know whether that would be legal."

Roy Storey, another farmer, said the creature followed him for a time and then "dropped to all fours and chased my pet dog into the swamp."

Residents of the district petitioned the sheriff to "catch this thing or we are moving out."[44]

### 1947: Skunk Ape Seen by Boy

Robert Robinson reports that in 1947, at Lakeland, Florida, a large, hairy, bipedal creature was seen by a four-year-old little boy, who stated he saw the strange creature standing behind an orange tree, watching him. He quickly went back into his home and related what he saw to his mother. Other incidents have happened at the Green Swamp which is directly north of Lakeland.[67]

### 1948: Chattering White-Haired Bigfoot on Road

Robinson also relate that in 1948, at New Port Richey, Florida, a white-haired bigfoot approached a man who had stopped his automobile to examine the remains of a dead animal on the road. The mysterious old bigfoot walked to within 20 feet of the witness and began chattering at him before it turned and fled. Old age can be tough in Bigfoot Nation—and there get to be fewer and fewer beings to chatter to. Defending one's roadkill can be a thankless pursuit as well. White-haired bigfoot and the white-haired smaller skunk apes are considered outcasts who venture close to civilization for the easy life of dumpster diving. They can sometimes be the most colorful and playful of bigfoot, who are known to be extremely shy. A white-haired bigfoot might stop to stare you in the eyes, and maybe give you a brief lecture about some of the laws of Bigfoot

**170**

Nation.[67]

## 1950: Bigfoot Chases Woman

In 1950, again in New Port Richey, Florida, a huge apeman terrified a young housewife as she was attempting to hang out her wash, and chased her around her yard. The frightened woman managed to lock herself inside her house and the creature disappeared.[60]

## 1955: The Hazards of Gardening in Bigfoot Nation

Some kind of swamp booger surfaced again on August 1, 1955 in Georgia near Kinchafoonee Creek on the Bronwood-Smithville Highway. It was reported that 20-year-old Joseph Whaley was alone on the Bronwood-Smithville Highway cutting grass and undergrowth with a scythe when he heard a noise and went to investigate it. He was suddenly was confronted by a creature that was covered in "shaggy gray hair" and about six feet tall. It had "tusk-like teeth and pointed ears" and seemed like a cross between a man and a gorilla.

Whaley said the creature was "grunting like a wild pig" and lumbered slowly toward him. He fought off the beast with his scythe, swinging it at the creature's chest and arms, and then retreated to his jeep. He tried to call someone on his radio but could not get through. Before he could start the jeep the creature reached through the window and scratched his arm and shoulder and tore his shirt. Whaley says he jumped out of the jeep and kept it between him and the hairy critter. He said the creature moved in a "lumbering and slow-moving manner" (not usually characteristic of bigfoot) and Whaley ran into the woods and then doubled-back to his jeep where he got it started and managed to drive away before the creature could return. Whaley later reported the incident to the Evansville, Georgia *Press* newspaper on August 22, 1955.[3]

The Fouke Monster was first shot at in 1955 by a woman named Lynn Crabtree according to her letter to *Fate* magazine (No. 28, page 28.[3])

## 1958: Bigfoot Grabs Truck Driver

In 1958, in Brooksville, Florida, a truck driver reported he was

**171**

asleep in a in large semitrailer on Route 41 when something with long arms reached in, grabbed him and pulled him out of the cab. When he started screaming, some nearby dogs heard the commotion and came running, barking fiercely. The thing promptly ran off into the nearby woods.[67]

### 1965: Fouke Monster Shot at by Boy

The Fouke Monster (later to be known as the Boggy Creek Monster) and the Crabtree family surfaced again in Arkansas when 14-year-old James Crabtree was approached by a 7- to-8-foot bigfoot while he was squirrel hunting in the woods near Fouke. The boy claimed he shot at the face of the bigfoot three times and the monster ran away.[3]

Also in 1965 it was reported that a man near Tarrytown, Georgia witnessed a bigfoot over 8 feet tall that appeared to have been injured and "mangled."

### 1966: Skunk Ape Chases Woman into House

In the spring of 1966 Mrs. Eula Lewis was chased by a hairy creature into her house in Brooksville, Florida, just north of Tampa. The Tampa-Sarasota area is often known as "skunk ape central" because of the proliferation of bigfoot/skunk ape reports and photos. Mrs. Lewis said that the bigfoot was swinging its arms as her dogs yapped at it and it ultimately chased her into her house.

Later, in the summer of 1966, near Elfers, Florida (also near Brooksville in the area just north of Tampa, in some brush by the Anclote River a local named Ralph "Bud" Chambers saw a bigfoot standing in trees and could smell a "rancid, putrid odor."

In the same area of Elfers and the Anclote River in December of 1966 two hunters saw bigfoot and reported it to the local newspaper.[3]

On November 7, 1966 it was reported that William and James Cagle saw a bigfoot near Winona, Mississippi. The two were driving in a truck when they saw a 7-foot bigfoot standing by the road. It had big red eyes and was waving at the men as they drove past.[29]

### 1967: More Sightings around Elfers, Florida

Perhaps it was the same bigfoot that jumped onto the car of four teenagers in Elfers in January of 1967. They described it as "smelly with glowing green eyes."

Also, the same local who had seen a bigfoot in 1966, Ralph "Bud" Chambers, saw a bigfoot in his yard near the Anclote River at Elfers during the summer of 1967.[3]

### 1969: Southern Florida's Incredible Manhunt

Southern Florida saw a wave of sightings around Davie, a small town west of Hollywood, Florida, near Alligator Alley. Reporter Duane Bostick wrote an article entitled "Florida's Incredible Manhunt for a Supernatural Suspect" for *Startling Detective* magazine (March, 1976) that reported that a bigfoot was encountered early in 1969 by a man named Charles Robertson in an abandoned guava orchard near Davie.

Bostick then reports that in the same area around Davie, a man named Henry Ring said he saw a huge black bigfoot that was treed by dogs in an orange grove. Ring said that the bigfoot escaped by swinging through the trees and diving into a canal.

### 1971: 8-Foot Tall Bigfoot Approaches Archeologists

*The National Enquirer* and other newspapers reported that in February of 1971 a group of archeologists in the Big Cypress Swamp in southwest Florida, near Everglades City, saw a bigfoot. H.C. Osborn and a group of other archeologists said they saw an 8-foot tall bigfoot with light brown hair with a strong smell approach the tents in their camp at 3 o'clock in the morning. The next day they found five-toed footprints that were 17-and-a-half-inches long.[29]

Then in June of 1971 near Greenville, Mississippi, Mae Pearl Young said she saw a 6-foot tall, black-haired bigfoot standing beside her daughter's home late at night. Her story was published in the *Delta Democrat Times* on June 22, 1971. She was quoted as saying that the bigfoot "...had a great big head ...broad shoulders with its hands on its hips."[29]

In August of 1971 a rabies control officer named Henry Ring was looking around an area west of Fort Lauderdale, Florida because of "animal" reports and said he saw a bigfoot with long dangling arms cross the road in front of him. *The National Enquirer* published his story on November 7, 1971.[3]

Also in 1971, near Davie, Florida, two police officers saw

bigfoot in a deserted building. Sgt. Harry Rose and Sgt. Joseph Simboli were investigating strange noises in the deserted house and watched the bigfoot escape from the house and swing through a grove of orange trees to get away from the officers.[3]

❦ ⟶ ❦

### 1971 to 1978: Boggy Creek and the Fouke Monster

The most famous of all the skunk and swamp apes of southern lore is the Boggy Creek Monster. Made famous by the 1972 feature film *The Legend of Boggy Creek*, the Boggy Creek Monster, known originally as the Fouke Monster, is one of the skunk ape version of the Amityville Horror.

The story of the Fouke Monster and Boggy Creek made local and international news in 1971 when in May of that year, the Ford family of the Jonesville area had a frightening experience with a large, hairy apeman critter. The *Arkansas Democrat* (May 3, 1971) reported that the creature pushed its "claw" through the family's screen door while Mrs. Ford was sleeping on the couch. Mrs. Ford's husband, Bobby, and his brother Don, pursued the creature into the woods. The local sheriff arrived and took casts of some unusual footprints. An hour later, the creature was back at the Ford's residence. When it was shot at, the hairy apeman disappeared from view again. On May 2, Bobby was outside when he was grabbed and pulled to the ground. After a brief struggle, he escaped his assailant. He was treated at a Texarkana hospital for scratches and shock. Another search found more footprints around the Fords' property.

The Legend of Boggy Creek

Later in the month, the *Arkansas Democrat* (May 25, 1971) reported that on the 23rd, several motorists reported seeing a six- to-seven-foot creature running across Highway 71 near the town of Fouke. John Green, in his 1978 book *Sasquatch: The Apes Among Us,* says that a 14-year-old named James

174

Lynn Crabtree witnessed a seven- to-eight-foot, reddish-haired animal in 1965 near Fouke. As reported above, Crabtree claims to have shot the creature three times in the face, but with no effect.

Said the May 3, 1971 *Arkansas Democrat* newspaper article about the Ford family encounter (headlined "Hairy 'monster' hunted in Fouke sector"):

> Miller County Sheriff's Department officers said early today a search of the area where a mysterious creature was spotted near Fouke early Sunday failed to reveal a clue.
>
> "Members of my department searched the area but didn't find a thing. I don't know what it could have been," Sheriff Leslie Greer said. Bobby Ford, 25, of Rt. 1, Box 220, Texarkana, Ark, who lives approximately 10 miles south of Texarkana on U.S. Highway 71, said the unidentified creature attacked him at his home shortly before midnight Saturday.
>
> Ford was treated at St. Michael Hospital for minor scratches and mild shock and released.
>
> "After the thing grabbed me and I broke free, I was moving so fast I didn't stop to open the door. I just ran through it," Ford said.
>
> The "creature" was described by Ford as being about seven feet tall and about three feet wide across the chest. "At first I thought it was a bear but it runs upright and moves real fast," he said.
>
> Ford, his brother Don, and Charles Taylor saw the creature several times shortly after midnight and shot at it seven times with a shotgun.
>
> "It first started Wednesday when our wives heard something walking around on the porch. Then Friday night about midnight the thing tried to break into the house again.
>
> "Last night it tried to get in again," Don Ford said.
>
> Elizabeth Ford said she was sleeping in the front room of the frame house when, "I saw the curtain moving on the front window and a hand sticking through the window. At first I thought it was a bear's paw but it didn't look like that. It had heavy hair all over it and it had claws. I could see its

eyes. They looked like coals of fire ...real red," she said. "It didn't make any noise. Except you could hear it breathing."

Ford said they spotted the creature in back of the house with the aid of a flashlight. "We shot several times at it then and then called Ernest Walraven, constable of Fouke. He brought us another shotgun and a stronger light. We waited on the porch and then saw the thing closer to the house. We shot again and thought we saw it fall. Bobby, Charles and myself started walking to where we saw it fall," he said.

About that time, according to Don Ford, they heard the women in the house screaming and Bobby went back.

"I was walking the rungs of a ladder to get up on the porch when the thing grabbed me. I felt a hairy arm come over my shoulder and the next thing I knew we were on the ground. The only thing I could think about was to get out of there. The thing was breathing real hard and his eyes were about the size of a half dollar and real red.

"I finally broke away and ran around the house and through the front door. I don't know where he went," Bobby Ford said.

"We heard Bobby shouting and by the time we got there everything was over. We didn't see a thing," Don Ford said.

Everyone at the house said they saw the creature moving in the fields close to the house. All said it cold move fast.

Walraven said he was called to the scene about 12:35 a.m. (Sunday, May 2) and searched the area without finding anything. "I looked through the surrounding fields and woods for about an hour. Then, I gave them my shotgun and light. A short time later they called back and told me they had shot at it again. I went back and stayed until 5 a.m."

Walraven said several years ago a resident of the Jonesville Community near Fouke reported seeing a "hairy monster" in the area.

"Several persons saw the thing and shot at it, some from close range. They said nothing seemed to stop it. They described it as being about seven feet tall and looking just like a naked man covered with brown hair," Walraven said.

All that remained Sunday morning at the Ford house

**176**

were several strange tracks—that appeared to be left by something with three toes—and several scratch marks on the front porch that appeared to have been made by something with three claws.

Several pieces of tin nailed around the bottom of the house had been ripped away and another window had been damaged by the creature, according to Ford.

"We plan to stay here tonight and see if we can get the thing if it returns," Don Ford said.

"I'm not staying here anymore unless they kill that thing," Patricia Ford said.

As for Bobby Ford, he said, "I've had it here. I'm going back to Ashdown."

That same year Fouke was invaded by tourists, bigfoot hunters and the movie crew for the low-budget movie *The Legend of Boggy Creek* to be released the next year.

An article run in the *Arkansas Democrat* on October 25, 1981, written by local resident Lou Farish, mentioned that in 1977 a farmer in nearby Miller County checked his pigpen and discovered the remnants of a small-scale attack on his pigs. Several of them had been ripped open and one carcass was found outside and away from the pen where it had been seemingly dragged and abandoned.

Farish also says in the article that during 1978, several areas of Arkansas were experiencing strange phenomena again. In March of 1978, footprints were discovered by Joe Cook of Appleton. Cook and his brother had been prospecting about 45 miles north of Russellville when they discovered the large footprints. They measured 17 inches in length and seven inches in width. Cook also made mention of several caves in the area. (Farish's ref: *Daily Courier*, Russellville, Arkansas, March 12, 1978)

Farish says that on June 26, 1978, 10-year-old Mike Lofton of Crossett, Arkansas proved his courage by shooting at a 7-foot "something" outside his home. The incident began as Mike was feeding his puppy when it began to tremble. He then saw this thing coming out of the woods. Young Lofton ran into the house and retrieved his father's .22 caliber rifle. He said he fired on the creature and it fled into the woods. (Farish's reference: *The News*

*The Skunk Apes of Swamp Nation*

*Observer*, Crossett, Arkansas, July 12, 1978)

The BFRO website (Bfro.net) mentions that there have been other Arkansas sightings including some from the 1930s when moonshining (illegal alchohol distilling) was a big business. BFRO says that the group had the opportunity of talking with Don Pelfrey of Covington, Kentucky in 1982. Pelfrey said he had spent several summers at the home of his relatives in Arkansas. He said his aunt and uncle live about 50 miles east of Hope near the Ozark Mountains and Black Lake. Fouke Creek (the "Boggy Creek"), which runs behind the house, was the center of activity over many years said Pelfrey.

His relatives (who wished to remain anonymous) had seen the creature on several occasions. They described the "monster" as a "gorilla type," except that it looked more human than animal. Its arms are longer than a man's and its face is covered with hair. The apeman allegedly leaves 17-inch footprints.

According to Mr. Pelfrey, one can see the dermal ridges on the prints. The ball of the foot is more flat than a human's and there is no indication of an arch.

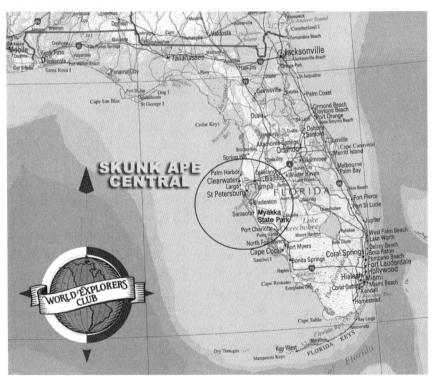

BFRO says that Pelfrey told them, "It is about 800 pounds and appears to be about 10 feet tall. It sounds like a bear with a screeching voice." He also told them that it leaves a bad stink like that of a skunk. In addition, he said that several animals of the property had been found in a mutilated state, such as chickens, a calf and dogs with large lacerations. He told them of an incident that occurred on his aunt's farm in July of 1977:

> My Aunt Martha had two prize hogs that she always hand fed until they were a couple of hundred pounds. Late one night, we heard such a calamity that we ran to the back porch and turned the light on. When we checked the pen, both hogs were missing. There was no sign of blood or anything else. While looking around the house, we found a huge path through the weeds leading into the swamp. We discovered the remains of the hogs about 500 yards away. There appeared to be large bites and scratches and the vital organs were torn out. It appeared that the hogs were killed for sport rather than food. The neighbors had two dobermans killed. Every bone in their bodies seemed broken. They were mutilated so rapidly, that by the time they got dressed and outside, the dogs were dead. I believe this creature has become more aggressive due to more people venturing into the swamps.

Pelfrey also told the BFRO investigators that the local authorities will not talk to anyone about the creature. In fact, Pelfrey claimed, they will chase you out of the county. (Bfro.net)

## 1974: Bigfoot Hit By Car in Hollywood, Florida

There were several incidents with one or more bigfoot on the night of January 9, 1974 around Hollywood, Florida. First, a man named Richard Lee Smith claimed that he struck a bigfoot with his car that evening while driving down Hollywood Boulevard just outside of town. The 7- to 8-foot dark-haired bigfoot had actually gone under the car, so it stood up to its 7- to -8-foot height, roared and then made a lurch toward Smith, who had stopped his car and gotten out. Smith jumped back into his car and left. Once at his house Smith called the police who then examined his car and found bloodstains and coarse hair. The police officers were all put on notice to look for the hairy giant.

Then an incident occurred at 2:20 a.m. on Highway 27 outside of Hollywood when patrolman Robert Hollemeyal saw a dark figure coming down the road at him. Hollemeyal got out of his patrol car and ordered the figure to halt. He then saw a 7-foot-tall dark-haired bigfoot coming toward him. He shot it twice with his revolver. The bigfoot screamed, jumped 20 feet and ran off ay about 20 miles per hour the patrolman said.[3]

These swamp apes and wooly boogers don't bathe much. Folks smell them coming from quite a distance. The local dogs go wild. Teenage girls run to their rooms screaming. Cops discharge their weapons into the 8-foot hairy critter on a dark road late at night. It is all like some B-movie gone horribly wrong. Trailer parks are known to attract tornados, rednecks, methamphetamine labs, and, apparently, skunk apes, smelly as they are. Swamp Ape Nation can be a dangerous place—where everything and everyone is on the wrong side of the tracks!

### 1975: Man Shoots at Bigfoot

On January 23, 1975, a rookie policeman named Kim Dunn said he saw a loping bigfoot crossing the road near Miramar, Florida.

Then on February 2, 1975, Richard Davis says he encountered a bigfoot near Cape Coral, Florida that was 9 feet tall. He shot the bigfoot once but could not shoot it a second time. Later in February near Gainesville, Florida, it was reported that bigfoot was hit by a car.

On March 6, 1975 a couple collided with bigfoot on a road near Lake Okeechobee in Martin County, Florida. Steve Humphries and his wife were driving at night when they collided with a bigfoot running quickly across the road. They stopped the car and the victim was gone, although the dents on their car showed a substantial collision.[3]

Then, on March 24, 1975, at a place called Black Point in Goulds Canal in Dade County, Florida, two men watched a bigfoot rock a

**180**

car. Michael Bennett and Lawrence Groom said they watched an 8- or 9-foot bigfoot rocking a blue car with a hysterical man inside the vehicle. That man exited the vehicle and yelled for help. Bennett and Groom said that when the lights of their car lit up the scene, the giant apelike man turned and ran into the nearby mangroves. They turned their car around and did not see where the other man had gone. They drove home and reported the incident to the Dade County Public Safety Department.[29]

On June 7, 1975 near Venice, Florida, a 12-year-old boy named Ronnie Steves said he was alerted in the night by the panicking of his ducks; he went outside to find a 6-foot bigfoot leaning on a post looking down at his ducks. Ronnie ran back into the house yelling to his parents in their bedroom, "There's an ape out there!" The police were called and they investigated the case. The next day the boy found huge footprints where the bigfoot had been. The whole story was written up in *The Sun Coast Times* a few months later.[29]

In November of 1975 seven young men, including 18-year-old John Sohl, saw three bigfoot while sitting around their campfire in Citrus County, Florida. They described the biggest as 8 feet tall. The group got out their flashlights and decided to search the area. Sohl got his camera and went off by himself. He set up his camera to take an automatic flash photo while he crouched by some bushes. It suddenly surprised a bigfoot who jumped up and knocked Sohl 15 feet to the side by a sudden sweep of his long arms as he ran away. Sohl thought that it was probably an accident as the startled creature fled. The photo was a washed-out blur.[3]

## 1976: Boaters See Bigfoot in the Everglades

In June of 1976 near Holiday Park, Florida, Mitch Bridges and a dozen other people were on a tour boat in Conservation Area Three of the Everglades National Park when the group saw a 7-foot-tall skunk ape standing on a grassy knoll in the swamp. Bridges said that it walked down into three or four feet of water and waded through the swamp at one point passing within 6 feet of the boat. Bridges said that it walked with a limp, was easily four feet wide and had a head like an ape.[1]

On June 18, 1976, the *Daily Herald News* of Punta Gorda, Florida, carried a story about several bigfoot sightings in the Grove

City area. The newspaper article said that in mid June of 1976 three youths near Grove City had two sightings of a "skunk ape" on the same night. They said that it was 7 feet tall with long reddish-brown hair and that it growled at them. The article went on to say that around that same time Deputy Carl Williams was investigating a pond near Grove City and when he shone his car light on the subject, he a saw "a big animal… hunched over." It was possibly drinking, had long brown hair and lumbered off into the woods.[3]

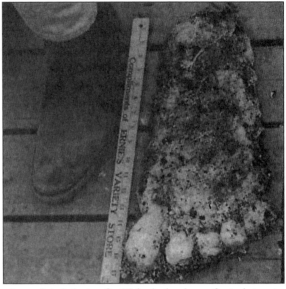

An undated photo of a 17-inch skunk ape footprint cast.

Also in June of 1976, a skunk ape was seen near North Fort Meyers, Florida by two brothers, John and Bill Holley, plus a friend. They said it was about 6-feet tall with long black hair and was standing in a clump of pine trees. This story appeared in the Atlanta, Georgia, *Constitution* on June 11, 1976.[3]

## 1977: Lurking Bigfoot in Central Florida

On January 20, 1977, the *Natchez Democrat* published a story about bigfoot sightings in southern Mississippi in the past month. The police station was then deluged with calls from locals who had seen bigfoot in the past year or so.[29]

The Mississippi swamp apes surfaced again when the Associated Press picked up on a story that occurred near Natchez on the Mississippi River on January 20, 1977. Said the *Arkansas Gazette* and other newspapers on that day under the headline, "'Hairy Creature' is Being Sought":

The police are investigating reports of a "huge, hairy creature" that reportedly was sighted by several Natchez residents. Those who reported the sighting to police Monday night said the "almost human" creature growled at a dog and fled when a patrol car approached.

The police said they found large footprints, broken tree limbs and other evidence that something was in the area.

Three occupants of one house said they looked out and saw "a huge, hairy creature, well over six feet tall, and dark, barefoot and naked." They said the creature walked with a limp.

This bigfoot was seen in the area of the mighty Mississippi River. That these creatures could be able to swim even very wide rivers is not surprising. In the American Midwest, at least, it is easy to conclude that bigfoot is equally at home in the water as he is on land.

In early February of 1977 a golf course superintendent just west of Delray Beach, Florida encountered a smelly, 7-foot-tall bigfoot at 1 a.m. He said that it was drinking water from a pond near the second tee of the golf course. Illuminated by the headlights of his pickup, the superintendent said that the bigfoot was covered with long, black shaggy hair and had very wide shoulders. It looked around and then lumbered into the woods. The superintendent then left a bunch of bananas at the edge of the woods and found them gone when he returned at 5:30 a.m. The city police laughed at the story and the County Animal Regulator speculated that it was a man in a gorilla suit trying to freak out lovers on the golf course at night.[3]

In April of 1977 at Moon Lake, Florida, three men in a truck saw a 9-foot bigfoot as they drove along a road during a full moon. They said that the bigfoot leapt across the road in one great bound and disappeared.[29]

On July 21, 1977, two men in Key Largo, Florida said they saw bigfoot in a field. The local paper, the *Florida Keys Keynoter,* ran a story on July 28 saying that Charlie Stoeckman and Charlie Stoeckman Jr. (13 years old) and a friend had seen a "skunk ape" three times that month.[3]

Another incident reported in the *Sentinel Star* of Orlando,

Florida (October 5, 1977) pretty much spells it out. Entitled "Lurking Bigfoot Trick or Threat?," the article said:

> Halloween is still three weeks away but strange creatures are already being seen around Central Florida this week. A 22-year-old hitchhiker reported sighting the legendary Bigfoot, saying the beast was tall, dark and stinky. It lurked in the darkness in a lightly forested area off U.S. 441 half a mile south of Belleview, he said.
>
> "I've got some information about Bigfoot," the tremulous voice on the telephone said. "I think I just saw it."
>
> Monday morning a security guard for an Apopka nursery told police a 10-foot-tall hairy animal with a chest full of reddish-gray fur and small ears attacked him, ripping off the terrified guard's shirt.
>
> Donnie Hall, 27, said he fired several gunshots at the creature in vain. The Bigfoot sighter—a Belleview welder who didn't want his name known—said the beast was brown and black. "I'm six feet tall and it was bigger than me. It smelled horrible, like garbage."
>
> Neither of the two creature sightings was substantiated. A Florida Game and Fresh Water Commission agent who examined tracks at John's Nursery in Apopka said they all appeared to be man-made. Marion County Sheriff Don Moreland chuckled about the Bigfoot report. "I've been in law enforcement for 20 years here and I don't remember any reports of monsters. Flying saucers, yes, but I don't recall any monsters."

The year 1977 was a good year for skunk apes skulking about in the night in Florida. On November 15 of that year the *Evening Telegram* (Superior, Wisconsin) and other newspapers reported the United Press International (UPI) report from that day entitled "Creature Sighted." The article said:

A skunk ape silver coin.

A 67-year-old Baptist minister who says he hasn't had a drink in 40 years tells how he stood eyeball-to-eyeball for 30 seconds with a great, hairy creature in the Ocala National Forest.

The Rev. S. L. Whatley, pastor of the Fort McCoy Baptist Church, said he spotted the thing out of the corner of his eye while he was cutting wood with a chain saw three weeks ago.

Whatley recalled Monday, "It was standing upright, in the middle of some palmetto bushes, and that sapsucker was at least 7-1/2, maybe 8 feet tall.

The minister said the creature "had dark, lighter-than-black hair on its head and chest, not much on its arms, and none on its face. It had kind of a flat face, a flat nose, its eyes were sunk in its sockets."

Whatley said he quickly went back to his truck to get an ax because "me and that creature was going to mix it up," but by the time he returned from the truck the creature had disappeared.

He hastened to add that he hasn't had a drink in 40 years.

## 1978: Police Officer Meets Bigfoot in Alabama

On on March 6, 1978, Mrs. Ruth Mary Gibson was at her rural home in East Brewton, Alabama when she heard a shrill screaming sound in the woods. She called her brother, Luke McDaniel, to come over to the house where he heard the screaming too. The horses and hogs were in a panic and the dogs had run off. Soon a local police officer, Doug McCurdy arrived and they saw something in the road. Later McDaniel saw the bigfoot in his car lights and described it as "...seven feet tall, weighed about 400 pounds and its eyes were solid red."[3]

In late March, 1978, it was reported that a man had seen a bigfoot on the Conecuh River in Alabama. The man said he saw a bigfoot bending over and picking something out of the water. This story was reported in the Fort Walton Beach newspaper, *The Playground News*.[3]

## 1979: Bigfoot takes a Volley of Bullets in Mississippi

In March of 1979 Tom Goff and his wife were in their home at Flower Lake near Tunica, Mississippi when they heard a ruckus outside. Investigating, they smelled a strong, foul odor and the next evening they spotted a 7- or 8-foot bigfoot in the woods near the house. The next evening, March 9, Tom and his son Rodney armed themselves and waited for bigfoot. When he showed up again they fired a volley of .22 bullets from their rifles and the bigfoot ran away. He came back later that night, however, and pushed on the front door, breaking the frame. The next day the terrified family found blood spots on the door and footprints 16 to 18 inches long.[3] This is just another episode in the mini-war going on at the fringes of Bigfoot Nation. Bullets will fly. Wooly boogers will cry. Bigfoot can only reply by terrorizing your cabin and tearing you limb from limb. It's a messy war, according to the newspapers (fake news, probably).

## 1980: Footprints Near Camp Ocala

A skunk ape story from Altoona, Florida was sent out by UPI on July 2, 1980 and picked up by the Houston *Chronicle* and other newspapers. Said the *Chronicle* story headlined "Police Think Mystery Footprints are Fakes":

> Most investigators figure it's a hoax, but there is enough doubt in their minds to order casts made of the size 18 foot-like prints found in a remote area of the Ocala National Forest.
>
> "I think it's a hoax," said Doug Sewell, chief investigator for the Lake County Sheriff's department. "There was no indication that something big enough to make those prints went back through the woods."
>
> Less sure, however, is Lake County Sgt. Dee Kirby, called out to make casts of the half dozen 17-inch-by-6 1/2-inch footprints found near a bulldozer in the vicinity of Camp Ocala, a federal job-training site.
>
> He said the prints showed a definite arching of the instep, five distinct toes and even some wrinkling along the instep. "The prints had a full four feet of distance between each of

one," he said, speculating that if they were real the creature that made them must be 10- to-12-feet tall and weigh close to 1,000 pounds.

The prints were discovered by a private contractor doing roadwork for the U.S. Forestry Service. Forestry officials also made casts of the prints, but doubted if they would investigate further.

Informal speculation centered on whether the creature was the infamous "skunk ape"—Florida's own version of Bigfoot and the abominable snowman—reportedly last sighted in the Everglades.

### 1986: Ginseng Hunter in Georgia meets Old Bigfoot

A startling encounter happened in August of 1986 along the Georgia-Alabama border, reported in *The News* of Summerville, Georgia with a byline of Tommy Toles. The story was about a ginseng hunter named David Brown:

> Brown was hunting ginseng below the crest of Taylor's Ridge when he thought a friend was following him. He turned and was shocked to see a heavy-looking creature with large eyes, a flat nose, a pointed head, and long arms that dangled to its knees. Brown was terrified and unable to move. The creature's left "hand" had long fingernails that curved "like corkscrews in a knot." Its left arm seemed to be useless and its left leg injured. The right hand had short fingernails and looked normal. Its body was covered with thick, long black hair that fell in locks, and Brown couldn't tell if it was male or female. The face was "monkey-like," thick-lipped, and toothless. The creature finally grunted and walked away. Brown threw up from fright and later reported the incident to police.[1]

Like many people who have

A drawing of a skunk ape by Matt Ellis in 2010.

sudden encounters with bigfoot, David Brown probably did not return to the area where he had his frightening encounter.

### 1989: Dumpster Diving in Alabama

The Birmingham *News* reported in October, 1989 that a woman named Barbara Demers and her nephew were driving along Ruth Road when their headlights illuminated a bigfoot crouching next to a dumpster. The glowing red eyes were larger than a quarter and the creature was stooping next to some scattered garbage. Demers stopped the car and the startled bigfoot stood up, crossed the road in one step and vanished into the woods.[1]

### 1992: Bigfoot Hurdles Guardrail in Texas

Bigfoot was reported in a letter to the *Dallas Morning News* in January of 1992, sent by a man calling himself Daniel Fisker from Hamilton, Texas. He said that he and his family saw a large hairy creature while driving home one night from Stephenville, Texas.

**188**

It was described as a bigfoot about 8 feet tall and having "long arms that extended down to its knees... a human face, showing four fang-like teeth, two on top, two on the bottom, and the rest flat like humans. It hurdled the guardrail and ran off into the night toward the brush along the river banks."[1]

### 1997: Tour Bus Sees Skunk Ape

Robert Robinson reports that in 1997, a group of people on a tour bus in the area of Ochopee, Florida all claimed to have seen a large, hairy apelike creature walking along the banks of the swamp. Local fire chief Vince Doerr managed to snap a photo of the hairy creature as it walked into the water.[67]

### 2000: The Myakka Skunk Ape Photos

In 2000, two photographs and a letter were mailed to the Sarasota County Sheriff's Department, sent by an anonymous woman. The photographs show what appears to be a large, hairy bipedal creature standing next to a large palmetto plant. In the letter, the woman claims to have photographed an ape in her backyard. The woman wrote that on three different nights an ape had entered her backyard

One of two photos of a skunk ape taken in 2000 by a woman from Myakka, Florida.

to take apples left on her back porch. She could only think that the creature was an escaped orangutan.

These photos are some of the best evidence for skunk apes, if that is what the creature is. He was described as larger than an orangutan, at least 7 feet tall with "dark brown reddish hair and an awful smell that lasted well after it had left."[68] You might say that, "if it smells like a skunk ape, it's probably a skunk ape." This area around Sarasota and Tampa is known as Skunk Ape Central with its many rivers and swamps. The Myakka State Park is very large and houses thousands of wild animals—including bigfoot.

One of two photos of the Myakka skunk ape.

### 2004: Peach Orchards and Bigfoot

The Alabama skunk ape surfaced again in 2004 when a story cropped up out of the town of Clanton on July 8. The local television station NBC13 of Birmingham and Tuscaloosa ran a feature on the nightly news and then posted this story on its website under the title "Bigfoot Legend Thrives in Chilton County: Man-Like Creature Lives in Peach Grove, According to Legend":

> Whether you're a believer or not, the legend of Bigfoot is alive and well in Chilton County.
>
> For decades people there have been talking about the strange creature that apparently has an affinity for the local peach crop.
>
> In the 1960s, some strange footprints were found in a

Chilton County peach grove. Now the original investigator reminisces about the time he spent tracking Bigfoot.

"In our opinion it was definitely not a fake. It was a real track," said James Earl Johnson, the former Chilton County investigator, whose case sparked a legend back in the 1960s.

"We checked the peach orchard, and there was a trail leading out of the peach orchard, and it was tracks—strange looking tracks, similar to a human but bigger and wider," said Johnson.

With nothing but a print to go on, picking a name for the elusive creature wasn't very hard. Since then, Bigfoot sightings have been reported across the country, and sketches of the creature vary depending on where the sighting occurred. The name varies as well. In Alabama, the creature is known as Bigfoot, while in northern areas, it's known as a Sasquatch.

"Supposedly, the legend is that a hairy man-like creature that walks on two legs at some point inhabited the bottomland swamp regions in Chilton County in Clanton, Alabama," said Bryan Wyatt, a Bigfoot researcher.

"I know one thing: [Bigfoot] likes Chilton County peaches," said Johnson.

Robert Robinson wrote that a woman named Jennifer Ward was driving on a rural road around Lakeland, Florida in the summer of 2004, on her way home in the afternoon with her two daughters asleep in the back seat, when something on the side of the road caught her attention. As her vehicle neared it, the creature noticed her and

A drawing comparing a bigfoot and a skunk ape by Matt Ellis.

stood to its full height—on two legs. Jennifer described the creature as standing six to eight feet tall, and said it was covered in dark hair about two inches long. The area around its eyes was whitish and its full lips had the color and texture of the pad on a dog's paw. This sighting took place right after Hurricane Charley.

A photo of a skunk ape taken in July, 2000.

⁘ —ᴧᴧᴧ— ⁘

## 2005: Fouke Monster Back in the News

The Fouke Monster surfaced again in 2005 when the *El Dorado News-Times* (May 31, 2005) ran a story on the monster and the most recent reports of its activities. Said the article:

> In Arkansas, when we hear talk of Bigfoot, we think of Fouke, and its highly-publicized trademark "monster."
>
> So prevalent are sightings and stories about Miller County's Fouke monster, it was featured in its own low-budget movie, *The Legend of Boggy Creek* (and the two ensuing sequels). Though they are known by a variety of other names, these mysterious creatures have been casually dubbed "Bigfoot," because of the abnormally large footprints found near some eye-witness sightings.
>
> Considering that only two counties separate Miller and Union County, it may not come as a surprise that Union County has had its own share of Bigfoot sightings— the most recent being May 7, 2005.
>
> According to the Bigfoot Field Researchers Organization (www.bfro.net) and the Gulf Coast Bigfoot Researchers Organization (www.gcbro.com) websites, Union County has had at least six submitted Bigfoot encounters. Most occurred in woodlands and bottoms along the route of U.S.

*Top*: One of the photos allegedly taken of bigfoot in November of 1995 by a forest patrol officer from Tacoma, WA. The officer preferred to remain anonymous and presented the photos to Cliff Crook of Bigfoot Central in Bothell, WA. *Below*: An automatic camera took the so-called Brents-Cam photo, circa 2001.

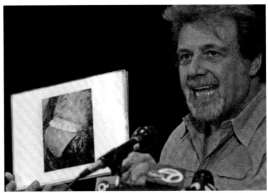

*Top*: The curious photo allegedly taken of sasquatch in April 2005 by a hidden camera at Moyie Springs in Idaho, near the Canadian border. The circled spot is a piece of bark spit in the air as the creature was apparently eating bark off a tree. *Above Right and Left*: Tom Biscardi of Searching for Bigfoot, Inc. showing a photo of the mouth of a bigfoot at a press conference in August 2008.

The "Tent Flap" photo of bigfoot from 2013.

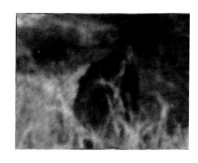

*Top Left*: Alleged photo of a Florida skunk ape taken on July 8, 2000 by David Shealy in the Big Cypress Swamp. *Top Right and Above*: No information is known about this curious photo that appeared on the Internet that seems to show some sort of ape crouching near a road with an ATV and rider in front. *Left Middle*: A 1997 photo taken by a firefighter in the Florida Everglades of what he believed was a skunk ape. *Bottom Left*: Alleged photo of a skunk ape from the Internet. Date and photographer unknown.

*Above*: A photo of a Texas bigfoot given to Donna Shelton at the Kountry Kubbard Restaurant in Lamar, Texas in the summer of 2009.

*Above and Below*: The interesting photos taken by Randee Chase, a backpacker from Vancouver, WA, on Silver Star Mountain in Gifford Pinchot National Forest, WA, near Mt. St. Helens, on Nov. 17, 2005. At first Chase thought it was a rock, but then it stood up and walked away. © Randee Chase.

*Top and Left*: Two photos of a bigfoot taken near the Hoffstadt Bluffs close to Mount St. Helens on May 9, 2002 and sent to the Bigfoot Research Organization (BFRO).

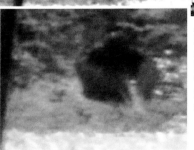

*Above:* A motion-sensing camera north of Remer, Minnesota took this photograph on Oct. 24, 2009 according to the owner, Tim Kedrowski of Remer. *Left*: On top is the "Backyard Bigfoot" photo taken in Kentucky in 2009. The bottom photo is an enlargement and enhancement of the original photo.

*Left and Below*: Two different photos taken in 2000 of a skunk ape lurking in a woman's back yard along the Myakka River in Sarasota County, Florida.

An advertisement for Flagstaff featuring bigfoot.

*Left and Below*: Two different photos and a close-up of a skunk ape taken by John Rodriguez in 2014. Real or fake?

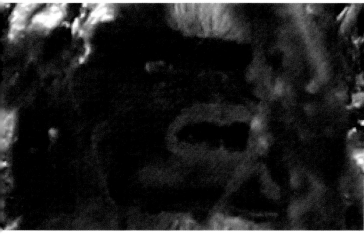

A footprint from the bigfoot that attacked
Darrell Whitaker in 2017.

*Above*: Two photos of a bigfoot by a river in Virginia taken in July of 2014.

167, but several have been reported near heavily wooded timberlands along the Ouachita River north of Smackover and to the east of El Dorado near Strong.

In a report (No. 11632) posted on the BFRO website, investigators were sent to El Dorado May 9th to interview the "young man" who reported the latest encounter—and to search the site on Victor Dumas Road where the sighting allegedly occurred.

In his written submission, the unnamed man told investigators that he and a friend were parked at the end of the dead-end road, sitting on the tailgate of his truck, which was facing the woods. Happening around 8 p.m., there was just enough sunlight remaining in the day to clearly see, the witness reported. Approaching the passenger side door of his truck to retrieve his cell phone, the man said, he glanced up to see on the left side of the road a fur-covered creature about 15 yards away. "With great speed, it ran across the narrow road, and paused when it got to the other side," he stated in his account. The man said the dark, hairy creature was stocky, hunched over and walked on two feet. Standing only about 5 feet tall, the creature ran with "great speed," according to this account. The other witness, who had remained seated on the tailgate, did not see the creature, but she claims to have heard the loud noise that was made as it darted off into the woods. A strong, foul odor, said to be reminiscent of a skunk or decaying animal, is often noticed even before a sighting occurs, according to information from the websites. There was no odor associated with the Victor Dumas Road sighting, according to the report. In his initial submission, the man made reference to the unusually short stature of the hairy being and posed the question, "Do you think this may be a young sasquatch?"

Sasquatch is just one of the many names of Native American derivation used to refer to bigfoot. The investigators' comments indicated they believed the man was "sincere."

It was also noted that the young man returned to the site with friends the next day looking for any signs to verify his experience. There was no related evidence found the day of the investigation.

Looking through the databases, Arkansas has 53 documented sightings. Miller County has the most on the BFRO database, followed by Saline County. Baxter County and Union County are tied. One of the more interesting accounts recorded in Union County occurred the summer of 1975. Two boys, aged 15 and 11, were riding on a motorcycle trail in the woods around Bayou D'Loutre just off Sunset Road (before the U.S. 82 bypass was built). The two boys had ventured deep into the woods, against their parents' wishes. They had just crossed a medium-sized creek when the oldest boy looked westward, into the sun. "I saw an 8-foot black figure staring at us behind a pine tree trunk, and then jumping behind it as though it was playing hide-and-go-seek," he wrote.

The creature was described as very thin for its stature. Its hair hung close to the body. Both boys decided it was time to leave. They jumped on their bikes and high-tailed it back the direction they had come. "I never looked behind me again, because I was near panic," the man wrote. After crossing the creek, the older boy, who was riding behind the smaller boy, started hearing the pounding of feet behind him. He claimed he could feel the vibration from the pounding of the last several steps through his handle-bars. The two peddled ever faster, as one of them saw a movement of black to his left. The two friends completed the rest of the shaky journey home without speaking.

Do they really exist..?

Charles B. Pierce's

*Boggy Creek II*
and The Legend Continues...

This man also claims to have met a man from Rogers, whose best friend saw a Bigfoot in the swamps near Parkers Chapel in the late 1980s. The man recalled how the two boys had smelled

194

horrible odors in those same piney woods and saw unusually large and peculiar piles of excrement that he couldn't link to any other animal.

In the summer of 1973, an 11-year-old boy had an encounter in Union County with something he believed to be a sasquatch. Camping with his family in the Ouachita River bottoms, near Eagle Lake, the boy volunteered to stay behind to gather firewood, while everyone else was out catching fish for dinner. The GCBRO website account claims that something started making gibberish noises, that he said sounded like a Tibetan woman auctioneer. It was loud and fast, reverberating through the bottoms like it was a large gymnasium. It happened three times, he said. The boy, now a grown man, said he has heard panther screams, coyotes, hoot owls, wolves, alligators and bears, but he, to this day, has never heard anything like that sound again.

Perusing various related websites, one can see thousands of documented sightings from areas across the nation. Most are investigated. A large map shows specks of color dotting states across the nation—indicating places where bigfoot encounters have happened. Audio tracks of odd howls and moans attributed to bigfoot can be accessed on one of the sites, which also includes an audio recording of an authentic 911 call from Washington state, in which a panicked homeowner requests law enforcement after he comes face to face with a creature in his own backyard.

Union County is far from alone in its mysterious encounters. Investigations have been launched by reports from Columbia, Ouachita and Drew counties in South Arkansas, North Louisiana, Oklahoma, Mississippi and Texas. In one GCBRO report, a Columbia County hunter shared encounters, second hand information from the past 20 years and claimed to have retrieved dark tufts of hair lodged high among broken tree limbs. In 1992, a Ouachita County woman cleaning a family cemetery, saw a tall, dark, hair-covered figure watching her from the wood line. "I stared—petrified—at the figure long enough to run through the possibilities of what it might be," she wrote in her entry.

After staring at the figure "for what seemed like an eternity," the woman turned her back and accepted her fate. "None came," she wrote. "I turned back to face the thing, and it was gone. I made a hasty retreat back to my car." The woman told investigators that her mother was raised in those woods, and never heard of any such encounters.

In the late 1950s, on a hot mid-August day, three siblings saw what they recognized as a bigfoot swimming in the pond behind their rural Drew County home. The 10-year-old brother ran back to the house to get a gun. He returned in time to fire a shot at the creature, who could stay under water for long periods of time and swim at a pretty good clip. They believed the bullet hit the target, but men who came and searched the pond and the surrounding area after the incident could find nothing.

And so the smelly skunk apes of the swamps continue to terrorize the backwoods communities and trailer parks of the south. As the grizzled skunk ape hunter in *Boggy Creek III* said to a reporter: "Yep, they're big—and hairy too."

## 2013: Bigfoot Caught Skinny Dipping in Florida?

Ken S. claims he was boating near Florida's largest island, Pine Island in Lee County, when he says he spotted something moving

One of two photos of a skunk ape taken in 2014 by John Rodriguez.

in the water near the shore. He grabbed his cell phone and managed to get a shot of whatever-it-was before it apparently disappeared behind the aquatic bushes nearby.

Pine Island is a very dense, impenetrable environment that would make for a perfect hideout for a large humanoid cryptid. The story first came to the attention of Toronto cryptozoologist and filmmaker Greg Newkirk who is a contributing editor to whoforted. com. (whofortedblog.com, 21 April, 2013)

In June of 2013 Mike Falconer and his son were exploring Florida's Myakka River State Park when they observed a distant figure walking around an open grassy area several hundred yards from where they were parked on the road. They both whipped out their low-rez cell phones, and the elder Falconer went to video mode and captured the alleged daylight footage. *The Huffington Post* later picked up the footage and posted it online. (HuffingtonPost.com, June 14, 2013)

### 2014: Swamp Ape Photographed?

In early 2014, Tampa, Florida fisherman John Rodriguez sent an account of seeing and photographing a bigfoot while fishing on the Hillsborough River near Tampa. He sent the photo to the *Huffington Post* and said:

One of two photos of a skunk ape taken in 2014 by John Rodriguez.

I fish for gar in the river and I bring my camera to take pictures of the birds and what not. I heard a squishing sound, looked over and saw this thing walking through the water and crouch down in the duckweed. It did not look like a guy in a suit—it was definitely an animal. I took this picture and got out of there as fast as I could. I've heard of Skunk Ape prints around Green Swamp [in Florida], but never anything like this. My whole life, never seen anything like it.

Analyst and former FBI agent Ben Hansen, one of the stars of the SyFy Channel show *Fact or Faked,* told the Huffington Post: "It's a relief to finally have a clear picture of the creature. Every other photo and video we get is usually too blurry or the Bigfoot too obscured in brush to allow for any useful identification. Thanks to the clear photo, I'm excited to announce that the photographer has captured a real-life... gorilla in a bigfoot suit!

"To be more precise, the face of a gorilla that has been digitally added to the photo with editing software. Although I originally suspected the creature suit was actually in the water when the photo was taken, I started to notice shadows in front of the Bigfoot that appeared to be an inconsistent length and shape with the rest of the photo."

Hansen went on to explain that digital photographs use a format called EXIF data, which stores technical information for each image

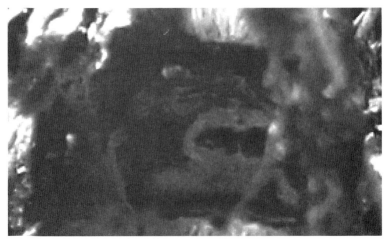

A close-up of a skunk ape taken in by John Rodriguez. The face of bigfoot?

such as shutter speed, whether a flash was used, the date and time of the image, etc. Hansen pointed out to the *Huffington Post* that the EXIF information of the Florida swamp creature picture appears to document that the image was digitally created on Dec. 26 with Photoshop.

Rodriguez took exception to Hansen's analysis: "I did not Photoshop this at all. Believe me or not. When I plug in my memory card, it asks to import and opens in Photoshop. I just changed the name and saved. It seems like people get publicly crucified for coming forward with this kind of stuff." Rodriguez also said he was hesitant to send the original picture to *HuffPost* because of the prevailing attitude of disbelief in the media. (Jan. 1, 2014, huffingtonpost.com)

## 2016: Alabama Family Threatens to Kill Local Bigfoot

The *Palm Beach Post* reported on April 19, 2016 that two Florida men claimed that they had a video of a skunk ape. The article said that two central Florida men, Mark Barton and Chris Conner, had combed the Lakeland area for clues concerning skunk apes. The duo said they didn't realize they had captured the image of the skunk ape until after they reviewed the footage and saw the brief "evidence." Both men said they believe these could be "massive creatures." "We have done re-enactments. I kind of pale. We're thinking 7 to 8 feet," Barton told local television channel Bay News 9 (said the newspaper report). The video can be viewed on-line and is interesting, though hardly conclusive.

In May 2016 a Gainestown, Alabama man said he and his family are "tired of dealing" with a huge, hairy hominid and were threatening to shoot it unless officials come to "capture and remove it." The man claims he was asleep on his cousin's sofa after a family reunion when he first encountered the bipedal creature in late 2015. At 3:30 am, he was awakened by the family dogs going crazy, one of them yelping like it was hurt. The man heard something climb onto the front porch and sat up to look out the window. He said, "… what I saw was unforgettable and unbelievable. It was maybe about 800 pounds and it smelled of cheese gone bad. It never turned so I could not see its face… It was squatting down right in front of me, I guess it was too big to stand straight up on the porch. I don't know why it was there but we had left the empty beer and soda cans and leftover food scraps in a couple of trash bags to be thrown out the next day. The lights were on so I could see it clearly."

The witness said the creature had brown and red hair, and its back, was very muscular. It had 16-inch feet and 5-feet-long arms. He was not able to get a picture despite observing the animal for about 20 minutes, as his cell phone was across the room charging. When the creature left, it leapt to the ground, crossed the 30-foot road in two strides and went down a ravine.

But, according to the family, the huge hairy humanoid has been lurking about ever since and has taken to terrorizing their pets, which they have to keep outdoors. "We know where it lives and how it travels, all we want is for someone to capture and remove it, or we will find it and kill it." Mike Brumfield, a longtime investigator, says he searched the area and found physical evidence such as "finger and hand prints" on a trailer located on the family's property, and has no doubt it was a real encounter.

Alabama has been a hot spot for Bigfoot sightings. In 2015, a woman in West Alabama and her granddaughter and a police officer encountered an unidentified, upright walking creature she believes could have been a Bigfoot. In 2013, a truck driver reportedly hit "something resembling a sasquatch" near Decatur. (May 30, 2016, cryptozoologynews.com)

### 2017: Skunk Ape Sighting Near Ocala National Forest, Florida

The National Cryptid Society's website has a case from late June, 2017 of a skunk ape sighting near the Ocala National Forest, north of Orlando in central Florida. The sighting was submitted by Rob:

I was driving down 182nd Avenue (known by locals as Forest Road 8) and I turned this corner and no more than 35-40 yards ahead I seen what I believe to be a Florida skunk ape (bigfoot of Florida). It was so quick I didn't have time to get my phone and snap a picture but it came from sunny hill preservation into the Ocala National Forest.

It took one stride to cross the road. Estimating it to be 7-9 foot tall about 3 1/2 foot wide long mammoth like fur. I

A cartoon about a skunk ape being interviewed in 2010.

stopped in the middle of the road astonished trying to see it through the woods and absolutely nothing there. No trace no noise, absolutely nothing. (www.nationalcryptidsociety.org)

## 2018: Skunk Ape Festival in Ochopee

The Skunk Ape Research Headquarters in Ochopee, Florida, held their annual Skunk Ape Festival in June. Their website says that the Skunk Ape Research Headquarters is run by the Shealy brothers—Dave and Jack. Dave Shealy, the younger and more outspoken of the two, is Florida's self-appointed skunk ape expert. Slim, in his mid-forties, he wears dark, wraparound sunglasses, a hat with a band of alligator teeth, and no shoes.

"There's never been a documented case of anyone ever being physically attacked by a Skunk Ape," he says, reassuringly. "But also, there's a lot of people that go into the Everglades that never come out." Dave has been studying the Skunk Ape "pretty much all my life" and describes it as six to seven feet tall and 350 to 450 pounds. He guesses that there are between seven and nine of the creatures around here, in a waterlogged and buggy wetland of buzzards, alligators, and towering sawgrass.

"Not everyone who sees a Skunk Ape reports it," says Dave.

## The Skunk Apes of Swamp Nation

"They don't want people to poke fun at'em, or to tell'em they're crazy. That's not the exception; that's pretty much the rule." But reports do get through. Dave recalls that in 2003 two European women were in the Big Cypress Swamp, photographing plants, when they were surprised by "a huge male Skunk Ape" with an erection. "It was what I believe was the mating season," Dave explains. The women escaped unharmed.

No doubt the smelly skunk apes of Florida, Alabama and Mississippi will continue to haunt the swamps and forests of Swamp Ape Nation. Perhaps they will even show up at the many skunk ape festivals that crop up in Florida and Alabama from time to time. It won't be just the swamp apes doing all the screaming and yelling. Some teenage girls in cut-off jeans are sure to be there and there will be plenty of screaming once they get up close and personal with those smelly, ugly critters. Some creatures should just not come in from the swamp!

Some think that Lincoln made a secret treaty with skunk apes.

# CHAPTER 7

# Bigfoot in the Southwest

The intrigue of a search for an unknown species
of man or animal… sparks the souls and
imagination of most people.
—*Robert H. Rines, Academy of Applied Sciences, Boston*

While most people know that sightings of bigfoot, sasquatch and skunk apes have been reported in the forests of Canada, the Pacific Northwest, the East Coast and the swamps of Florida and other southern states, many are not aware of the plethora of sightings in the mountains of New Mexico and the eastern forests of Arizona. This Arizona bigfoot is called the Mogollon Monster (pronounced mug-ee-OWN). The American Southwest is made up of deserts, mountains, forests and canyons. Much of it is wilderness and it is an ideal habitat for the elusive denizens of Bigfoot Nation.

The Mogollon Monster made news all over Arizona on September 2, 2006, when newspapers in the state reported on bigfoot activity at the White Mountain Apache Nation which comprises a large part of east-central Arizona. This area of the state is heavily forested and lies along what is known as the Mogollon Rim. The Rim stretches from Flagstaff, through small towns to the south like Pine and Strawberry, into Payson, Show Low and the White Mountain Apache Nation and then to the Mogollon Mountains in New Mexico. The Mogollon Mountains and Mogollon Rim are named after the Spanish governor of New Mexico from 1712 to 1715, Ignacio Flores Mogollon.

This area contains the largest ponderosa pine forest in the world and is the sort of habitat that bigfoot is said to prefer: dense forest with plentiful rivers and streams, and a near complete lack of human towns and cities. Indeed, this vast area, larger than many eastern states, could contain many hundreds of bigfoot. Areas around Payson, Flagstaff, Stoneman Lake, and the tiny towns of Pine and Strawberry have experienced bigfoot reports for many years, and I personally know several people who say they have briefly encountered bigfoot in this area. Let us look at a chronological history of bigfoot in the Southwest.

**The Mogollon Monster**

The Mogollon Monster is described in the same way that most bigfoot are described: it is an apelike creature that walks on two legs and is over seven feet in height. The creature is said to be covered in long black or reddish brown hair, except on the face, hands and feet.

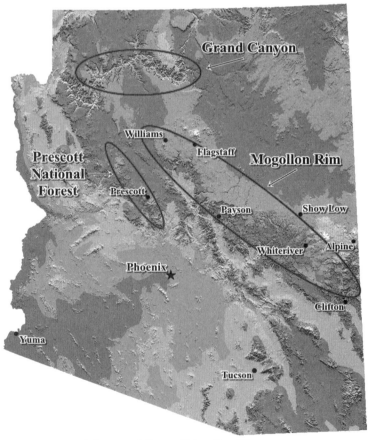

Arizona and the vast Mogollon Rim area.

Like other bigfoot and skunk apes of the swamps of the southern states, the Mogollon Monster is said to have a strong body odor that smells similar to a skunk or dead fish. Some investigators have theorized that bigfoot actually takes the scent glands from skunks that it kills (and probably eats) and uses them to create the horrible smell as a form of protection, including using the smell gland on infant bigfoot.

The Mogollon Monster has his own Wikipedia entry:

> Stories say the creature is nocturnal, omnivorous, very territorial and sometimes very violent. It is generally reported to: walk with wide, inhuman strides; leave behind footprints measuring 22 inches in length; mimic birds, coyotes and other wildlife; emit unusual whistle sounds; explore campsites after dark; build "nests" out of pine needles, twigs, and leaves; and hurl stones from locations that are hidden from view. The creature has also been said to decapitate deer and other wildlife prior to consumption. In numerous reports, the monster has been said to emit a "blood-curdling" scream, described as sounding like a woman in "great distress." Accounts of the creature regularly describe an "eerie silence prior to the encounter, an appreciable stillness in the woods that commonly surrounds predatory animals."

## 1903: Hairy Beast Seen Near the Grand Canyon

Wikipedia and *Weird Arizona*[59] mention this very early report of bigfoot in Arizona, when it was still a territory:

> The oldest known documented sighting of the Mogollon Monster was reported in a 1903 edition of *The Arizona Republican* in which I.W. Stevens described a creature seen near the Grand Canyon as having "long white hair and matted beard that reached to his knees. It wore no clothing, and upon his talon-like fingers were claws at least two inches long." Upon further inspection he noted "a coat of gray hair nearly covered his body, with here and there a spot of dirty skin showing." He later stated that after he discovered the

creature drinking the blood of two cougars, it threatened him with a club, and "screamed the wildest, most unearthly screech."

### 1923: Cowboy Shoots Rifle at Bigfoot

In her book *The Mogollon Monster, Arizona's Bigfoot,*[69] Susan Farnsworth says that an early incident occurred in November of 1923 when a hunter and trapper named Jake Waite encountered the monster near the small town of Escudilla, which is near Alpine, Arizona on the New Mexico border. Waite was tracking one of the last grizzly bears in Arizona, known as Clubfoot, as it had chewed off a front foot that had been caught in a steel bear trap.

Waite described an animal that was stalking him and his horse. At first he thought it was a bear, but when he caught a glimpse of the animal walking on two legs like a man, he thought it might be a person. Dismounting from his horse to get behind a boulder for safety, he called out to the person, whom he thought was trying to steal his horse: "If you are a man, speak up!"

When no answer came Waite called again: "I am armed and I will shoot!"

Finally, when no answer was given, Waite shouted, "I'd hate to kill you over a horse!"

Suddenly the creature, a giant apelike man, ran for the horse and Waite fired his rifle. The creature fell but then got up immediately and kept running for the horse. Waite fired two more times but it did not seem to affect the monster. He then emptied his rifle into the huge, hairy creature.

As he reloaded his rifle he saw that the creature was now retreating. He emptied his rifle into the creature again. It let out a bloodcurdling scream, but it never went down. With only two shells left, Waite decided to save them in case he would need them later.

When he got back home to Alpine he tested his last two bullet cartridges by firing them into a double stack of two-by-four wood pieces. He found that his cartridges barely penetrated one two-by-four and he realized that the powder in the shells had gone bad. The Mogollon Monster was not bulletproof after all—Waite had been firing bad cartridges.

### 1924: Bigfoot with an Armload of Corn Picking Turnips

A report from the Bigfoot Co-Op and Peter Guttilla says that Mabel Fulcher of Flagstaff said that her family had a ranch at the foot of the San Francisco Peaks five miles northwest of the city. Mabel says that in July of 1924 she and her mother saw a heavy creature about 7 feet tall that was covered with light brown hair. She and her mother watched while the hairy creature held an armload of the farm's corn while it pulled up turnips from the garden. When they went outside to yell at the bigfoot it ran through a wheat field and jumped a rail fence to make its way to the nearby pine forest—still clutching its armload of turnips and corn![1]

### 1926: Bigfoot Attacks Cabin near Springerville

Susan Farnsworth, who wrote in her 1966 book about the Mogollon Monster tells the story of Lillian and her family in a cabin on the Little Colorado River east of Springerville in the spring of 1926. Lillian's husband, Jake was out for the day when her children—Billy, Fred and Jerry—came running toward the cabin from some woods near the house. Lillian was standing to one side of the cabin and as the children ran toward her one of them yelled, "Mom! There's someone watching us!"

Lillian asked who it was and Jerry said, "It's a big hairy man and he ain't got no clothes on!" Lillian then saw that a large hairy creature walking on two legs was coming towards the cabin.

"Hurry boys," she said grabbing a broom. "Get in the house!" They all ran to the cabin door where the bigfoot intercepted them. Lillian hit it with the broom and they ran inside the cabin and bolted the door. The cabin did not have windows and after letting out a scream the bigfoot began to circle the house. Lillian grabbed a shotgun that was kept next to the fireplace.

She was afraid that the bigfoot would force the door open and pushed a long bench against the door. They could see through small cracks in the logs what was happening outside. The bigfoot approached the door and began to push on it when the family dog, Lady, still outside, could be heard growling at the bigfoot. Lady suddenly lunged at the bigfoot and tore some flesh off the creature. The bigfoot howled and gave the dog a sweeping blow with one of its long, powerful arms. The dog attacked again and was again thrown off the porch, yelping in pain.

Lady attacked the bigfoot a third time, this time from behind, locking her jaws on the back of the neck and shoulders of the bigfoot. The bigfoot screamed and flung his arms but could not shake the dog away. Screaming the bigfoot ran off the porch back towards the woods with Lady still clamping down on the creature's back neck. Eventually the dog let go and fell to the ground, seemingly lifeless. The bigfoot continued to run into the woods.

Lillian was afraid to venture out from the cabin immediately, but eventually went to see the dog, telling the boys to lock the cabin door behind her. The dog was dying with broken bones, some protruding from her skin. Lillian was grateful that the dog had given her life to save the children and her. At that moment she heard a sound and looked up with her shotgun ready. To her relief it was her husband Jake returning home, soon to hear the astonishing story of a bigfoot trying to steal their children![69]

**1938: Eyes in the Dark**

A father and son were out camping and inspecting traps in the Bigelow Springs area to the east of Springerville, on September 28, 1938 when the father, Jonathan, left his 10-year-old son, Marvin, at their camp to mind the fire while he inspected some traps. Marvin dozed off and awoke to find that it was dark and the campfire had died down. He piled more wood onto the fire and then smelled a strong foul odor from some animal. Whatever it was it was crossing upwind of the camp. His father had told him to keep the fire big if he needed to scare animals away. Marvin also had a single-shot .22 rifle that his father had given him, and a pocket full of bullets.

He began hearing noises around the camp and got his rifle ready in case something happened. Then large rocks started landing on or next to the campfire, effectively smothering it. Marvin was standing near their vehicle trying to see into the darkness when another large rock came flying out of the darkness onto the campfire. He could see now a shadowy figure move from some bushes to hide behind a tree. As the fire burned down he could see two eyes behind a bush looking at him. Marvin's firewood was nearly out and he called to the figure in the dark, "Whoever that is they better cut it out. I'm armed and I will protect myself."

The eyes moved again and were briefly seen and then vanished. Marvin was preparing to take a shot between the two eyes next time they showed up in the bushes across from the dying campfire when he heard a noise behind him. It was his father returning to the camp. Marvin explained what had happened to his somewhat skeptical father, but then they noticed that the iron Dutch oven pot with their meal in it was now missing. Inspecting the area where the iron pot had been the father saw large footprints in the ground that were not from a bear or other animal. Just then the father and son heard a bloodcurdling scream that sent chills down their backs. Jonathan told his son they were leaving immediately and left their things at the campsite while they drove to the local sheriff's office. They returned the next day and found the empty iron pot on the hillside overlooking the campsite.[69]

**1939: The Apemen of the Borrego Desert**

I include this incident because it occurs in the desert of southerneastern California, a very arid area not far from Arizona and New Mexico. About five miles southeast of Borrego Springs is the Borrego Sink area. The Borrego Sink is the lowest part of Borrego Valley, receiving runoff from Coyote Canyon. Vegetation on its flanks is typical of desert growth in alkaline soil such as mesquite, desert thorn and bunch grass. In 1939 a prospector was confronted by a pack of gigantic silver-haired beasts with red eyes that glowed in the dark. Although they menaced him for some time, they appeared to fear his blazing fire and kept a distance.

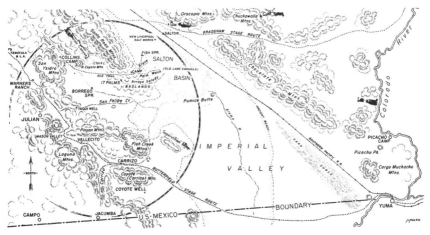

Mike Marinacci in his book *Mysterious California*,[64] says that Southern California bigfoot expert Ken Coon once interviewed the man who said he'd seen sasquatches in the tangle of dry gulches known as Borrego Sink. The witness was a local storeowner who wished to remain anonymous, and he told Coon that back in 1939 he was prospecting around the area and was camped there alone at night, when he was confronted by a pack of hairy, two-legged creatures. The apemen were covered with white or silver fur, and had red eyes that glowed in the dark. They surrounded him at his camp and threatened him for a bit, but were frightened by the blazing campfire. [64]

No one paid much attention to the old prospector's claim until 30 years later when Harold Lancaster, "a well-respected desert wanderer," confirmed to skeptics that some kind of strange beast was roaming the Anza-Borrego desert. He claimed that while camped in that same area, he was startled to see a "giant apeman" approaching. Lancaster grabbed his shotgun and fired a warning shot. The apeman "jumped a good three feet off the ground," then hightailed it back into the early morning shadows.[63]

Other apemen, or perhaps the same ones, were lurking in nearby Deadman's Hole. According to Marinacci:

> Back in the 19th century, this wooded hollow witnessed a string of unsolved murders that were blamed on a rampaging Sasquatch.
>
> It all began in 1858, when an unidentified man was slain here. Twelve years later, a Frenchman who had just settled in the Hole was murdered in his cabin. Two more locals were killed at the Hole: prospector David Blair, who was found dead of "knife wounds" in June 1887; and a young woman named Belinda, who was either shot, strangled or mutilated three months later.
>
> The rest of the story is vague and controversial. In March 1888, two hunters from Julian went up into Dark Canyon, just west of the Hole, and were allegedly attacked by "an immense unwieldy animal" that was over six feet tall, covered with black hair, with huge feet and a humanlike face and head. The hunters had been exploring a little cave full

of human and animal remains when the creature surprised them. Cornered, they shot it dead.

The beast's body was then supposedly taken to either Julian or San Diego, and exhibited publicly at a police station on April 1. The *San Diego Union* covered the story, and blamed the beast for the recent murders at Deadman's Hole. The next day, though, the paper ran a retraction, dismissing the whole thing as an April Fool's Day joke and belittling credulous readers who had trudged down to the police station to see the monster. If the whole incident was a joke, it was in extremely poor taste, considering that it made light of real, recent murders.

Ugly rumors and feelings still surround Deadman's Hole. Local sportsmen tell of "bad vibes" around the hollow, and Indians give the area a wide berth. Nobody quite knows why the wooded glade still inspires such feelings of dread.[64]

## 1940: Georgia O'Keeffe and the Ghost Ranch

West of Santa Fe and Espanola on Highway 84 is Abiquiu, New Mexico and north of that town is the Ghost Ranch. The Ghost Ranch was owned by Arthur Pack when the accomplished painter Georgia O'Keeffe (1887-1986) first came to northern New Mexico in 1917 with her sister. The soon-to-be-famous artist described her instant love for northern New Mexico by later saying, "When I got to New Mexico, that was mine."

O'Keeffe moved from her home in New York City to New Mexico in 1929 and in 1934 she found her way into the Ghost Ranch. Although she never owned Ghost Ranch, O'Keeffe eventually purchased a small home from Arthur Pack in 1940 and later a home in Abiquiu. She spent many years exploring and painting the Ghost Ranch environs.

The 21,000 acres that comprise Ghost Ranch were part of a land grant to Pedro Martin Serrano from the King of Spain in 1766. The grant was called *Piedra Lumbre* (shining rock). However, the locals preferred to call the area the *Rancho de los Brujos*—meaning Ranch of the Witches (or Warlocks) since the area was said to be haunted by evil spirits. The name "Ghost Ranch," was commonly used in English. Arthur Pack bought the ranch in 1936.

The Ghost Ranch logo.

According to the official brochure that they give out at the Ghost Ranch, the area is haunted by several entities. There have been frequent reports of six-foot tall "earth babies" covered with red hair howling at night, and a ghost cow with the ghosts of men killed in battles between sheep and cattle ranchers, and also the spirits of rustlers who once lived in Ghost House.

There were many bones to be seen in this high desert country and O'Keeffe was entranced by them, painting them, displaying them, and shipping a barrelful back to New York. O'Keeffe made a drawing of the skull of a steer and presented it to Arthur Pack as a gift. He promptly adopted the artwork as the logo for the Ghost Ranch. Ultimately, the Ghost Ranch was given by Arthur Pack and his wife to the Presbyterian Church in 1955.

It seems that the hairy "earth babies" were the Southwest's version of bigfoot making their standard wild screams at night, scaring the crap out of everyone for miles. Bigfoot screams are like the high-pitched wailing of the banshee, and those who have heard it say that it is very frightening and seems to be the awful sound of something supernatural. The ghosts of Ghost Ranch are bigfoot, ready to howl like banshees under the full moon.

### 1945: Bigfoot Invades a Boy Scout Camp

In the mid-1940s there was a well-known story circulated around northern Arizona about a Boy Scout camp near Payson that had a frightening encounter with a bigfoot one night. A scout named Don

Davis, 13 years old at the time, was camping with other scouts near Tonto Creek close to the small town of Pine, when something in the night woke him up as it rummaged though the boys' belongings. Not knowing who would be doing this in the middle of the night, Davis called out to the noisemaker who then came and stood near him. Later, Davis, who died in 2002, described what he saw:

> There, standing still less than four feet in front of me was a monster-like man… The creature was huge. Its eyes were deep set and hard to see, but they seemed expressionless. His face seemed pretty much devoid of hair, but there seemed to be hair along the sides of his face. His chest, shoulders and arms were massive, especially the upper arms; easily upwards of 6 inches in diameter, perhaps much, much more. I could see he was pretty hairy, but didn't observe really how thick the body hair was. The face/head was very square; square sides and squared-up chin, like a box.[59]

Another similar story is about a scout in a mummy sleeping bag with the drawstring drawn tightly over his face. During the night he woke up and found something scratching at his bag as if trying to find out how to get into it. Looking out through the hood the scout saw the large creature picking up several other scouts who had been asleep in their bags, as if to carry them away. The scouts screamed and struggled and bigfoot dropped them and ran away. This story, whose exact date is unknown, was told at many a campfire around Payson in the 1950s.[69]

### 1951: Rancher Sees Bigfoot

An incident in the BFRO database concerns a rancher in the early 1950s in the foothills of the Pinaleno Mountains near Stafford, Arizona in the eastern part of the state. A rancher was riding the range of his ranch on horseback checking on his cattle herd, and he saw a large, dark brow,n furry, upright creature walking on two legs that "was not a bear." He said he has seen bears his entire life up there on the range and insisted, "this was not a bear." He said that when the creature was aware that the rancher had spotted him/her it turned and ran uphill up a steep tree-lined canyon.

## 1955: Saved by the Mogollon Monster

A curious story is told by Susan Farnsworth that she says took place on November 22, 1955 on the South Fork of the Little Colorado near Springerville. Twelve-year-old Mike White was on a camping trip with his family and there was some snow on the ground. It started to snow again and the boy made a few sledding trips down an embankment near the woods. He then caught a whiff of a foul smell coming from the woods. He suspected that something large was moving through the woods above him. He decided to make one last sled trip down the hill and then head directly back to his parents' nearby rental cabin. He had heard about the Mogollon Monster and the Boy Scout camp and was starting to become afraid.

Just as he started to launch his sled, something large began crashing through the forest directly toward him. Mike slid down the hill on his sled and when he hit the bottom he jumped up too quickly and stumbled on a rock. He fell onto the surface of a nearby pond that had a thin coating of ice on it. He stood up again to run in fear and slipped on the ice and fell again, this time crashing into the shallow pond. Just before he blacked out he saw the hairy face of the Mogollon Monster looking at him through the hole in the ice. His mother later found him on the porch of their cabin, safe but wet. Mike is sure that the Mogollon Monster saved him from drowning that day.[69]

Nonetheless, there is still a disturbing pattern here of bigfoot often trying to capture children or teenage girls. Why was the bigfoot crashing through the forest at Mike? He could have kept hidden instead. Did the bigfoot decide to save the boy, rather than kidnap him? It is hard to say what the motives are behind the shocking incidents that occur in Bigfoot Nation.

## 1962: Rock Throwing and a Frightened Dog

Farnsworth also tells the story of Kent and Sarah Johnson, who along with their daughter Lacy, were hunting near Greens Peak on the White Mountain Apache Reservation, 30 miles east of Springerville. Kent, an avid hunter, had Sarah let him off at a certain spot on a remote logging road and told her to drive up the road for a mile or so and wait for him.

Sarah drove the car down the road to a spot where the road split and stopped the car. Suddenly the family dog, a cocker spaniel that loved to chase squirrels and rabbits, went crazy barking and trying to get out of the car. With a leash on the dog, Sarah and Lacy opened the doors and let the animal out of the car. The mother and daughter noted an odd odor in the air and the dog continued to pull on her leash, gagging and coughing as the collar choked her neck. Suddenly the leash broke and the dog ran barking into the woods toward the foul smell.

They called for the dog and walked a bit into the forest. The dog came running back and they saw something that they thought at first was a log, somehow being dragged by the dog. It turned out that the log was actually a bigfoot, chasing the dog from a distance.

The dog collapsed in their arms when it returned to Sarah and Lacy and suddenly a large rock came flying from a distance and landed on the hood of the car. Just then Kent arrived to ask what was going on. They showed him the dent in the hood and told him to get in the car. Just as Kent got in the car a large rock—big enough to kill him—landed where he had just been standing. The family drove away and vowed never to return to Greens Peak.[69]

Here is an interesting example of an excitable and inexperienced dog suddenly charging off to see what stinky animal is in the vicinity and then retreating in deathly fear. It would seem to indicate that dogs who have smelled a bigfoot before will be reluctant to attack the animal or even to track it, as David Paulides has shown in his

A drawing of the Mogollon Monster.

half a dozen books.[41]

## 1963: Something Violent at Stoneman Lake

Farnsworth also tells us of some curious incidents that happened near Flagstaff and Stoneman Lake in August of 1963. The area was not home to the busy Interstate 17 that exists now at the time, though even today the dirt roads leading from Stoneman Lake along the Mogollon Rim are fairly remote spots. Reports from various newspapers told of a truck driver, traveling with his wife, who had parked his truck by the side of the highway near Stoneman Lake to spend the night. The truck driver was later found pummeled to death and the wife was found nearby, having escaped from the attacker, "brutalized" with several large claw marks down her back and legs. She described the attacker as an apelike creature with long hair. The police speculated that her husband had been killed with a club that may have had spikes in it because his body was badly torn apart. The police speculated that it may have been a bear or a "crazed hermit."[69]

This curious incident, apparently quite famous around Flagstaff in late 1963, seems to indicate sexual assault. With her husband beaten and torn apart outside their truck the woman was dragged and beaten and assaulted. She somehow survived and escaped. Sometimes it is dangerous to be a woman in Bigfoot Nation—even while standing next to your husband!

## 1965: Small Bigfoot Seen North of Winslow

Early bigfoot investigator John Green says that he received a letter from a schoolteacher in Arizona who said that in the fall of 1965 he was driving north of Winslow when, "I was startled to see what I thought was a charred man climbing over a low fence or guardrail into the road."

He turned his car around and went back to the spot where he saw that it was "not a burned man at all but a glossy pelted thing that ran like a man mocking an ape. More man than an ape in his run, but more ape than man in his looks."

The creature was about three feet tall with glossy black hair and long arms. No ears could be seen in the 15 to 20 seconds that he viewed the small bigfoot, probably an infant.[29]

In October of 1965 a hunter named Lenny Wilson was hunting with his father, Jack, along the Mogollon Rim in an area called Bear Flats. He was separated from his father and found that as he moved through thick bush something was following him and making him walk faster and faster until he found himself running. He suddenly realized that this thing chasing him was possibly driving him into a trap—the area had many ravines and rock spires and he could easily fall into a ravine hidden by brush and drop six feet onto a sharp rock.

He stopped at a clearing in the thick bush and decided to face his pursuer with his rifle. The bigfoot came at him through the bush, but he could not see it. He called out a warning, saying that he would shoot. When no answer came and the creature seemed to be circling him in the bushes, looking for some advantage to attack, Lenny let fly a shot directly at where he could see the creature must be. It gave out a scream and as he was loading another bullet in his bolt-action rifle he could see the creature pushing the bushes away from him and running away from the clearing.[69]

## 1968-69: Bigfoot Shot in Chuska Mountains

In the summer of 1968 a couple were driving north of Anthony, New Mexico (in the extreme southeast of the state close to the Texas border) when they encountered a bigfoot. They were about six miles north of Anthony just after midnight when they saw a thing "larger than a dog" and looking like "an ape with long black wavy fur" eating an animal that had been killed on the road. The woman who made the report also said that a friend in the same area had heard scratching on the window of her home and then saw two hairy bigfoot in her yard when she turned on the outside light.[29]

It was reported in a letter from a Mrs. Cheeseman of the Navajo Nation that two Navajo shepherds in the wooded Chuska Mountains of New Mexico had shot at an 8-foot bigfoot that they had suddenly encountered. The creature ran wounded into a canyon while two other bigfoot helped it.[3] The Chuska Mountains continue to be a remote and mysterious location in the heart of the Navajo Nation.

## 1970: Bigfoot Runs Beside Car near Zuni

The Gallup, New Mexico *Independent* newspaper reported on January 21, 1970 that four youths from Gallup were driving in an area of the Zuni Reservation, south of Gallup, when suddenly a bigfoot was running along side their car, which was going 45 miles an hour. Armed with guns, they shot at the bigfoot and knocked it down. It then got up and ran away. They estimated the height of the hairy creature to be about 5 feet, 7 inches tall.[29]

**1971: Dumpster Diving in Flagstaff**

A report on January 23, 1971 in the northern Arizona newspaper the *Daily Sun* concerned two students at Northern Arizona University in Flagstaff claiming that a bigfoot had looked in their parked car at 1:00 a.m., probably while they were involved in some sexual activity. In a state of shock they went to the police station and reported it.[3]

Flagstaff has a huge forest of ponderosa pines around it that expands along the Mogollon Rim into New Mexico. It also extends to Prescott, once the capital of Arizona. That bigfoot goes dumpster diving in Flagstaff, Prescott, Payson, Snowflake and many other towns along the Mogollon Rim shouldn't be a surprise. And, while dumpster diving in Flagstaff you never know—you might find a couple of students in a hot and heavy session in a car. Basically, anything goes in Bigfoot Nation.

**1973: Bigfoot Chases Car near Flagstaff**

Ann Slate and Alan Berry report in their 1976 book, *Bigfoot*,[30] that a group of researches headed by Kent Lacy were camping at a spot called The Buttes in the Mohave Desert in late 1973 when they saw a hair-covered figure at night that they presumed to be a bigfoot. They also said that a very strong "rank odor" accompanied the encounter.

A BFRO report says that west of Flagstaff in December of 1973, during a snowstorm, a man traveling with his wife and infant saw bigfoot when they stopped to read a map. In the late afternoon, while traveling on Route 66, he pulled off to the side of the road to gain his bearings and check his map. He thought he might be lost because he hadn't seen another vehicle for miles and didn't even see any tire tracks in the snow covering the highway. He was driving a VW Beetle, which he left idling on the south side of the highway. While looking for the map, he glanced up to catch sight of what appeared

**218**

to be a large, bulky, two-legged figure running toward their stopped car from the rear. He mentioned that the figure had unusually long arms and legs for a man. The head appeared pyramid shaped but rounded on top. It appeared to be covered in black or brown dark fur and no clothes were observed. He thought it was about 10 feet tall. Feeling threatened, he quickly put the car in gear and tried to accelerate away from the fast approaching figure. The witness stated that the creature actually chased his car and came within 15 feet of the rear of his vehicle before he reached a speed of 45 mph and began to put some distance between himself and the figure. The figure remained on two legs for the duration of the encounter and at one point even raised its arms over its head.

On December 27, 1973 near Palmdale, California, a desert mountain community northeast of Los Angeles, a young woman and her brother reported seeing a bigfoot that was "twice as tall as a man" walking across the desert. When it spotted the duo, the bigfoot ran off very fast.[3]

### 1975: Bigfoot Runs Behind Car

A letter from Yarnell, Arizona to Dennis Gates discussed in John Green's *Sasquatch: The Apes among Us*,[29] said that in summer of 1975 a man driving in the area saw a bigfoot running down the road behind his car. He stopped his car and got out to look at the creature, which then ran away. The next day he saw it again on the mountainside, "lumbering along, its arms swinging and extending below its knees."

Susan Farnsworth, in her second book with Mogollon Monster expert Mitchell Waite, says that on October 27, 1975 two hunters, Lance and Steve, were in the Greens Peak Wilderness near the White Mountain Apache Reservation when they encountered bigfoot activity. Steve saw a bear and another creature fighting, and heard the ferocious roar of the bear and the shrill scream of the adversary—which he at first mistook to be the scream of a woman.

The bear suddenly took off and ran defeated down the mountain, and everything was quiet. Steve cautiously moved toward the area and then discovered a small hollow that had six dead deer lying inside, each without a head. He stared at the sight for some moments and then realized that this was a stash of dead deer hidden by a

**219**

bigfoot, and the bear had been coming to steal some of it. Realizing the danger he was in, he quickly went in search of his friend and the two of them immediately left.[70]

### 1976: Deer Hunter Sees Bigfoot

A report to BFRO says that the witness encountered bigfoot near Pinon, New Mexico in November of 1976. Pinon is in the southwest part of the state in the area of the Mescalero Reservation. Said the witness:

> I and a couple of cousins (primos), were deer hunting in Otero County in the area of Weed, New Mexico. I am a loner by nature, so I went off to do my own hunting. They went a different direction. As I climbed the side of a mountain I spotted some turkeys running uphill, so I gave chase so to speak. As I got to the top, I started going down the other side; it was very thick with pinon trees. As I went further down I saw a small meadow in the arroyo. I was on my knees because of all the thick trees. Anyway as I sat there, tired of walking, I was looking towards the meadow, and from the left side of the meadow I saw something walk out from the tree line, and up the edge, and back into the tree line. It never saw me and I did not stick around for it to see me. What I saw was tall, maybe six and a half to seven feet tall, [had] black long hair all over its body, and walked like a man. It was heavyset and appeared muscular. Its face was also covered with hair.

### 1979: Bigfoot Seen on Hopi Reservation

A newspaper story about a bigfoot sighting at the Hopi Indian Reservation in northern Arizona on February 11, 1979 appeared in the *Phoenix Republic* newspaper with a byline of Maggie Wilson. A Hopi man by the name of Kendrick Outah had told the newspaper that the first sighting of the bigfoot was near a local church at Polacca. The creature disrupted church services because every dog in the village began barking at the same time causing a great commotion. The police were called and found smears of fresh blood on a church bus and large human-like footprints that led through a wash and then disappeared where First Mesa's sheer cliff walls make their precipitous rise.

Kendrick Outah also said that another man had heard strange noises in the night and had gone out to investigate when he saw a very large, hairy creature standing near a tree. There had clearly been multiple sightings over the period of a day or two and Kendrick said that another witness said that the creature had "a head the size of a pumpkin."[3]

## 1980: Campers See Screaming Bigfoot by Tree

The Carlsbad, New Mexico *Current-Argus* reported on October 28, 1980 that two men, Gene Bryan and Mike Waldrop, were camping at Sitting Bull Falls with their families when there was suddenly a "loud and horrifying scream" in the darkness around their camp. They saw a tall hairy creature standing by a tree.

The same newspaper reported on November 2, 1980 that Marion Dean of Artesia, north of Carlsbad, saw a 7-foot-tall dark-haired bigfoot with white eyes standing in an alley near her apartment.[3] One gets the rather spooky vision of bigfoot haunting the alleys of remote towns in the west like some bigfoot stalker in search of prey. Could we actually attribute some missing people, even in towns, to sasquatch kidnappers? It has been reported before.

## 1981: Morning Sighting in Lukachukai Mountains

A report to BFRO says that on November 7, 1981 a man encountered a bigfoot in the Lukachukai Mountains of Arizona, just northwest of the Chuska Mountains on the Navajo Reservation. The town of Cove is in these mountains and has had numerous bigfoot sightings. Says the witness:

It was my first day of the 1981 Navajo deer season. I have hunted these Lukachukai Mountains for deer through my teenage years with brother T., uncle DJ, and cousins. I was twenty years old then. It was about 7 A.M., November 7, 1981 when our hunting crew reached the top of the mountain, southwest of Cove, Arizona. The weather was cold with shifting fog; the ground was frozen from the drizzle the night before.

Two cousins and I were to walk the upper mountain ridge that arced to the northwest. I packed my daypack and loaded my rifle. By then my cousins had already walked ahead of me, on a well-used trail, which rounded a hill to a saddle which splits the mountain range.

I wanted to catch up with them, so instead of following the trail, I climbed up the hill and over. As I reached the top and began to go down the other side I stopped and yelled my cousin's name to locate them.

I first heard crashing of oak brush, below me 40 to 50 yards to my left. I could not believe what I was seeing walk downhill on two legs. The oak brush was about armpit high on the thing. By then the smell had reached me, which was musky, wet smelly hair, an undescribable scent. I was shocked. The thought of shooting it came to mind, as I watched it through my riflescope, but it walked too similarly to a human. I did not shoot. I watched it walk down to the big trail below, about 70 to 80 yards and into the forest. I then hurriedly made my way down to the north, towards the forest road we came up on, and stayed on the road back to meeting area to the northwest end of the ridge.

I think it followed, because of the movement I could hear in the oak brush while walking on the road. I shot once to scare whatever was moving in the oak brush.

What I saw, was a very large black hairy being that walked upright on two legs. The upper body was broad and muscular. The hair appeared coarse. The smell was bad. I can only say, what I saw that day was a bigfoot.

The nearby Chuska Mountains, which are actually in New Mexico, is a much larger area and is known for its bigfoot sightings, some mentioned here.

**1982: Deer Hunters Find Tracks North of Williams**

According to a BFRO report, in October of 1982 a "Dave A" and his nephew were hunting in a mountainous area north of Williams, Arizona and found numerous bigfoot prints of different sizes. These tracks were observed when they had hiked a considerable distance from their campsite. The report said that the approximate location is in a mountainous area north and west of Williams, and between twenty to thirty miles south of the Grand Canyon. Dave believed that a family of bigfoot lived in the area.

## 1983: Fisherman Sees Bigfoot near Sedona

A BFRO report says that in July of 1983 a teenager (13) encountered a bigfoot near Sedona, Arizona, at the Oak Creek Canyon Slide Rock area where they were camped along the river. The boy took off on his own to fish along the creek surrounded by heavy forest. Then he began to hear noises:

> I heard footsteps. Not your typical steps, but HEAVY thumping steps. When I turned to look I saw nothing and the thumping seemed to stop. When I decided to get back to the more serious business of trout fishing I heard it again. I looked around again and this time when—It—stopped I heard very heavy deep breathing. I was scared and flattened my back against a tree, trying to peer around. I searched for the source of the noise, but could not locate it. I waited, I tried to make myself small, I was only 13. I stayed still for 20 minutes, my back pressed flat against the tree trying to look around without moving much. All the while I could hear that thumping walking sound and sometimes breathing. It sounded soooooooo close. Finally it stopped. I regained some courage, shrugged it off as my very good imagination and started fishing again, but I was still nervous. I felt "watched." Again the thumping and breathing. And this time to my left I saw it. A shadow in the dark woods, but an unmistakable one. I saw a dark brown, black body. Maybe three-inch fur. Shaggy looking. Six to seven feet tall. Moving away and at an angle. Approximately 35 to 40 feet away. As soon as I saw him he was gone. The woods were thick.

He also noted in the report that several times during the night and once during the day he found his dog in the back of the tent shivering uncontrollably and refusing to come out. This sighting

223

took place very near Sedona, but in 1983 the Slide Rock area did not receive the amount of visitors that it does today.

### 1989: Bigfoot at Sedona Sky Doorway

Peter Guttilla, tells of an encounter near Sedona in the summer of 1989 that is particularly bizarre. The story comes from a local man named Albert Rosales who says that an unnamed friend told him that while touring some property under construction in an area outside of town in the vicinity of Red Canyon and Loy Butte he saw "something that looked like a window suspended in mid-air." He also claimed that standing near this "window" on the rocky cliffs were two bigfoot-types who were 9-feet tall and seemed to be guarding the site. Frightened, the witness immediately fled the area. While this may just be a late night talk radio story, there is occasionally this element of bigfoot and interdimensional doorways.

While some bigfoot may play a role in military experimentation or extraterrestrial bio-manipulation and control, even holding rayguns wookie-style, most researchers into Bigfoot Nation feel that bigfoot is a powerful and frightening half-human animal—the missing link—who is afraid of fire, grunts and whistles for communication, and is largely incapable of firing rayguns or piloting spaceships.[1]

A report filed with BFRO says that in August of 1989 two forest technicians in the Chuska Mountains on the Navajo Reservation heard a bigfoot.

> One summer morning of the year 1989, I and a forestry technician were just finishing up a routine spotted owl survey in the northern part of the Chuska Mountain range. After calling for owls at a call point, just before sunrise, we began to walk back to the vehicle when we heard a loud, deep yell/roar from down below our position. The habitat was a mixed conifer stand within a deep dark canyon.
>
> Since there are sheep camps throughout the Chuska Mtn. range, it did cross our minds that perhaps someone (a human) was yelling, but the distinct factor that myself and the technician had agreed upon was that the yell was very deep and long (lasted approx. 5 seconds). After the vocalization, the echo itself retained the deepness of the sound as it

travelled through the canyon below us. It was definitely not a human that had the lung capacity to make such a sound.

The forestry technician surmised that the bigfoot may have been responding to their sounds, since they were calling with the imitated vocalization of the Mexican Spotted Owl. He said, "I've listened to several audio clips of recorded sasquatch vocalizations and can see where one may have mistaken us for another creature of its kind."

## 1992: Deerhunters Observe Bigfoot near Clint's Well

According to a story in the monthly Flagstaff, Arizona magazine *Mountain Living* (August 2004), in an anonymous article on the Mogollon Monster entitled "Yeti or Not: Northern Arizona is Bigfoot Stomping Ground," in the fall of 1992 two deer hunters observed an 8-foot bigfoot at their camp at Blue Ridge Reservoir near Clint's Well (between Flagstaff and Pine). The bigfoot took two licks of bacon grease from the hunters' Dutch oven before heading into the forest.

## 1993: Bigfoot Peeping Tom at Campground

As reported in an earlier chapter, in September of 1993 the *Payson Roundup* reported several curious bigfoot encounters at a campground near Woods Canyon Lake. The newspaper said that an unnamed visitor from England was hiking along the Mogollon Rim when he encountered a bigfoot. He returned to the campground—terrified—and left the camp ground. A short time later another couple at the same campground, Greg and Charlene Eairhart along with another man went target shooting and while Charlene was "answering the call of nature," she "had the feeling that someone was watching... I looked up and that's when I saw it." She described the creature as very large and human in appearance with extremely long hair of "a burnt orange color" that fell below the waist.[1]

## 1995: Campers Hear Screams on Mount Graham

A BFRO report says that some friends heard the screams of a bigfoot in September of 1995 when they were on Mount Graham, east of Safford, Arizona. The buddies were camping on the top of Mt. Graham near Route 366 in an undeveloped campsite just past the turnoff for Riggs Flat Lake. Said the witness:

> The first night, we were sitting around our campfire at about 10:00 pm when we all heard a loud unidentified bloodcurdling scream. It was like nothing we had heard before—not human or any other animal like an elk or something that we had heard before. The noise came from about 200-300 feet in the distance. We heard the scream about two or three times over the course of 15 minutes. We all commented about the noise like, "What was that?" But, we just kind of laughed it off.
>
> Later that night, at about 2-3 am, we were sleeping in the tent when we heard "something big" creeping behind our tent. It was definitely bipedal, because we could hear the pine needles crunching under the footsteps of whatever it was. You could also tell it was big and had some weight to it. We were so creeped out that I grabbed my 9-mm pistol and cocked it, and when we got the nerve we stuck our heads out of the tent and looked around. Nothing was there.
>
> The next morning I looked for footprints, but couldn't see any because of the pine needles covering the ground. The next night the same thing happened at about the same time—something big on two legs was walking outside of our tent. When we looked out it was gone.

Reports from around the Southwest indicate that it is good to be armed when camping in Bigfoot Nation. Also, note that the witness points out how pine needles on the ground keeps the bigfoot from leaving footprints in this part of the country.

A report in the *Mountain Living* magazine (August 2004) says that in 1995 a cowboy driving on Highway 89 in Chino Valley, Arizona hit a bigfoot with his pickup truck one night. The bigfoot got up and ran into the forest. One might think that it sustained some injuries. Such accidents may account for reports of bigfoot with a limp or a mangled and broken arm.

**1996: Encounter near Flagstaff**

A respected doctor from Flagstaff reported that on April 16,

1996 he encountered bigfoot in a canyon south of Flagstaff. He was hiking in the afternoon in a remote canyon when he found a curious rectangular structure made out of intertwined branches and rocks. The structure had five circular entrances to it, two big holes and three small ones. When something made a deep-chested growl from inside the structure he fled in terror.

**1997: Two Hunters nearly Shoot Bigfoot**

Another report in *Mountain Living* magazine (August 2004) says that in 1997 two hunters near Flagstaff came across a newly-made path in the woods and then saw a tall, hairy animal standing on two legs like a man. "My friend was going to shoot it and I said 'no," said the anonymous author of the report.

**1998: White-Haired Female Bigfoot on Road**

In 1998, the same doctor involved in the 1996 incident was driving back to Flagstaff near Lake Mary on a dark, rainy September evening when he saw a white-haired, female bigfoot crossing the road in the rain. This is a spot where a lot of game in the area cross the dirt road. It could be seen very clearly in the headlights and the female bigfoot had large breasts and a broad ridge on the top of her head. The bigfoot had 6-inch-long hair covering its body including the breasts and all the standard features of bigfoot, with the long arms and such. He went back to spot the next day and found prints and a long strand of white hair which he keeps to this day. Others had seen a white-haired bigfoot in the area including some Navajo friends. Some Navajo believe that a blue bigfoot lives in the San Francisco Peaks near Flagstaff.

The doctor had a third encounter, on March 5, 2006 when hiking in remote canyon near the first encounter. After going through some small ponds that were frozen, he encountered a sandy trail in the canyon that led among the trees to "the perfect cave" along the cliffs. It was an isolated and remote spot and when he investigated the cave he suddenly realized that it was probably occupied already. Then in the back of the cave he saw two large red eyes with dark hair all around the large head. He immediately turned and walked out of the cave and away from the box canyon and back several miles to his car. He said he knew a group of six hunters who reported that they heard "children talking" on Howard Mountain near Lake Mary. On several occasions they heard what seemed like a young boy and a young girl talking but could never find the source, and the voices would move to different places.

In January of 2013, the doctor walked out of his home one cold night and heard a strange sound coming from the direction of a Flagstaff water plant. It started as a low-pitched thumping sound and then was suddenly a high-pitched giggling sound, then it became a very odd metallic whistling-whooping sound. Thinking that it somehow had to do with bigfoot, he found out two days later that bigfoot had been seen near that water plant during the afternoon of the same day by Flagstaff city workers doing a monthly check on the remote well. That bigfoot makes strange whistling and giggling sounds is one thing, but the weird metallic-sounding whooping makes one wonder what is going on?

The Prescott *Daily Courier* had a story on July 27, 1998. "Arizona Man Searches for Bigfoot." The article profiled Lyle Vann of the tiny forest town Paulden, between Jerome and Williams. Paulden is surrounded by miles of wilderness. Vann, a former Hollywood cowboy extra, moved to the tiny settlement after 25 years in California and claimed to have seen bigfoot around his Paulden property, and even to have photographed them. The reporter, Andy McGinnis, said:

> Somewhere in the shadows lurks a beast. To a man who can see the creature, the existence of Bigfoot is no joke and you can laugh if you want. Lyle Vann sees him—or them—everywhere. And they're watching, working, involved in an existence out of some science fiction novel.
>
> Vann's home on the outskirts of Paulden, Arizona is kept and colorful; a peacock lives on the roof, while others live in cages in the back. Vann enjoys looking at them. He lives on the ranch with his wife, Jacquelen, and his Rottweilers. They hope to add a llama someday.
>
> Bigfoot visited the ranch recently, and Vann took a picture. Vann has hundreds, maybe thousands of pictures of Bigfoot on the wall of his basement and in all his albums. He points them out excitedly, describing in detail the

appearance of each one and the circumstances of the taking of the photograph.

"See his face!" Vann says. "Here's an eye. Here's an ear." The photograph is decidedly soft focus, and the areas which look like shadows, rocks and tree limbs, are in fact, Bigfoot creatures, or perhaps the aliens who control them, Vann says.

Vann is an earnest bigfoot hunter, but his photos are not convincing to the average investigator, including those from the Prescott newspapers. He currently runs the Arizona Bigfoot Center out of his ranch in Paulden and was still active as of 2018. Lyle Vann, like the bigfoot that surround his ranch, has chosen to live in the shadows of Bigfoot Nation.

## 2000: Bigfoot Encountered on Jacarillo Apache Reservation

The story in the *Mountain Living* magazine of August 2004 says that in 2000 a father and son were hiking around Sunset Crater northeast of Flagstaff and reported hearing angry huffing sounds threatening them from a ridge above the crater.

In May of 2000 there were several encounters on the Jacarillo Apache Reservation near the town of Dulce, New Mexico. A retired police officer from the reservation named Hoyt Velarde, who had been with the Jacarillo police for over 32 years, said that while he was investigating an electric fence, nearly 10-feet high, he came face to face with a dark-haired bigfoot that he estimated was about 14 feet tall. It was leaning down to touch the top wires of the electric fence.

Hoyt said that he turned the fence off while making his thrice-weekly inspections of the fence on a 4-wheel ATV. He says that the top four wires of the fence are never live, but he had the entire fence turned off for his inspection. One part of his fence must be inspected on foot as it is over a small hill that the vehicle cannot climb. Hoyt says that he had just walked over the hill and saw the giant bigfoot standing there testing the fence, about 35 feet away. They stood staring at each other for some seconds and then Hoyt ran back to his ATV and the bigfoot ran in the other direction. I have personally inspected the site and interviewed Hoyt. His interview

**229**

can be seen in the 2009 documentary *Mysterious Creatures of the Southwest* (available from Adventures Unlimited as a DVD). Hoyt also surfaced in January 21, 2017 investigating mysterious claw marks on a camping trailer (see 2017).

The *Mountain Living* magazine story of August 2004 says that on Christmas Eve of 2000, a 7-foot bigfoot was seen in the Jack's Canyon area, near Winslow, Arizona, by two people. "Bigfoot raised his hands and shielded his eye from the headlights," one man said. "Then he ran away."

### 2001: Berry Picking Bigfoot at Chevelon Lake

A report in the *Mountain Living* magazine (August 2004) says that in June of 2001, a driver was looking for a campsite along Road 7 near Canyon de Chelley on the Navajo Reservation where he saw an 8-foot bigfoot standing on the side of the road. The man said that the bigfoot crouched down and hid behind a four-foot juniper.

Chevelon Lake, near Heber Arizona, is one of a number of lakes on the Mogollon Rim including Bear Lake, Woods Canyon Lake and Knoll Lake. Chevelon Lake is quite remote and is a deep canyon lake that requires a relatively steep hike of three-quarters of a mile to get to the water's edge from the parking area. There are ample trout and crayfish to be caught and a thick forested area of trees and bush around the lake.

In August of 2001 a couple named Richard and Alice were

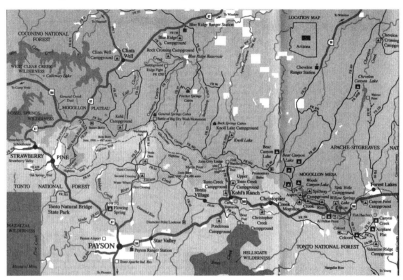

taking a hike along Chevelon Lake looking for blackberries when they came to a large patch. While the two of them separated with their baskets of berries, Richard took to fishing in the lake and suddenly saw a bigfoot family shoving berries into their mouths by drawing the branches full of berries to their mouths and eating them. Frightened, Richard dropped his fishing rod and drew a pistol he was wearing and fired off several shots in the air to scare the two large bigfoot and an infant away.[70]

A BFRO report says that on June 17, 2001 a bigfoot sighting was made in the western Chuska Mountains, near the Canyon de Chelly National Monument. Said the witness:

> I was driving along the washboard dirt road (7) that heads east along the south side of Canyon de Chelly looking for a place to duck into to camp for the night. I was about 7-10 miles east of Chinle driving at about 20 mph. It stepped out from the left side and walked across the road right in front of me, about 40 feet away or so, right at the edge of the bright part of my headlights, walking briskly but in no hurry crossing the road and slightly away from me at the same time so that it was probably 5 feet ahead when it reached the other side of the road. As soon as it crossed the road and the little swale of a ditch, it bent over just as it was behind a bush as if to take cover as soon as possible. At first, all I kept thinking was, "I just saw an ape of some kind," but I quickly realized what it had to be. It wasn't particularly large, about six feet tall or so, but very solid for its size and uniformly covered in dark brown hair. It never looked at me. I only saw it for about three or four seconds but I saw it clearly. I ended up going back a little, turning north on a paved road that leads to the edge of the canyon, just a mile or so, and turning off into the woods a little to sleep in the back of my truck for the night just two or three miles at most from where the sighting occurred.

## 2002: Why Did Bigfoot Cross the Road? Part III

A report submitted to the Bigfoot Research Organization was about an incident that occurred on September 17, 2002 near Rock

Springs, New Mexico, just north of Gallup going toward the Chuska Mountains. The witness, an electrical worker, was on Highway 264 when:

> About 20 yards from the truck I saw something walk out from behind a juniper tree that is located on the west side of the dirt road. Right when it stepped out into the lights of the truck, it hesitated and it looked towards me. I stopped the truck at that moment. It then started to walk faster, picked up its stride a little more. It took about 4 steps walking across that road; it did not cross the road in a straight manner, it crossed at an angle on the road and walked behind another juniper tree that is located on the east side of the dirt road. I had stopped the truck as soon as it had stepped out onto the road, my visual contact time with what I now refer to as "the Creature" was about 15 seconds. I waited there to see if it would come back out or if I could see any type of movement, [but] I did not see any. I sat there for a while thinking: what did I just see? My mind went through an elimination process, I thought, that was not a horse, a cow, a deer or an elk, 4 of the large animals that are prevalent in this area. The creature had a shiny brown hairy coat, it was approximately 7 feet tall—its face was like a monkey's and the eyes were big and black, like a big teardrop shape. Its head was small and it came to a long point towards the back. The torso was skinny, narrow shoulders, the arms and legs were about 3 to 4 inches in diameter, it had elbows and knees but I did not see any hands, fingers or a type of foot or toe structure. The hand and foot area were just rounded off, like nubbed. The only closest description would be like the way an amputee's arm or leg might look, rounded off. It took about 4 steps for it to cross the road; its gait was long.
>
> I sat there about 30 seconds wondering if I should start driving forward towards the highway or turn around and use the other turnoff further west. Also at that time, a chill came over me and I hurriedly locked both doors, I did not even want to look out toward my side window because a fear had come aver me at that point. I just revved the engine

and drove fast towards the highway. I drove fast down to the pump house and found the problem, it was a power outage to the well site. I had to go back to Ft. Defiance to pick up some fuses. I did not want to go back out to the area alone, so I had the dispatcher contact the Electric Line standby and I went back to the well along with him and I got the well back in service.

The next day, my co-worker and I went back to the site and found the footprints. He had a digital camera and he took some photos of the footprints. The footprints were about 4 to 5 ft apart; we tracked it to the east into the brush area. That night I went home and drew what I had seen and told my children of the incident.

According to *Mountain Living* magazine (August 2004), in October, 2002, the *Mojave Daily News* reported that a bigfoot was seen crossing Highway 95 near Bullhead City in far western Arizona. The witnesses speculated that it was just coming from a swim in the Colorado River.

**2003: Screaming Heard by Hunters**

A report to BFRO says that on September 28, 2003, a man and his friend were hunting at a waterhole near Sawmill, Arizona, on the Navajo Reservation, just west of the Chuska Mountains, when they heard strange sounds. Said the witness who was behind a hunting blind with his friend:

At 8:30 pm, the sun went down behind the ponderosa trees. We decided to crawl out of the blind and break the blind down. As we were taking the portable blind down, we heard a high-pitched scream that came from about 200 yards NW of the water hole. We stopped and listened thinking it was a bull elk. Again, the scream came 30 seconds after the first scream. Right then, I said, "That don't sound like a bull elk at all." As I said that, another scream came which seemed to last a lot longer.

It was about 8:30 in the evening and since they were a bit

spooked, they decided to leave. The Chuska Mountains are a wild area where bigfoot sightings are common.

## 2004: Bigfoot Reaches through the Window

There were several bigfoot reports in 2004 around Seligman, Arizona, west of Williams and Flagstaff. It was the talk of the town for many months.

A report to BFRO said that in late July in the town of Mescalero, just north of Alamagordo, New Mexico, a bigfoot was seen skulking through the streets. Mescalero is on the Mescalero Apache Reservation, and as on many reservations there are many trailer homes and power shortages. Said the report from an unnamed man (all the reports on BFRO are anonymous):

> Around 11:00 p.m. my sister-in-law ran in to my mother-in-law's house from outside and said that she saw something very tall walking on the trail below the house. She said it was walking back and fourth on the trail below before it came up to the house and stood at the corner looking at them sitting there. That's when she and her friends ran inside and told me.
>
> We checked outside around the front but saw nothing. So they went in her room after that. My girlfriend and I stayed in the living room and watched TV. When we heard some noise in the dinning room I said, "What was that?" She said, "I don't know," so I jumped up to see. Some of the girls came out to see what the noise was. It was like somebody throwing stuff around in the room. When I got to the dining room I saw a large hand reaching in the window. It reached across a table by the window and pulled out a bowl that had some food in it. We all got scared and I called the conservation office. Nothing else happened after that.
>
> This thing has been hanging around this town [Mescalero] for about 2-3 years now. About 2 years before that, a bigfoot followed my brother-in-law home from a friend's house about 12:00 am. He saw it down the road, about 150 yards away. He got scared and ran home. When he got to the door he started pounding on it. He didn't know

it had followed him, but when he looked behind him he saw that the bigfoot was standing there looking at him, about 10 feet away. When they opened the door my brother ran inside. He said the thing left after about 5 minutes.

Another sighting was about a year ago at the same house. My mother-in-law went out to get her clothes off the line. There was snow on the ground. It was about 8:00 a.m. She saw two sets of tracks, a very large set and a smaller set, like it had a smaller one with it. The tracks went between the house and the clothesline. Some of her clothes were on the ground. The tracks went down to the trees below her house. Now I live in a trailer home up the highway. The closest house is a mile away. One time I could hear loud screams one canyon over from where I live.

One night my girlfriend and I were here without any power and no dogs. We were going to bed and we heard a sound like a rumble on the side of our room. It was like somebody bumped our trailer with a car. It happened just once. I figured it was a bigfoot because we've heard it around here.

Bigfoot reaching in the window and grabbing the fruit out of a basket is everyone's nightmare where a hungry bigfoot has been lurking lately. He knows that he is not going to be invited in—with his bad manners and all—but he wants to be part of scene if he can. Besides, it's his nation too!

### 2005: Bigfoot Frightens Campers near Sedona

A report submitted to the Bigfoot Research Organization was about an incident in July of 2005 that occurred at the Lo Lo Mai Springs Campground by Page Springs, which is near the New Age mecca of Sedona, and also very near the northern Arizona home

A photo of a bigfoot standing by a tree near Williams, AZ taken Oct. 26, 2005.

**235**

of John and Cindy McCain. Said the report:

> I was in Page Spring,s Arizona on Oak Creek in July 2005 with my kids, camping, and my daughter and I saw something. I saw it twice. Also, a friend of mine and I had some bad feelings in a particular area there. He was camping further down the creek. What I saw was odd. It was grey, 4'-5' tall, slender, fast moving, able to hide, and made a screeching noise twice, once when I think it hit something while moving and again, far away when tons of dogs were barking. Could hear stones clicking, walking and breathing nearby after I went into my tent for the night. Our peaceful camping trip turned into us being frightened.

It is interesting to note how close this incident was to the home of Senator McCain. One might think that the Secret Service would be especially vigilant in protecting him if they suspected that a bigfoot was somehow on the property!

A report to BFRO detailed an encounter on November 3, 2005 at Borrego Pass near Crown Point in western New Mexico. The man wrote:

> I was traveling southeast from Crown Point, NM, on the eastern part of the Navajo Reservation. I was headed home. As I was going through a small canyon (pass) when in the headlights of the vehicle I observed an animal traveling east to west across the highway It appears to about 6-ft. tall and big; it was walking on two legs and went into a small gully. I pulled the vehicle around and shone the light up the gully and I could not relocate the animal. Due to the darkness and only seeing it through the headlights I could not make out the hair color; it appeared dark.

## 2006: White Mountain Apache Nation Sightings

It is reported on the BFRO website that there was a sighting of a bigfoot in the afternoon of October 26, 2006 near Concho, Arizona.

**236**

The driver, a doctor, said that he was heading for a ranch at 2:30 in the afternoon when an animal, that he thought was a dog, come up to the road in front of him. It then stood up on two hind legs and ran across the road. He estimated that the bigfoot was 6 or 7 feet tall.

The September 2006 White Mountain Apache Nation reports are particularly interesting because a number of Apache Nation police officers were involved, and reports were made to the police department that tended to show the seriousness of the encounters. Local television news crews were dispatched to interview witnesses

**Sworn Affidavit**

On this date: 8/21/2006, I, ▮▮▮

of P.O. Box 218, WMR, AZ 85941

do subscribe and swear to the following;

During the time period of: Summer 2004 / Summer 1982

and at the following location(s) Reservation Lake area on WMR - Ft Apache Reservation in Arizona.

did experience and/or witness the following: ▮▮▮ *(handwritten narrative, largely illegible)* ... was a big tall black hairy being walking ... when my vehicle ... I was traveling @ 58 m.p.h. and acknowledged what it was Big Foot ... the Being (Bigfoot) was gone. Next day we went back to check for foot prints but was grazing area ...

**Certification:** I, ▮▮▮, have given this statement of my own free will and certify under oath and under penalty of perjury that the statement written above is true and complete to the best of my recollection and ability

A 2006 affidavit to the White Mountain Apache police that a bigfoot was seen in 1982 and 2004.

on September 2, 2006, and this story appeared on Tucson's Channel 3 website, azstarnet.com, under the headline "Apaches Go Public with Bigfoot Sightings":

Footprints in the mud. Tufts of hair on a fence. Ear-piercing screeches in the night. These are only fragments of the stories now coming from the White Mountains in Eastern Arizona.

For years the White Mountain Apache Nation has kept the secret within tribal boundaries. "We're not prone to easily talk to outsiders," said spokeswoman Collette Altaha. "But there have been more sightings than ever before. It cannot be ignored any longer."

It is a creature the world knows as "Bigfoot."

"No one's had a negative encounter with it," said Marjorie Grimes, who lives in Whitewater, the primary town on the reservation. Grimes is one of many who claim to have seen the creature over the last 25 years. Her first sighting was in 1982. Her most recent was in the summer of 2004, driving home from the town of Cibecue. She becomes more animated as the memory comes forth. "It was all black and it was tall! The way it walked; it was taking big strides. I put on the brakes and raced back and looked between the two trees where it was, and it was gone!"

Grimes' son Francis has a story. Their neighbor Cecil Hendricks has a story. Even police officers have had strange encounters. Officer Katherine Montoya has seen it twice. On a recent Monday night dozens of people called into the tribe's radio station, KNNB, to talk about what they'd seen. Others came in person.

…Tribal police lieutenant Ray Burnette puts it in terms of public safety. "A couple of times they've seen this creature looking through the windows. They're scared when they call."

As in all alleged sightings of a bigfoot creature, tangible evidence is scarce. The "Patterson film" from 1967 is the most-often-seen video. It shows a tall hairy figure striding through the woods of the Pacific Northwest. For nearly 40 years this film's authenticity has been debated; it has never been discredited.

In the White Mountains last year, investigators found footprints, several tufts of hair and other material at the scene of a sighting. Tribal police made plaster casts from the prints and sent hair and plant samples to the Department of Public Safety for analysis in its state-of-the-art crime lab. Test results showed the hair was not human, but animal in origin. Further testing to determine what kind of animal was not done.

…Back on the reservation, Lieutenant Burnette wants

## WHITE MOUNTAIN APACHE
### Game and Fish Department

Law Enforcement
Investigation Report
Phone (520) 338-4385
Fax (520) 338-1712.

Case # 0507070419
Date 7-22-05  Time 1000 A
Received GF·8
How Received Page out

### COMPLAINT

Nature of Complaint: Sighting of a large unidentified primate.

When Occurred, Day of Week: Tuesday  Date: 7-19-05  Time: 7 or P.
Exact Location of Occurrence: R78 AND 78H JCT.
Suspect (s) Name (s): N/A
License # and Description of Vehicle: N/A
Complainant: N/A
Name  Address  Phone

Witnesses:

### INVESTIGATION

Details of Investigation: On 7-19-05 I WAYNE B. Amos received a phone call from ranger Raymond D. Valentino requesting assistance with traffic in the area of Paradise Creek. A report was made by a male subject of seeing what he believed to be something that look like Bigfoot. Upon arrival I made contact with male subject John Morris. ____ began to tell me that he and his wife were driving down the R78 road heading west, when they saw what appeared to be a large hairy animal step out of the tree line walking like a human. As they stopped their vehicle the animal noticed them and went down into a squat position and began to look back and forth several times. At this time ____ told her husband that it was a gorilla. ____ tells his wife, "NO" and then observes the animal stand up and begin to run east. He describes the run as right hand and right leg moving forward together and left hand and left leg moving forward together. ____ states he exited his vehicle and started walking south of the road to

Report Given to:

A 2005 report of a bigfoot lurking about the White Mountain reservation.

outsiders to realize that the department takes these calls seriously, and so should you. "The calls we're getting from people—they weren't hallucinating, they weren't drunks, they weren't people that we know can make hoax calls. They're from real citizens of the Fort Apache Indian Reservation."

Another report came from the same area on November 6, 2006, published by *The Arizona Republic* with the headline "Ft. Apache reports spur Bigfoot hunt." In the article it was mentioned that a police report had been made by White Mountain tribal Officer Katherine Montoya (who was mentioned n the Cannel 3 story), who responded to a call at 2:30 a.m. on August 14 when Barry and Tammy Lupe of Whiteriver called 911 to report an unhumanly large prowler peering through their window. Officer Montoya reported what she witnessed when she arrived at the Lupe residence:

It stood approximately 6'7" tall. It appeared to be about 220 pounds or more. It had exceptionally long arms; it did not appear to be wearing any clothes, and just appeared black. When it turned towards me, the most obvious feature was its eyes. The skin around his eyes was a lighter color than the rest of the face. It appeared almost white while the rest of the suspect was black. I could smell a distinct odor, like a stinkbug. You know, when you squish a stinkbug it smells. It never made any sounds until it crashed through the fence [while running away].

Officer Montoya's suspect was, by her own admission, a large, hairy, stinky apeman. Officer Montoya had just met the Mogollon Monster.[11]

In the same area, with the nearest town being Strawberry, Arizona, a man named John Johnson reported on July 10, 1999 to Oregonbigfoot.com that he had camped with a friend a few days earlier, and they had a sasquatch visit their camp. Johnson claimed that they heard strange screaming noises like a banshee's one night. On the next night he and his friend heard what sounded like pounding on a hollow log. This occurred off and on through the night and the next morning they discovered an old tree that had been torn into pieces by some powerful being. Said Johnson, "You would have to be Hercules to do this to a tree." (Oregonbigfoot.com file #00503)

Strawberry, and nearby Pine, are two small towns along the steep cliffs that make up the Mogollon Rim, a heavily forested area with rocky cliffs, outcroppings and lakes. They are also a hotbed of bigfoot sightings and the topic of the Mogollon Monster is a common one in the area.

A doctor posted a story on the Unexplained Mysteries forum (UnexplainedMysteries.com) about an encounter in the area in 2006:

I'm a doctor in Northern Arizona. On a trip from Show Low to Concho on the afternoon of Thursday, October 26th, 2006, I saw a sasquatch about 1/2 a mile in front of my car. It entered the road from the right, ran across the road, down the shoulder on the other side and into the brush. My first thought/comment was, "What the hell was that!" thinking that it certainly did look like a sasquatch, but I didn't believe that they might be in Arizona of all places. Perhaps in the Pacific Northwest or even in the mountains of the eastern US, but Arizona? That certainly would have never crossed my mind! ...until my wife looked up this site on the net which contained several references to sasquatch by the local White Mountain Apaches.

...The interesting thing is that no matter how much a person doubts the existence of something, no matter how much other people try to explain it away as your eyes playing tricks on you, no matter how much people try to rationalize somebody else's experiences, once you've seen something crystal clearly on a bright, clear day yourself, you know. You realize that the comments of others is simply their ignorance and need for denial. It no longer matters to me what anybody says about sasquatch, there will never again be a single doubt in my mind. Once you see one, it takes it out of the realm of possibility and firmly into the realm of knowing. I don't consider myself a "believer." It's not a matter of believing. I now know.

### 2007: White Mountain Apache Sighting

It was reported in an article in the *Fort Apache Scout*, a newspaper of the White Mountain Apache tribe, in its May 26, 2009 issue (Vol. 46, No.3) that bigfoot was spotted on Sun Creek Mountain in early May, 2007. Said the article, which ran for several pages in the newspaper:

> ...Armon Armstrong went looking for elk antlers at the beginning of this month. "I came upon it walking the other way, about 75 yards away on top of Sun Creek Mountain," he said. The area is near the vicinity of Christmas Tree Lake in an isolated opulent wilderness. A wilderness so thick with assorted vegetation, animals, water, it's a natural habitat for this creature. "It was tall, probably around 8-foot high as it walked through bushes full of thorns like nothing. Its stride is far apart and it was going at a fast pace," said Armstrong. Knowing that he saw bigfoot for the first time, Armstrong high tailed out of that area as fast as he could. The way he walked up that mountain is the way he made his way back down. "I ran very fast and was tired. I ran all the way back down the mountain to the truck," he said. "You could just tell that it had muscular arms. Its arms went down to about the knees and its hair was just black."
>
> At the same time when Armstrong was traveling back down the hillside, Fernando Nosie and another guy were on the bottom side of the hill where bigfoot was traveling. Not knowing that Armstrong was gone from the top, the two lads were in the front trail of a massive being unknown to humans.

The article goes on to say how famous bigfoot hunter Tom Biscardi showed up and Armstrong, Nosie

A photo of a bigfoot in November, 2006 by Dave O.

and others returned to the area for an episode of the television show *Searching for Bigfoot*. An interesting end to the article was a plea for anyone who has seen bigfoot in the area to contact AK Riley of the White Mountain Police Department and a telephone number was given. Finally, Bigfoot Nation is getting the hotlines that are desperately needed.

## 2007: The Chevelon Lake Bigfoot

Susan Farnsworth and Mitchell Waite chronicle a number of more recent encounters in their 2011 book *More Mogollon Monster, Arizona's Bigfoot.*[70] They mention that a number of sightings have been made around a series of lakes on the Mogollon, particularly Chevelon Lake. One story they tell is that of a man named Mike who had some encounters in February of 2007. Mike had a camper, a shell that would normally be on a pickup truck, sitting on the ground at a place called Chevelon Retreat.

Mike owned the remote parcel of land and had placed the camper on two wooden skids to use as a cabin in the woods. He would occasionally visit his land and camper from Heber, where he lived, but soon after he had put it up he arrived there one day to find that it had been turned upside down and was off the wooden skids. He could not right the camper himself and therefore used the winch on the front of his pickup to place the camper back correctly on the skids.

When this happened a second time, he suspected vandalism. After righting the camper again with the help of the winch, he decided to set up a trail camera that would photograph the vandals who were pushing over his camper. He also nailed some two-by-fours to the side of the trailer to make it more difficult to push the camper over and off of the two pallets.

When Mike again returned to his property he was relieved to see that the camper had not been tipped over. He found that his trail camera had taken a photo, however. In it was a fuzzy dark animal that he thought at first was dog, and then a bear cub. But when he noticed that the animal had hands instead of paws, he knew that the Mogollon Monster had been visiting him. The authors surmised that the bigfoot was trying to get at the nests of packrats that were using the wooden pallets as ideal nesting places. With the strength that only bigfoot has, this Mogollon Monster (one of many) would push the camper over and then grab the packrats in their nests as an easy meal.

The authors note in another story in the same area, from 2006, that a hiker in a remote rocky cleft surrounded by bushes discovered a freshly killed deer that had been torn apart limb by limb, with the head torn from the neck as well. The hiker realized that only bigfoot could rip a deer apart in that way, and the creature must still be nearby. The hiker hastily beat a retreat back to the main trail fearful the entire time that he might be ambushed by the monster himself.[70]

### 2008: Woman Sees Bigfoot near Little Colorado River

A report to BFRO says that on July 12, 2008, a woman from Phoenix whose family like to vacation on the Mogollon Rim had a bigfoot encounter on a rainy afternoon near Christopher Creek. They were on a side road off Forest Road 300, the main Rim Road, and it had been raining off and on all afternoon, so the family was reading or napping in their camper van when the woman heard a large animal in the forest outside the trailer and grabbed her camera:

> Not five minutes after I had put my camera down and resumed reading a branch about 4 feet long and 3 to 4 inches round came shooting out of the trees directly at the van like a javelin. It hit the side mirror dead on center, pushing it in towards the van. (It is hard to even move this mirror by hand. The force it took to force it in towards the van had to be tremendous). The force was such that it shattered the side mirror into many pieces. There's still a dent on the back metal portion of the mirror from the impact.

They did not see anything more, but that night she could hear a large animal sniffing at the slider window of the van where she was sleeping. The sniffing and huffing noises went on for about five minutes, and suddenly stopped. She did not hear the sound of the animal moving away from the van. In the morning they found that their kitchen had been raided and some food taken, but not by some animal crashing around and tearing bags and knocking things over, but crackers had been removed from their plastic pouches and

**244**

sausages taken out of tinfoil without tearing it. They returned to the same spot a week later and loud screaming was heard in the afternoon by them and some target shooters. The Mogollon Monster doesn't like hunters or target shooters!

The Mogollonmonster.com site (now defunct) records a sighting near Springerville, Arizona by a woman named Donna who reported her encounter on December 25, 2008:

> We spotted it on the old Bigelow homestead. It was walking down the treeline along the Little Colorado River on the south side of the creek. It was huge—about 8 feet tall. It didn't seem too worried about us either. We were on the road a good 100 yards from the creature, and we were in our truck. We had just dropped down off the plain on the South Fork access road. We wanted to look at the old abandoned house. Then we spotted it. It was large, looked black. There was no clothing, so it was not a man. We watched it until it moved back into the tree line. A good 4 minutes, but we had no cameras with us. It was about daybreak.

## 2009: Bigfoot Seen on Forest Road near Reserve

It was reported in early 2009 that a forest service employee was driving north on a remote forest service road outside of Reserve, New Mexico designated FR41, that dead ends at Cienega Canyon. He spotted a tall bigfoot along the road near the canyon and the end of the road. Cienega Canyon is in the rugged and remote San Francisco Mountains, a largely uninhabited wilderness in a little-populated section of New Mexico—a great spot for denizens of Bigfoot Nation to avoid people if they so desire.

A report to BRFO says that a man and his wife from Oklahoma were camping in their mobile camper near the Red River outside of Taos, New Mexico when a bigfoot looked inside the bedroom window of their travel trailer. It was 4:30 a.m., and the couple were going to get an early morning start for their trip home:

> My wife had gotten up first and then I got up and went into the bathroom. My wife opened the door and said that someone was standing outside the entry door to the

bedroom of the trailer. I went back to the room and saw a large shadow in the window. The window is privacy glass so they couldn't see inside. I could see a chest, a head and about half of the arm. I reached into the nightstand and took out my pistol thinking that it was someone. I then started toward the back of the trailer to the main entry door. While I was doing this, my wife thought to take photos. She took 3 photos which does show the shadow of whatever it was very well. When I was at the other end of the trailer I opened the door and turned on the outside light at the same time. There was nothing there, I did hear what sounded like someone walking very quickly in the distance. I went around the trailer but couldn't see anyone. It was at this time that I realized that the window on the door is too high for someone to have been standing there. I took pictures to show how high it is. We waited until daylight to go back outside, I looked around the front and side of the trailer and noticed what appeared to be large tracks in the gravel.

Blurry photos are posted on the BFRO website, plus photos showing the camper and the height of the windows.

### 2010: Daylight Sighting of Bigfoot on Rim

In May of 2010 it was reported to the BFRO website that a father and son were camping together on the Mogollon Rim and saw a bigfoot in a broad daylight sighting. The father and son were camping near Forest Lakes, Arizona near forest road FR115. It was about 6 p.m. and still very light outside. Said the father in the report:

My son and I were just getting ready to leave the campsite. As soon as I stood up from my chair, I saw what looked like a VERY large man in a ghillie [gorilla] suit walk across the opening in the trees to my left. I had a clear sight and it was VERY large. I could see the arms swaying, and my son was able to see the legs separate as it stepped. It didn't seem to be in any rush, and seemed to be walking rather casually (kinda slow) but it covered a lot of ground in very few steps. As I said, I could see both arms swaying, and it was not carrying a rifle or anything else that I could see. [It] …would have been at least 7 1/2 feet tall.

BFRO also reports that on August 15, 2010 a bigfoot disturbed a camper in a high country forest with strange noises. Says the report:

At about 12 AM, I was awoken to the sound of two sticks cracking together near my RV trailer. The knocking sounded as if somebody had two girthy sticks, maybe about 2 inches in diameter, and they were banging them together at a perfect 2 second interval. Sometimes

A.K. Riley looking at bigfoot footprints on the White Mountain Reservation on March 31, 2010

the sticks sounded a little different as if a knot had been struck but the timing was never flawed. …I have never heard a known animal make this sound, let alone in perfect repetition for the duration that I heard it. But that wasn't the strangest part; the sound was translating through the forest quickly and without making additional sounds. The sound was emanating from an area on the backside of my trailer and receding away. It would then come closer and recede again. This was happening over and over. I would say that it was probably about 20 to 30 yards at the closest and went out an additional 50 to 70 yards away. My campsite was near a primitive road and the sound seemed to parallel the road but I can't be sure.

After lying in bed, listening to this for about 2 minutes, I decided that I needed to do something about this thing that was disturbing my camp. Familiar with the observance that bigfoots knocked wood, a bigfoot did come to mind instantly, but I felt that as the patriarch, I needed to investigate and protect my family. My family members were all three asleep …I did not turn on any lights and was absolutely silent, feeling around for my clothes, shoes and pistol. Once dressed, I moved silently to the trailer door, being careful not to shake the trailer or create any noises. This was actually quite easy because there is a door adjacent to my bed. I waited until the cracking sound had receded as far away as it sounded like it was going to get. And remember, the sound was emanating from the opposite side of my trailer. I slowly opened the door, again careful not to make a noise. The knocking sound continued. This is the part that freaks me out the most: as soon as I stepped outside, the knocking sound that seemed as far away from me as possible, stopped.

Now the story does not stop there. I had a lousy flashlight (unlit) in one hand and my pistol in the other. I proceeded around the front of my trailer to the other side. Once I was on the other side, I was confronted by the pitch black woods in which I was certain that there were a couple of unknown creatures. Having the distinct feeling that there was something to the rear of my trailer, I shined the lousy flashlight directly towards the rear. This only lit up the two very large pine trees that were about twelve feet in front of me. Shining the flashlight did however elicit a response. As soon as I shone the light, directly in front of me, but on the other side of the trees, perhaps about 20 to 40 yards away, something let out a "whoop, whoop." It was clear, it was distinct and it was amazing. Before this incident, I had never heard on TV that bigfoot made a "whoop, whoop" sound, so I am certain that this was not in my head. At that moment, I knew that there was something different from an elk, a bear, an owl, etc that was disturbing my camp. And I also knew that there was more than one. I felt that this was an alert call signaling any additional creatures to leave the area.

**248**

His wife came to the door of the trailer just then and the creature silently disappeared. He said that he thought about the bad odor that was often said to come with bigfoot but he says he did not smell anything at all. The next day he looked for tracks but could not find any. He did find two thick sticks from a ponderosa pine that made a similar sound when he banged them together as the one he had heard in the night.

### 2011: Bigfoot in the Headlights in the Chuska Mountains

A report to BFRO stated that on March 5, 2011 a man said he was driving north of Thoreau, New Mexico, east of Gallup, when he saw a figure by the road:

> …The time was about 8 p.m. As I was traveling on hi-way 612, right when I was exiting the sharp curves, I noticed a figure moving by the road on the right side. I thought it was a very tall person at first but when I looked I noticed that it wasn't human. As I got closer it started to cross the road and almost hit my truck. It stopped and I did not want to stop because the road was ice packed and I didn't want to get stuck or run off the road. I saw the creature a few feet thru my truck's passenger front window. The creature's face looked ape and humanistic. He was probably 7 feet tall because when he got real close to the vehicle I couldn't see his face. He stood way over the truck. I was overwhelmed with fear at this point and just kept going home.

Another report said that on July 16, 2011 an unnamed man and his family were driving through the Chuska Mountains of New Mexico when a bigfoot was encountered on the road. As aforementioned, the Chuska

A bigfoot photo taken near Sedona in March 2010.

**249**

*Bigfoot in the Southwest*

Mountains are a high, forested and isolated mountain range in the Navajo Nation, near the Arizona border. Said the man in the report:

> We were going to the Chuska Mountains on the Navajo reservation for a family reunion. We just left the main paved highway through Narbona Pass, between Sheep Springs, NM and Crystal, NM. We went south on a dirt road, Indian Service Route 32, into the Chuska Mountains. We were about 5-8 miles into the mountains, when we came upon a small hill that curved towards the east, then to the south. As we approached the hill to go up, the road quickly turned right/south. As we reached the top, we saw the full moon and it lit up a flat green pasture that was on top of the hill.
>
> As we made the turn to the right/south I noticed a big black figure standing. As I looked at it, it stood with the full moon behind it, so that all I could see was a black-outlined form. I kept my eyes on the figure while making the turn right. I said to my wife, "Did you see that?!" She said, "What?" I said, "Something is standing over there by the road."
>
> As I looked, I noticed that the figure was standing by a small pond, which was about 10-15 feet from the road. I could see the figure's reflection in the pond, along with the full moon. I would say when I first saw it, it was about 75 feet away. As we got closer, our headlights turned to the right, away from the black figure, but I still could see it, because the moonlight was so bright. It just stood there, still, as if it was waiting for us to leave. I told her [my wife] I was going to pull the truck onto the edge of the road. The road being dirt, and because of the rain, it had been plowed, so there was a ridge of dirt on both sides of the road. So, I pulled the vehicle left towards the "Bigfoot" to flash my headlights on it.
>
> As my headlights flashed the "Bigfoot" it turned. We could see the legs (two) turn, the arms (two) turn, and it started running away from us up a small hill into the trees. It was a quick, smooth run. I mentioned to her that it ran Ninja-like, smooth and stealthy. In less than 5-6 seconds it was in

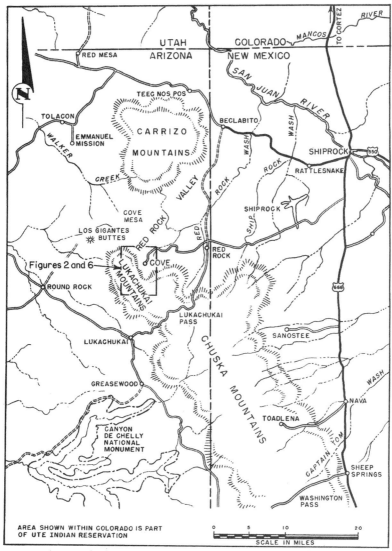

A map of the Chuska Mountains of Arizona and New Mexico.

the trees. As it was turning and running, we didn't see any clothing—buttons shining from the headlights/moonlight—we saw a huge mass, a body running on two legs; we never saw any eyes. We noticed the legs and arms, and for sure it ran on two legs up the hill.

We were about 30 feet away from it when it ran up the hill. We could see that it was not a bear or human. It stood at least 7-8 feet tall. It was wider and taller than a person. After

**251**

it ran away, we were in shock; we sat quietly in the truck, still for about 15 seconds. Then, all of a sudden my oldest daughter screamed and said, "Daddy, what was that." I was shocked that she was awake the whole time. I thought only my wife and I saw it. But, she was terrified, asking me, over and over, "Daddy, what was that?" I couldn't say anything but tell her it was a Bigfoot.

My wife and I aren't crazy nor were we believers of Bigfoot until now. In fact, we were the biggest skeptics. But we can't deny what we saw. I have to believe it, because it was real.

Welcome to Bigfoot Nation! Also in July of 2011, a mother camping with her children heard possible late-night vocalizations in the Knoll Lake area of the Mogollon Rim. Said the witness in her report filing with BFRO:

It was in the middle of the night on a trip when I took my three kids camping. I was awoken by strange noises. The noises sounded like an angry female with a smoker's voice screaming in short bursts. Probably 5- to 10-second bursts every 10 to 20 seconds. The camping area where we were was near Lake Knoll, Arizona. ...I did not sleep the rest of the night. I heard other noises later that night. It sounded like multiple animals fighting but it was more animal sounding... maybe wild bores or something. I asked some of my hunter friends and they could not explain the first sound that I heard. Other than those noises, there was not a sound to be heard. It was dead quiet. (www.bfro.net)

### 2012: Campers Awakened by Screams near Grand Canyon

On October 6, 2012 it was reported to BFRO that two friends on a motorcycle camping trip heard strange sounds around their campsite south of Jacob Lake near the North Rim of the Grand Canyon. They were sleeping in their tents when, at about 2:30 a.m., they were awakened by screams. The sounds made the hair on their necks stand up and went on for about five minutes. They were convinced that it was bigfoot making the vocalizations.

## 2013: Screaming Bigfoot Leaves Behind Bush Teepee

A report was made to BFRO by a father who heard strange screaming on August 22, 2013 while camping with his family north of Woods Canyon Lake near Payson, Arizona. They were close to forest road FR117. Wrote the father about the moonlit August night in his report to BFRO:

We decided to go to bed around 10 pm. I put some more wood on the campfire hoping it would burn all night. As we were in our tent the moon was like a big nightlight, then we fell asleep. At about 3:10 am I woke up to a sound that was unlike anything I have ever heard. Both our dogs sat up and were very still. It was as if someone was screaming thru a loud PA system; it was very clear. I woke my wife so she could hear the sound but it had stopped—then again it started. We were both laying there trying to figure out what could be large in size that would make a sound so loud and long it was echoing in the canyon to the north of us. …The next morning after breakfast I took one of our dogs out for a walk in the direction, the screams came from and saw nothing. But about 200 yards in the same direction I found what looked to be a possible shelter made from dead trees about 12 to 15 feet long and 4 to 5" in diameter. They were set up, standing like a teepee there was one tree laying on the ground next to the structure I tried to lift it and found it was so heavy that I don't think two large men could pick it up, much less stand it up like the rest. One other thing I saw was, the trees were saw cut but there were no tree stumps around, so the trees had to be carried there from else where. If someone did this for fun they had to work hard to do this and I cant see why. The first night we were there no one was camping anywhere near us, but the second day we were there some campers set up about 1/2 mile to the north on the other side of the canyon. That night our dogs were on edge, looking out away from camp and growling. My wife said she could hear something large moving around in the woods to the west of us—but when shining a spot light in that direction she didn't see anything. I put some more wood on our fire then we went to bed. The next morning we got up and made breakfast, took our time cleaning up our campsite, then packed and left for home.

Another report on the BFRO website is from a high-level healthcare professional who was driving from Denver to Albuquerque, New Mexico on October 18, 2013 and stopped at a gas station in Las Vegas, New Mexico at one in the morning to get gas. He was travelling with his wife who went into the gas station, just off of Interstate 25, and he decided to urinate in the desert in back of the station. A he walked back to the car he saw a bigfoot that was 8- to 10-feet tall, covered in dark brown matted hair. Said his report:

> As I turned and looked over my left shoulder, I saw an enormous, lurking animal. The animal was crouched over, almost as if taking cover in the sparse and cold vegetation. In fact, I think the creature watched me the whole time, and did not make so much as a noise. However, the creature noticed when I saw it. The creature stood up, and quickly lumbered into the dark, away from the direction of the parking lot. The one attribute of the creature that resounded with me was how heavy the footfall was. It sounded like somebody dropping a sack of potatoes over and over again. And it was fast. I observed the creature for about 8-11 seconds, from the moment it realized I saw it, to watching the animal dart into the wood line. Due to radiant light from the parking lot, I could make steady detail of the fleeing creature.

He said that the creature had a strong, foul odor and "massive, human-like hands." Although he had a concealed handgun in

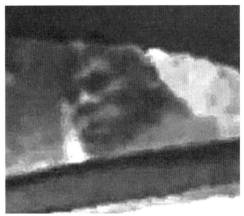

The "Tent Flap" photo of bigfoot from 2013.

his possession, he was "scared stiff" and couldn't sleep for several nights after the sighting. It took him weeks to tell his wife about the incident.

## 2014: Female Hiker Sees Bigfoot

The Pine Barrens Institute reported that, in 2014, a 28-year-old woman was hiking through the Canyon Point Trail along the Mogollon Rim when she came across an odd-looking creature on its knees drinking water. Curious as to what the creature was, the woman decided to take a photo of it. As she reached into her bag to grab her camera, the creature quickly turned its head in her direction and stared directly at her. Now extremely frightened by the large unknown creature staring directly at her, she began to try to scare the creature off. She started waving her arms and yelling as loud as she could. The creature stood up on its two legs and took off running into the canyon. The woman described the creature as having a human-looking face with no hair on it, a thick nose, small lips, brown-red eyes and a body covered in hair.

A report of an encounter with the Mogollon Monster near Sedona, Arizona on June 29, 2014 was given to the Bigfoot Research Organization. A father, his son, and another friend were frog hunting just after midnight on a moonless June night when a smelly bigfoot apparently began throwing rocks at them and even charged them briefly. Said the anonymous report:

> We entered the creek which is known as Beaver Creek. We all had our gigs and 100 lumen lights, and were walking upstream after we entered the canyon in which the creek was located. As we entered the canyon I noticed a strong, musky, stinky smell, but I did not say anything because this could have been skunk or javelina which are common in the area. After walking for about 200 yards, my son, who was in front, stopped and said he heard something walking away from him up the creek. I asked if it was a deer or elk. He told me he could not see because of the underbrush, but said it sounded like a heavy person.
>
> We continued for a few more feet and we all then observed three large rocks thrown from the thick brush

above our heads, about 20 yards in front of us over the creek to the opposite side. We all stopped and then heard branches crashing as something crossed the creek in front of us. We looked in all direction with our lights but the brush and trees were too thick to see. I stopped and hit my gig against a tree three times. We then heard branches breaking upstream. We then crossed the creek and stopped. A rock was then thrown toward us and landed in the creek five yards in front of us. I advised my son and my friend that we needed to go, but as we turned to go back out, something very large ran toward us from up the creek bottom in the thick bushes, breaking large branches. We searched with our lights but could not see anything. We then walked out and made it back to the truck.

The man also noted that it was unusually quiet at the time, without the normal insect and animal noise one would expect around a bushy creek in the summertime.

The alleged sighting prompted an investigation by BFRO member Chuck Jacobs. Jacob says that 9 days after the incident, the depressions in the grass were still at the sighting spot. "It was not possible to get an accurate measurement of the foot size, but the length of the stride was clearly longer than what a human could achieve," said Jacobs. He added that they were able to estimate the height of the purported creature, and set it at about 8 feet. "That would be standing erect," he explained. Jacobs determined that the figure couldn't have been a human being given the extremely large size of it. Additionally, he observed, "it moved faster than a human could run."

**2015: Bigfoot Taps on the Window**

A woman reported that on July 12, 2015 she was awoken at a cabin by whooping sounds. She and her two children were staying at a remote cabin 12 miles down a dirt road at an undisclosed spot on the Mogollon Rim. Wrote the woman in her report to BFRO:

It was a Sunday afternoon and I went to stay at a cabin we rented, with my two children, for the night. We were escaping the heat of Phoenix and it was a beautiful day, clear, sunny and no rain or clouds.

That night we were asleep in the cabin but I kept waking up because I was on a very uncomfortable cot. As I lay there trying to fall asleep again, I heard what sounded like a "whoop." This was followed by a clear wood knock sound. They were about 8-10 seconds apart. I lay there listening and about 1 minute later, I heard the same "whoop" and again, followed up by another knock about 10 seconds later. They seemed to both come from the same direction (SE of the cabin). I was the only one who heard it as the kids were asleep, and I didn't tell them as I didn't want to spook them. The sounds sounded close, I'm guessing within 50 yards since I was able to hear them while inside the cabin.

... about 10:30, earlier that night, shortly after we climbed in bed, I was trying to fall asleep while the two kids were playing games on their Ipods. All of a sudden a rap noise hit the window on the south side of the cabin. Immediately, the kids look at me and say, "What was that?!" The sound was like a small pebble hitting the window. Again, it was clear and no wind. I played it off to the kids that it was probably just a moth or bug hitting the window, and it may have been just that. But then I heard the whoop and knocks later in the night and wondered if something was watching us. Whenever we camp, we always set up a camera trap, for the fun of it, to see what wanders into the camp. I did so on this night, too, and it was set up in front of the cabin, but it had zero hits on it.

As we drove down the road to the cabin we saw only 2-3 other camping parties along the roughly 12-mile stretch to get to the cabin. It was Sunday afternoon about 2PM when we drove to the cabin. But when we left

A 2016 photo of an Arizona bigfoot by Adam Bird.

the next morning about 7AM, they had all left—assumedly the previous afternoon since it was a Sunday. So we were the only ones in the area 12 miles back in the woods. We passed one truck near the main road as we left Monday morning but that was it.

It is interesting that they had set up a camera trap, and that there was no male present at the cabin, just a young mother and two children. With all the other campers having left, perhaps this was the only cabin worth being curious about. Sometimes a camping trip is just a camping trip. Sometimes a camping trip is a trip to Bigfoot Nation.

### 2016: Camper Sees Bigfoot on Mogollon Rim

It was reported that a camper spotted bigfoot while camping in the Coconino National Forest near Strawberry, Arizona on June 26, 2016. The eyewitness claimed he was camping in a USFS campground in the Mogollon Rim area when he spotted the beast. "I had finished reading a book when I looked across the campground and I noticed a very fast moving dark figure, heading from north to south," he said. The man went on to say that he initially believed the figure was a "large kid on a bicycle," because "it was moving too fast." Then, he explains, he realized that what he was looking at was something unusual.

"It was a very large bigfoot. It only lasted about three seconds, but I was lucky to see it at all." He added that the dark figure was about 125 yards from his viewpoint, and he was not able to identify "facial details." He said the hair was almost black with a slight reddish tint.

"It ran with a slight

A petroglyph near the Zuni Reservation.

258

forward slant to its body. Its head did not bob up and down like a human runner's head at that speed." (cryptozoologynews.com)

## 2017: Bigfoot Punches Trailer near Dulce

A report from the Sasquatch Chronicles Blog (sasquatchchronicles.com) said that on January 11, 2017 investigators had looked into a report that a ranch near Dulce, New Mexico on the Jacarilla Apache Reservation was having visitations from a bigfoot which was terrorizing the ranch, and they believed

A 2018 advert featuring Arizona's bigfoot.

it was trying to kill and remove their horse in order to eat it. The bigfoot then attacked a camper trailer and left a big dent of knuckle marks by the door when it could not get inside.

Retired Jacarilla police officer Hoyt Velarde investigated the trailer marks as well, and was satisfied that a bigfoot was responsible for the marks as the family claimed.

## 2018: Mogollon Monster Medals to Be Awarded

The *Payson Roundup* (central Arizona) announced that the 6th Annual Mogollon Monster Mudda would be held at the Payson Event Center on June 2, 2018. Named in honor of the Mogollon Monster, it was voted the "Most Outstanding Event in the State of Arizona for 2016" The paper said:

> 2018 marks the 10th Anniversary of the Payson, Arizona Mountain High Games. Making an exciting comeback is the 6th Annual Mogollon Monster Mudda 5K Mud Run. The course make up will be developed using mountain trails with natural and man-made obstacles.

For the $60 cost, participants receive an event T-shirt, a 3" Mogollon Monster medal, race bib, timing ankle bracelet, and other goodies. The celebrations of bigfoot are many and far-flung! And, they are giving out medals!

As we approach the year 2020 we can expect to hear more from bigfoot in the Southwest. The Mogollon Monster will still raid camps once those campfires start to die down. The monster's late-night antics of will be told at Boy Scout camps for years to come out there—on the rocky rim of Bigfoot Nation.

# CHAPTER 8

# Post-Millennial Nation

Well, I'm a King Kong man,
I'm a Voo-Doo man
Y'no, I'm an Apeman!

—The Kinks, *Apeman*

The heyday years of the late 20th century were now over. It was a whole new world. Bigfoot had been looting camping areas, logger camps and edge-of-civilization dumpsters for decades now. Berry pickers and hunters had reason to be afraid. Too many unexplained disappearances and deaths. Fortunately, bigfoot was never blamed for the 9-11 attacks, and the general machinery of the military, the FBI, and local police forces were willing to let Bigfoot Nation remain in the shadows.

What good would it be to claim that Bigfoot Nation was using chemical weapons in its now well known campaign of stinky assault? Let's face it, none. Bigfoot needs to be ignored if possible, though the relentless advertising campaigns that pervade all aspects of the pop culture in America and Canada make it difficult to discount the hairy giant. Canada has gone so far as to honor bigfoot with its sasquatch stamp, and several states in the USA have seen lawsuits or legislation concerning bigfoot.

Still, the curious and largely nocturnal bigfoot turn up from time to time. As we have seen, they often wander onto the highway and wave at truckers, who thought that they had seen everything! Other bigfoot are just out there on the fringes of normal society when some hiker happens to meet them at the berry patch. Let us look at some of the bigfoot reports starting in the year 2000.

**2000: Female Hiker sees Bigfoot in Colorado**

The *Denver Post* carried a story about Julie Davis, an experienced hiker, who encountered bigfoot in the San Juan National Forest on the afternoon of August 5, 2000. Said Davis in the *Denver Post* article:

> It was gigantic—it must have been 8 feet tall. My first thought was, "I'm looking at something I've never seen before." I didn't even think Bigfoot. The notion that these animals were out there in Colorado never crossed my mind. It had very, very broad shoulders—huge shoulders. Its face was almost completely covered in fur but human-like, on the human side of halfway between a human and gorilla. I've had a lot of time to get to know what bears look like up close. This animal was bigger than any bear.

Then, the creature made a "low mumble" and a second, somewhat smaller creature came out of the woods, peering intently at Davis. Then they both turned and ran into the forest. Davis decided to stay an extra day at her camp in order to see the creatures again but they did not return.[10]

**2001: Bigfoot Chattering Like a Bear**

On April 18, 2001, the famous Canadian sasquatch researcher Rene Dahinden passed away in Richmond, British Columbia at the age of 70. Born in Switzerland in 1930 decided to emigrate to Canada in 1953.

In May of 2001 a man named Gordon Bomersback said that he saw a bigfoot just after he passed through a toll gate in Hope, British Columbia. He said it was covered in dark brown hair and he watched it for about 10 seconds.

In September, near Mission, British Columbia Mikel Crowther saw a sasquatch while he was out bear hunting. While sitting on a tree stump at 10 in the morning he heard possible footsteps behind him. He turned and saw a bigfoot stepping over a fallen tree a few dozen feet from his position. He said he cold hear it "chattering" to itself, much like a bear chatters and growls when it's angry—low grunting noises. When it was straddling the log, it saw Crowther and suddenly froze. Crowther and the sasquatch looked at each other for a few moments and then the creature turned and walked away. He smelled a strong odor. It was covered with shaggy salt and pepper brown hair. He estimated that it was about seven and a half feet tall.[7]

In her book *Who's Watching You?*,[8] author Linda Coil Suchy tells of a graphic designer from Eugene, Oregon with the initials C.D.F., age 32, who told Suchy that he had an encounter with bigfoot just southwest of Eugene in August of 2001. He wrote:

> I used to haul bundles of newspapers late at night/early morning for the local. One area I drove through was a fairly new road in southwest Eugene, Oregon, just east of Willow Creek Road. The area is protected wetlands near the Hynix semiconductor plant.
>
> ...I had to relieve myself anyway so I got out and walked around the van to the side of the road and gazed at the sky while doing my business. I was looking up when out of the lower half of my vision I saw something move. It couldn't have been more than 20 feet away.
>
> I saw a huge, hairy, broad-shouldered figure stand up, turn its back to me and calmly walk off into the brush. If I hadn't already just peed I would have marked my territory in my pants! I very quickly dashed around the van, hopped in, and took off.
>
> The creature was at least seven feet tall, though it was hard to tell because where it stood was lower than the road where I was. But he was taller than me, and I am six foot one. It had no neck; its head and shoulders were mountain shaped into one angled peak. As it moved, it sort of moved its arms in a breast stroke motion to get through the brush. I could hear the branches and twigs breaking as it pushed its way through.
>
> Later I wondered who had been more frightened, me or the bigfoot? ...I never returned to that spot, I even took another route every day after that to purposely bypass the area.[8]

A 32-year-old man from Albany, Oregon claimed he saw bigfoot on a remote logging road in the Cascade Mountains in November of 2001. He told Linda Coil Suchy:

> I did see something one cold, rainy night, deep in the Cascades. I had my wife with me, and it was around 10 p.m. We were in my Dodge D-50 4x4 on a logging road that heads deep into the Cascade Mountains. We were probably 35 miles in from the main line snow peak, somewhere around tree line, which is very high up; only four wheel drive vehicles can get through up there.
>
> It was just starting to get foggy when we saw it—a bigfoot. It was running up the road in front of us. My truck was in second gear, and when I tried to speed up to get closer for a better look, it suddenly bolted off into the trees. It was only about forty feet in front of us; it was foggy but we knew what we had seen. This bigfoot was approximately seven feet tall and well over 300 pounds. This thing was big and it moved fast. It was running upright, its arms swinging, and it was covered in dark brown hair that was wet from the rain. It looked like a giant gorilla.
>
> Funny how it disappeared so fast. When I stopped on the road exactly at the spot where it left the road, I shut the truck off. We couldn't hear a thing, just dead silence. Yet I had this feeling it was watching us, maybe from behind a tree, just waiting for us to leave. The experience very much freaked us out and we quickly left the area and returned home.
>
> We never told anyone until now, because we knew no one would believe us. To this day, my wife does not go with me to the mountains. I have never returned to that spot, yet I remember it so well I could take a person back to the exact spot where we saw it. This experience is forever burned into our memory. Bigfoot stays in your mind for a long period of time. This is my story, I now believe in bigfoot![8]

### 2002: Forest Highway Pit Stop startles Bigfoot

Linda Coil Suchy tells of an encounter with a sasquatch near Grand Forks, British Columbia in July of 2002. She says that a 15-year-old boy and his friend, Landon, were camping with his family and said:

> ...By the time we unpacked, lit the fire, readied the sleeping and got the food cooked and eaten, it was around 9:30 p.m. and the sun had just set. Landon suggested that we take a walk around the campsite to see what was there. We grabbed our flashlights and headed out.

> We followed a dirt path heading deeper into the forest; we had been walking for some time when all of a sudden we heard heavy breathing to the right of the path. We both immediately stopped, thinking it was a bear (we each lived by a big park where bears had been spotted several times so the two of us were extremely paranoid). We stepped way back putting distance between ourselves and the creature and shone our flashlights into the dark bushes and trees.

> ...The creature that we first thought was a bear had been crouching or kneeling and as we shined our lights on the bushes, it grunted and began to slowly rise to stand on two legs. It kept getting taller and taller behind the bushes. I remember thinking, "When is this creature going to stop getting taller?" When it was fully erect on two legs it stood about eight feet tall; I know this because Landon and I were close to six feet and this thing was more than two feet taller than us. It was covered in dark brown hair and had the posture and body structure of a human.

> With our mouths open, the two of us could not move; we could only stare while this huge creature, through the dark hair covering most of its face, stared back at us. Then it turned and ran swiftly into the dark forest. We were scared out of our minds and too afraid to follow it.

> We headed straight back to the campsite to tell my parents everything that happened, but they didn't believe us. We were so terrified neither of us slept a wink that night, although we secretly hoped it would come

One of several photos of bigfoot taken near Mount St. Helens, May 9, 2002.

back, if only so my parents would believe our story. Landon and I still talk about that night; we know what we saw.[8]

A BFRO report from a German with the initials G.R. says that on August 4, 2002 he and a dog made a quick pit stop on a highway near Bellingham, Washington and met bigfoot. The man was on his way to Bellingham from Spokane when he decided to make a pit stop and urinate on the side of the road. The dog, Kane, suddenly became very agitated and started barking and the man saw a hairy figure vanishing into the woods near the car. Says the witness:

> So I got "Kane" on the leash and we walked to that position and after about 20 yards the dog stopped, pressing out all his muscle, and started growling. I tried to pull him with me but he wouldn't move an inch. I had a little flashlight with me and pointed it towards the woods but couldn't see anything. Then I realized this awful smell (smelled like ferrets but much more intense). The dog then started backing up and I thought it was time to get outta here! We were back at the car when all of a sudden the bushes and trees behind us started cracking and bursting towards us. We got in the car and hit the gas.

## 2003: Bigfoot Encounter behind Campsite

A BFRO report says that in July of 2003 some campers encountered bigfoot on Mount Baker, near Van Zandt, Washington. The time was between 3 and 4 p.m. and it was still daylight. Said the witness:

> Two friends and I decided to go camping in my "backyard" which happens to be 10 acres in the foothills of Van Zandt. It was getting to be later in the afternoon, about 3 pm or so, and we decided to find a place to pitch a tent. By this time we were about 80-90 feet above the house and in the woods at this old single room trailer that is left up there, locked. In the front there is a fire pit and so that's were we decided to pitch the tent. My two friends, one a guy about 20 years old, the other a girl about 17 years old decided to

go and grab some wood from just nearby. Not but a minute after rounding the trailer, I heard both scream and run back around the trailer with sheer panic on their faces. It freaked me out just looking at them. They both swore up and down they saw a very large, hairy, upright "thing" move very quickly out from behind a tree into thicker brush near by. …
We decided to stay anyway and within a couple of hours it was pouring rain with thunder and lighting.

In late summer of 2003 three women were hiking during the day on Bowen Island, near Vancouver, British Columbia and suddenly met with a bigfoot on the trail. The three women had gone for a walk on the trail when all of a sudden a bigfoot jumped onto the middle of the track at some distance from them and stood there looking at them. The three women stared back at the bigfoot in disbelief. Then the tall hairy creature ran off into the forest and disappeared.[7]

## 2004: Bigfoot Runs with Truck in Washington State
In June of 2004, a 52-year-old truck driver reported that his friend, Joe, while driving on Interstate 90 over Snoqualmie Pass in Washington state, saw a bigfoot. Joe was driving the 18-wheeler between exits 48 and 51. According to his friend:

As Joe was driving slowly along, he saw a strange hairy creature about eight feet tall with long arms standing on the right side of the road. It reminded Joe of a large ape, with an egg-shaped head.

As Joe was about to pass the "ape creature" he began looking out his passenger side mirror, when suddenly the creature began running alongside the truck, as if it were trying to keep up with him.

The creature got closer and closer to the passenger side door, its dark brown, mangled hair blowing back from its face and body as it ran. At one point when reaching the passenger side window, it turned its head left and looked directly at Joe.

Joe saw one of its eyes and described the color as darker than dark. It was the scariest thing he had ever seen in his life. It frightened him so much he said, "I almost messed my pants right there." After a few minutes, the bigfoot swerved to the right, leaped over the road barrier and was gone.

Joe was so terrified that he never stopped at the town of George where he was supposed to do his logbook, and instead drove nonstop to Spokane.[8]

Welcome to Bigfoot Nation! A BFRO report says a witness had to stop his car because of a bigfoot on the road on August 7, 2004 near Leavenworth, Washington. Said the witness in his report:

August 7th between 10:00 and ll:00 AM. Saturday— was driving on Highway 2 toward Leavenworth. I was about 10 minutes out of the town. The car in front of me saw it first. He had to stop his car or he would have hit it. Then, I stopped my car behind the first car. The animal came from the right and was on the left side of the road, I only saw his back. He was dark brown with golden highlights (from the sun shining on the coat). He then walked into the bushes on the left side of the road. I didn't report it at the time because I didn't really believe it.

### 2005: Seeing Bigfoot from the Windowsill

A report to the BFRO website said a man living in Duvall, Washington on June 23, 2005 saw a bigfoot from his window sill. Said the witness:

I was sitting on my windowsill at 11 at night. I lived next to a large wetland/swamp area. My backyard was a large hill in front of the wetland. I was sitting on my windowsill and saw a large figure come out of the wetland, walk down the hill, and then re-enter the wetland at the bottom of the hill. The figure was probably 7 feet tall (I doubt it was 8 or 9) dark in color, and very large in build.

Also, on November 17, 2005, a backpacker from Vancouver, Washington took a series of four photos on Silver Star Mountain in Gifford Pinchot National Forest. He says he doesn't know what

The photo taken by an automatic camera at Moyie Springs, Idaho in April 2005.

the figure was, but he does not believe it was another hiker or backpacker. The photos are inconclusive, but they are potentially relevant. The figure you see could be a bigfoot. See the color section to view these photos.

It was in 2005 that an astonishing photograph of a bigfoot was taken by a trail camera at Moyie Springs in northern Idaho. Little is known about the photo except that it was sold to *The National Enquirer*. The color photograph shows the head and upper body of a bigfoot in the snow. He is near a fallen log with snow on it and his dark, hairy body has blobs of snow on it as well. Most notable about the photo is the grimace that the animal is making, as if in pain, and his teeth can be seen. The photo seems to be a genuine photo of bigfoot and no one has claimed to have hoaxed it.

### 2005: The DuPont Monster strikes in Illinois

An October 10, 2005 article in the *Chicago Tribune* chronicled the recent bigfoot sightings around Seneca, Illinois, a town on the Illinois River in an area of thick bush and wilderness, but not very far from Chicago. The area is near a DuPont chemical plant with a large wilderness area. Said the article:

> For better or worse, Seneca has become a veritable Sasquatch Central following a flurry of investigations

conducted by a member of the California-based Bigfoot Field Researchers Organization, which bills itself as "the only scientific research organization exploring the Bigfoot/Sasquatch mystery."

"My mind's open to anything. After all, they just found another planet. So, who knows? Anything's possible," lifelong Seneca resident Jim Maier, 61, joked. The rumors also create questions. From how and why Bigfoot stories can begin in a place such as Seneca—about 70 miles southwest of Chicago—to the reasons behind our powerful fascination with tales of things that go bump in the night. "Bigfoot is one of those things that people like believing in," said Dr. Christopher Bader, an assistant professor of sociology at Baylor University in Texas. "Because, how boring would the world be if we thought we had discovered everything?"

Since Stan Courtney of the BFRO first visited Seneca, he has deemed reports of four separate Bigfoot encounters near town credible enough to post on the group's Web site. Two of the alleged encounters happened in early June, and the others date back to 1979 and 1983. Courtney first posted two Bigfoot reports on the group's Web site July 9, prompting the *Daily Times*, a newspaper in nearby Ottawa, to publish a story about the rumors. After that story ran, Courtney said he received information about other Bigfoot encounters. He posted two more reports in late August. All four of the supposed sightings were within a mile of each other in a densely wooded area just south of the Illinois River along Seneca's narrow and twisting DuPont Road. Three occurred in Grundy County, while the fourth was in LaSalle County. One account involved two Bigfoot creatures.

"We heard some commotion over in the woods, and we were looking down into the trees. …At first, I didn't know what to think," a man identified only as "Tom" is quoted as saying on www.bfro.net, the official Web site of the Bigfoot Field Researchers Organization. "If anything, it could be a man in a suit. "Then I saw the second one in the clearing as plain as day. I guess I don't know how to explain it, but I just knew it wasn't a man at that time."

"Tom" believes the creatures he saw in June near Seneca—allegedly covered in hair, standing more than 8 feet tall and reeking of a pungent odor—to be Bigfoots.

To many longtime Seneca residents, such stories are actually nothing new. Tales of a towering, hairy creature stalking the woods along DuPont Road date back four decades, they say.

The BFRO website has reports of several sightings around Seneca that year. One was on June 10, 2005 when three men had a daylight encounter with bigfoot. Said the witness:

> … I'm on top of the hood of the car. Something caught my notice out of the corner of my eye to the right of the silhouette. Out in plain sight, plain as day there was an actual fur bodied [creature], walking. Probably 10 to 20 feet away from the silhouette I saw a smaller one and this one was starting to walk where the trees thin out. It started to make its way to where the trees get thicker, and just walking.
>
> So at this time, I tell John, "There's another one." And he says, "Where, where?" And I point in the general direction, I jump down off the car and run into the woods after it. It didn't run until I got about 20 feet in; that's when its pace picked up. It brought its elbows real high as it was running. And then I lost sight of it, because I didn't know that the ground actually sloped down. By time I got back to the hill I couldn't see it.

In another report with BFRO, dated June 2, 2005, a snake hunter encounters bigfoot during the daytime:

> I was just out snake hunting the roads, and I saw a spot and thought I would go up and look for some snakes. I heard like a rustling, kind of like something was further in front of me. There was a tree line there and it breaks off into an opening. Right outside of the tree line I saw the back half from the waist up of this bigfoot. It turned ever so slightly, it didn't face me, but it turned towards my direction a little bit,

kind of like it acknowledged me there and then continued to walk off.

Another story from that year was of a romantic couple having sex in the backseat of a car in an area known for sighting of the DuPont Monster. Suddenly the face of a bigfoot appeared in the window of the car. If the windows were open, it would have been an even more terrifying sight. Apparently the woman had been wearing a tampon and this was tossed outside the car prior to the passionate session of sex in the backseat. The DuPont Monster apparently smelled the discarded tampon and came to investigate. Sticking his head in the window he might have wanted to say, "Hey, what's up?"

The terrified couple stopped whatever they were doing and drove to the police station where they reported the incident to the police. Earlier that year someone had witnessed a bigfoot in a barn west of Seneca.

**2006: Woman Tries to Speak with Bigfoot**

In his book *The Hoopa Project,* author, researcher and retired California police officer David Paulides tells a number of interesting tales from the vicinity of the Hoopa Indian Reservation in northern California, an area with a great deal of activity. Paulides says that Josephine Peters, a retired herbal specialist who lives on the Hoopa Reservation, had a close encounter with a huge bigfoot at the front gate of her home in late January of 2006. She had seen a bigfoot back in 1963 and was aware of other tales of the hairy creature.

Josephine told Paulides that she heard her dog barking outside at approximately 10 p.m. one evening, and when she went outside she saw the dog run behind the house and then hide beneath the house in the fear. She then saw the silhouette of a large bigfoot standing behind her truck which was parked near her house. She apparently motioned for the bigfoot to come closer, and spoke to it as well. She was not afraid of the bigfoot and she told Paulides that the creature walked up to the picket fence, up the short walk from her front door and stood there staring at her. She tried to speak to the creature but it remained silent. She said that it had calm, green eyes. She told the creature that she did not have any food for it and then went back inside where she got a half loaf of bread and returned to the fence.

The bigfoot was gone and she left the bread. An hour later she went back to check on it and the bread was gone. She told Paulides that she has left other food out for bigfoot and believes that he will not eat cooked food like wet cat food or dog food.[36]

Probably the scariest thing that can happen on a school camping trip is to suddenly realize that you are a tourist visiting Bigfoot Nation. Julio Barrera Jr., age 13, of Plumas Lake, California located 30 miles (north of the city of Sacramento on the Feather River), told Linda Coil Suchy that he saw a bigfoot while at a school camp in the summer of 2006 at nearby Sly Park in the El Dorado County forest:

> That night, when I was supposed to be asleep, I was looking out the window of our cabin. About 40 to 50 feet away, I saw a huge hairy creature standing behind two oak trees. It stood like a human and looked like it was about six or seven feet tall. It kept bending over picking something up; I couldn't tell what it was because it was dark outside.
>
> I ran and tried to tell the cabin leaders but they wouldn't listen to me; they just told me to go back to sleep. I went back to look again and the creature stepped back into the forest. It looked black from the dark, but I knew it might have been a darkish brown color.
>
> The next morning, my friends and I went outside to check it out, and the area and trees smelled real nasty like wet with a sour food smell, which almost made me puke.[8]

## 2007: Bigfoot Seen Fishing from Log

Bigfoot was active in British Columbia, as usual, in 2007. In January a hunter named Chapman reported a 10-foot-tall bigfoot walking along the tree line of a ridge where there had been clear-cutting near Harrison Hot Springs.[7]

Then on March 30, 2007 near Ucluelet on Vancouver Island a motorist said they saw a bigfoot laying on a log that was over the Kennedy River. He first thought that it was a bear but then saw that it was an apelike creature with its arms hanging down into the river as if to catch fish by scooping them up as they swam upriver. He said that he distinctly saw its facial features and they were those of an ape. He said that the whole body, including the face, except for the mouth and eyes, was covered in dark brown hair. He estimated that if it were standing it would be about 7 feet tall.[7]

On September 27, 2007 a hunter encountered a bigfoot and foul odor near Canal Flats at White Swan Lake in British Columbia. He said that he had just sat down on the stump of a tree to have a snack when he was overcome by a powerful and noxious odor—worse than a skunk. He looked upwind and saw a tall, dark-haired bigfoot standing about 50 yards away. He said it was massively built with thick muscles and a broad body. Although the hunter did not feel threatened, he looked down to steady his rifle and when he looked up again the creature was gone. He said the whole episode lasted about a minute and a half and that the odor did not linger after the sasquatch had disappeared.[7]

### 2008: Biker Meets Bigfoot on the Trail

A report to the BFRO website by a trail biker says he encountered a bigfoot on August 27, 2008. While he was on his mountain bike going down a trail about 17 miles north of Chelan, Washington the witness said:

> I came around a left-hand bend in the trail, which was proceeding up a ridgeline slope of moderate grade. The trail was well packed and damp, as a rainstorm had preceded my biking trip by two days. This weather pattern was unusual for Central Washington in the late summer month of August. I was biking alone, and the section of trail preceding my unidentified animal sighting was downhill and allowed me to ride quickly, making little noise. As I proceeded around the left-hand bend in the trail, my vision was drawn to a motion on the ridgeline that continued to my upward left. What I saw was a tall (approx 8 ft), dark brown, longhaired animal running rapidly in a bi-pedal manner from the exposed ridgeline in a northwesterly direction. He remained in my line of vision as he ran through a moderately dense high alpine forest. It was astounding to me how quickly and quietly the animal was able to move for his sheer body size. I immediately stopped my bike with the initial sight of this animal. After stopping my bike, the animal remained

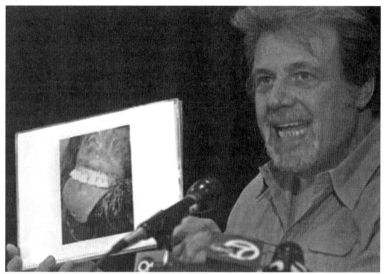

Bigfoot hunter Tom Biscardi holds up a photo of a bigfoot mouth in August, 2008.

within my sight for approx 10-15 seconds as he was running rapidly away from my intrusion.

There was no mistaking this animal's height as I am 6' 4", and my estimate of 8 ft. may be a moderate estimate of actual height. There also was no mistaking the bi-pedal pattern of running exhibited by this unknown animal. After seeing the animal run through the forest, I dropped my bike where I stood, and walked quietly down to the point where I saw him cross the trail. The tracks of this animal showed poorly as the ground on either side of the trail was densely vegetated with low-lying grasses and shrubs. It was remarkable to see such a large animal move so quickly and efficiently through the density of the forest. I looked for broken twigs, branches, or hair and found none. I failed to find tracks within the trail.

### 2009: Woman Sees Silver-Haired Sasquatch

On April 4, 2009 a woman reported that she was driving near Langley, British Columbia at 12:30 a.m. when she saw something in her headlights as she approached 18th Avenue. It was a bigfoot with silver-white hair with dark gray mixed in it. The hair was very long like a shaggy dog's and draped in a perfect arch below the legs. She said that it was probably less than 6 feet tall, but very stocky. It

**275**

Keith Quinlan

Sasquatch running at Peace Camp
on Mt Elphinstone,
seen april 2009 [signature] . 18/12/2010

A 2009 drawing by Keith Quinlan of a bigfoot walking through fallen logs.

disappeared into the darkness after crossing the road. When asked how she felt about the experience she said, "I feel wonderful. I think of it as a gift." For some, Bigfoot Nation is a place of fear, while for others, it is a place of wonder and elation.

Also in April of 2009 a man named Keith Quinlan reported seeing sasquatch walking through fallen timber near Gibsons, British Columbia. Quinlan said that he witnessed the bigfoot taking very long or very short paces through the fallen timber, depending on where he could step, in a "slinky manner." It would bend its body and swing its legs forward very quickly. He saw the locomotion as highly animal-like, although he thought that a very athletic person could also walk in this flexible manner. Quinlan drew a sketch of

Tim Peeler demonstrating an encounter with Knobby the bigfoot on his North Carolina property on June 5, 2010.

Tim Peeler drawing an image Knobby the bigfoot.

**277**

the bigfoot slinking through the forest which reached sasquatch researcher Christopher Murphy.[7]

## 2010: Couple Sees Bigfoot at Mountain Overlook

A man motoring with his girlfriend on Mount Sicker near the town of Duncan on Victoria Island, British Columbia spotted a bigfoot on June 6, 2006. The couple had driven in a Jeep to a lookout near the top of Mount Sicker in an area that had been clear-cut. It was about 9:30 in the evening and just beginning to get dark. They got out of their vehicle to stretch and saw a tall figure about 300 feet away with long black and brown hair. It was walking on two legs, had very long arms and was between 8 and 9 feet tall.

He said to his girlfriend, "I think I just saw a sasquatch." They joked about it and returned to the car where they sat talking for 10 or 15 minutes before they heard a loud grunt outside the vehicle. It was dark now and they could not see the animal that was making the grunting sound, which occurred several times again, but came from a different direction each time. Eventually they left the area and filed a report that was investigated by Canadian sasquatch researchers. They also mentioned in their report that another odd thing happened at the same time as the grunts —a small black and white bird kept squawking and swooping around them the whole time.[7]

※ —◦— ※

## 2011: Return of the Boggy Creek Monster

Newspapers in Arkansas spoke of the possible return of the Boggy Creek monster. A story at naturalplane.blogspot.com on June 10, 2011 quoted a letter to the site that said:

> My brother and his wife had a shocking event on May 5th, 2011 when they were driving home to Genoa, Arkansas from a visit with his in-laws in Texarkana. He was driving eastbound on Tennessee Rd (County Rd. 16) at around 7:30 pm and had just gone by Mosely Rd. when a creature suddenly jumped out of the trees and brush, crossed the road and blended into the thick woods. It was headed in the direction of Old Bitty Lake.

They both had a decent look at it and say it was about 6 foot tall and very stout with huge legs and feet. It was covered with very long reddish-brown hair that had dirt and debris stuck to it. When they stopped the car to look in the direction it went into the woods, they got a whiff of a horrific stench (the windows were open).

I had heard the tales of the 'Fouke Monster' since I was a young girl but never bought into the hype. We actually lived near the Mercer Bayou at one point and talked to several people who verified the stories. My brother doesn't dare identity himself since he feels that it may cause problems but he felt there was a need for a warning.

I do believe him because he has never lied to me and is a very trustworthy, hard-working man. He is also a very experienced outdoorsman and knows the swamps and backwoods of southwest Arkansas like the back of his hand. But this has left him shaken, to the point where he was at a loss for words when talking to me. That is VERY unlike him.

It was reported on Cryptomundo.com that a posting on Facebook by Thomas Terry ("Tom") Graham of Medford, Oregon, of State of Jefferson Sasquatch Research, and also a member of Team Bigfootology, said that on May 14, 2011, on a hillside four miles from O'Brien, Oregon, he and his research companion encountered a seven-foot tall white sasquatch. The hairy hominoid saw them and bolted up a steep incline. Graham gave out about four calls and it called back as it went into the trees and forest. Further investigations are ongoing at the site. The State of Jefferson is a proposed new state that would be formed from the territories of northern California and southern Oregon that have been trying to separate for years.

It was reported in the *Tipp Gazette* on December 21, 2011 that two Tipp City, West Virginia women were driving on a local mountain highway in broad daylight and witnessed what they described as a bigfoot walking up a truck ramp. The creature disappeared into the

Two photos from a Sept. 9, 2010 Vermont trail camera. Left: coyote. Right: bigfoot?

woods before the startled women could stop and snap a photo. One of the witnesses, Terri Bessler told the *Tipp Gazette*: "It was huge, there is no way it was a person… if it was a real person, it was the biggest person in the world…"

Understandably reluctant to claim they had seen a fabled "bigfoot" the women estimate the creature was a bout a half mile away from their car when they spotted it. They observed that the creature was a solid shade of black and appeared to be unclothed. The other witness, Crystal Krieger, told reporters, "We weren't sleep deprived or juiced up on caffeine," and they didn't expect everyone to believe their story, but urged area residents to keep their eyes out for the huge, elusive humanoid. (Tippgazzette.com, Dec. 21, 2011)

### 2012: Hiker Has Afternoon Encounter in Washington

Tulalip is a group of Native American peoples from western Washington state who settled onto reservation lands after signing the Point Elliott Treaty with the former Washington Territory on January 22, 1855. The reservation is the western half of the Marysville Tulalip community and it lies west of Interstate 5. A BFRO website entry says that on June 10, 2012, the witness was hiking on the Tulalip Reservation:

After I got to the top of the hill I walked down a little

further and at my 2 o'clock I heard a large branch snap like how a twig snaps under a man's foot, and the brush crashed and I heard what sounded like a baseball bat hit a tree. When I looked at where the noise came from and I saw to my horror a rock come towards me from out of the bushes, and my eyes caught the hand throwing the rock. When I noticed the hand I saw it jump in the air and do a 180 spin so it would be faced away from me when it landed, and I swear to god it threw the rock so freakin' hard that the entire rock didn't spin at all when it was being chucked. It bonked the stump on the side of the trail and I kept staring at it because I thought at first it was a ghost or maybe somebody behind the stump that I just saw do a ninja move. Then I realized that it was facing away from me towards the swampy brush, because the stump I was looking had a muscley buttocks and I could see on the top of the stump what looked like a v-shaped tuft of hair similar to Howard the Duck. I was yellin' and shoutin' at it but it just stood there and kept looking away from me, and I knew that this thing is not going to move unless I go over there, and at that point I left the forest by going back where I came from.

Bigfoot sightings are not uncommon in the Kuskokwim delta region of the Yukon. On May 29, 2012, two teenaged boys and their mother from the village of Kasigluk went egg hunting on ATVs. When they reached a certain lagoon, the eldest son ran ahead to see if anyone else was already working that area, and returned to say that somebody was already there. According to the mother's report: "So we decided to go check somewhere else when that 'somebody' started running at an incredible amount of speed. ...That 'somebody' was all black from top to bottom, kind of hunchbacked, like it had no neck and its head was cone-shaped. Its long arms went past its knees and it was incredibly tall.

"At first we all asked each other, 'Who is that?' Then after about 10 seconds as it was walking with long strides, it would occasionally look towards us. The way it walked was fast and no human could cover that amount of tundra in the same amount of time. I asked, 'WHAT is that?'

"All that time we were awestruck and dumbfounded as to what we were witnessing. Then as it was going to disappear from our view finally I said, 'I think we just saw Bigfoot!' As it passed in our full view it had covered the whole entire hill in a matter of about a minute. It seemed to be just walking but with big strides."

The bigfoot was approximately 75 yards away at its closest approach. The witnesses claimed that they watched it for about two minutes. The sighting occurred at around three p.m. on a slightly cloudy day. (deltadiscovery.com, 23 January, 2013)

## 2013: Bigfoot Throws Rocks at Workers

A BFRO report says that several families in the Stanwood, Washington area were experiencing bigfoot activity in 2013. The entry said that in November of the that year contractors on a property said that rocks were being thrown at them from the forest and they had begun to hear strange noises including a deep growl from an unidentified source. The son of the report filer had seen bigfoot, plus they had found tracks; they had horses stampeding, heard vocalizations, and creatures moving around the property at night. The area has rolling hills and many heavily wooded areas that provide a corridor for animals to travel through undetected. The wooded areas lead directly to the foothills of the Cascade mountains. There are several houses in the area and some have heard screams, howls, and what has been described as Samurai Chatter. No doubt the activity will continue in this corner of Bigfoot Nation.

In February of 2013, Nederland, Texas native David Arceneaux saw two bigfoot at the Oak Bluff cemetery in Port Neches, Texas where he goes every month to visit and clean the gravesites of a relative and friend who are buried there. On this visit he received more than your standard cemetery fright.

Interviewed by the *Port Arthur News* (Texas), he told reporters, "I heard a bloodcurdling scream and a lady nearby asked me if I was OK. I told her it wasn't me… We walked over to the water and looked to the left then straight ahead." What the two witnesses observed amazed them. Two bigfoot-looking humanoids were throwing rocks into the water that borders the cemetery. One appeared to be standing underneath a tree, a second creature was down on its haunches. The second creature stood up and Arceneaux grabbed his cell phone and snapped a photograph.

"All of a sudden they started walking then running through the woods… When they began to run, the lady said 'I'm leaving' and [she] left. I stayed a few more seconds and then thought there may be a way for them to cross here so I left, scared." He told reporters that he was able to see their faces "plain as day." According to reporters "…he did not come forward with his story sooner because he worried about what others would think of him. He has shown this photographic evidence—which was taken at a far distance with a cell phone—to friends and family and only had one person scoff." (ottumwacourier.com, 20 Feb., 2013)

In October of 2013 a Tehama County, California man said that he had a new neighbor who seemed unfriendly. Ken S. contacted KRCR-TV in Redding, California and then contacted Tom Biscardi and his "Searching for Bigfoot" team. He told Biscardi of his predicament and the Bigfoot hunter team paid Ken a visit.

It all began around the first week of October when Ken was nearly struck by two rocks that were thrown just over his head while he visited a sandy creek located on his remote 200 acres of land. A short time later Ken took his visiting brother to the site, and his brother let out a series of whooping calls. After about five minutes of the whooping, two or three return whoops were heard. "A few days later they took my couch and dropped it and dragged it 20 feet towards the house," Ken told a reporter from KRCR. (dailymail. co.uk, Oct. 23, 2013)

## 2014: Virginia Bigfoot Photographed—Neanderthal in North Carolina

In June of 2014 an interesting claim was made by a Virginia man and his father, who allegedly snapped what could be among the clearest photographs of bigfoot. The father was fishing in the afternoon with a friend when he spied the hairy hominid lurking on the shoreline. He grabbed his cell phone and snapped two pictures before it lumbered off into the underbrush. Evidently, this was not his first encounter with something strange in the area. His father and a friend had run into bigfoot there 25 years earlier. (whofortedblog. com, July 1, 2014)

In November of 2014 a North Carolinian named Bernard Tillman,

Two photos taken in June 2014 of a bigfoot fishing on a river in Virginia.

66 years old, was taking his dog out when they encountered what he described as a 10-foot-tall, humanlike creature. "I was taking our dog for his daily ride. It was 6 p.m., [and] we were approaching a small creek on the downgrade of the road. I was looking at the 4-feet saplings where they had cut all the trees down." Tillman thinks they may have surprised the creature. "There he stood; we must have surprised him because he was just standing real still—the sun was setting between me and him," he said about the alleged 30-second encounter. "He was huge. He was massive in the back and chest. His hair looked black. From the side profile, his neck, his head, his nose and his lower jaw... he looked just like a Neanderthal." (cryptozoologicalnews.com, Jan. 8, 2015)

Jim Smith, founder of the Alabama Bigfoot Society told reporters that in October, November and December of 2014 four people claim to have seen a "very large black Bigfoot" along Alabama State Route 22 in the Tallapoosa County area. Sightings of the creature over the years have prompted locals to dub the creature "Big Joe."

The first report of the 2014 sightings was filed by a woman who was driving on Halloween night when she and her passengers spotted the creature. Smith described her sighting report: "There is a hunting trail that goes into the woods," he said. "When they came upon the curve, they...saw the black Bigfoot walking through the woods." Smith investigated the report about a month later when he went to the area. Much to his surprise and elation, he became the latest of several witnesses.

It was around Thanksgiving week when I first saw him. When I came around the curve, that's when I saw him. He wasn't that far from the road, but he was walking down through the woods. He was very muscular, he was very large, he was very wide, and he was also black.

Another witness, traveling east on the same highway, said the creature he spotted was "almost dark." "He only got about somewhere around 70 to 80 yards from this sign. The sign is reflective, like all road signs are, and that's when my lights hit it. I could see this very tall Bigfoot." The man claimed that as he approached the beast, it strode across the road and that it "took only three steps to cross it" before disappearing into the woods. It would take an average human at least nine steps to cross this section of road, according to Smith.

The alleged Sasquatch was described by the witness as having "flowing hair" on its neck and head. Smith noted, "The Bigfoot's head was [up to] this yellow sign, so we measured and that would have made this particular Bigfoot...about 9 feet tall." (Dec. 14, 2014, cryptozoologynews.com)

In Kingsport, Tennessee in 2014 a man dialed 911 to request law enforcement help because "a bigfoot was trying to break into his [Bloomingdale Road] home." Police took the panicked man's claim seriously and dispatched officers. When they arrived, there was no sign of the creature which had evidently run off into the nearby woods. (Jan. 20, 2017, cryptozoologynews.com)

## 2015: Bigfoot Throws a Tree at Workers

A video taken in 2015 was uploaded by NvTv on February 4, 2018 showing workers at a construction site in Alberta, Canada watching a bigfoot. One of them had seen the creature in the trees and grabbed his video camera. The bigfoot, a giant dark figure toward the left of the screen can be seen throwing a young tree at the workers like a huge javelin. One of the men says, "Holy shit! He just threw the fucking tree!" Then the other one says, "I see him now!" The footage, zoomed-in and repeated in slow motion (beginning at the 1:04 mark), is fascinating and it would seem unlikely that a bear could hurl a tree in the manner clearly seen in the video. The bigfoot appears to be huge, with a very wide chest and a height of perhaps

10 feet or taller.

A bigfoot was accused of destroying cars at an Oklahoma used car lot in September of 2015. Fred Griffin, the general sales manager at Green Country Ford in Vinita, Oklahoma, called the local police in mid-September, to report strange damage to nine cars in his lot. While vandalism is a common occurrence in car lots, Griffin had never seen anything quite like this.

Said Griffin, "The mangled cars have paw prints, fine, course hairs mixed in all the mangled parts and what look to be bite marks. That whole front clip was just ripped plumb off with teeth marks all over it and hair matted to it. It was just totally destroyed."

Griffin says that the damage done to his cars by the mysterious beast, or beasts, now totals in the tens of thousands of dollars. The mysterious beast has attacked the car lot four times and nothing was captured on surveillance cameras. He says everyone has their own ideas ranging from bigfoot and chupacabras to bears, mountain lions or even a pack of wild hogs.

Michael Bergin from the Oklahoma Department of Wildlife Conservation admits being puzzled by the car damage. "I can't even fathom what that would be, because there's nothing about a vehicle that usually attracts an animal, especially biting a vehicle, tearing off a bumper, puncturing tires or anything like that. That's not indicative of any form of wildlife species that I know of."

Local police were concerned enough that they set traps to capture the motor vehicle monster. Griffin thought about hiding in the lot overnight, but instead sent samples of fur, blood and saliva to a forensic company for DNA analysis. (mysteriousuniverse.com, Sept. 15, 2015)

**2016: Bigfoot Goes to Washington**

The *Washington City Paper* featured a story on June 9, 2016 about a bigfoot sighting in the Patuxent Research Refuge in Laurel, Maryland. The witness (named Jeremy) was driving on Brock Bridge Road near the airfield known as Suburban Airport when he spotted an animal in the brush. "I saw what I thought was a bear, so I pulled over to take some pictures." But when he got a closer look, he noticed that the animal, which he estimated was six or seven feet tall, was walking on two legs. "Bears usually walk on all four feet.

I know they can walk on two, but he was wading through water on two feet, which I thought was strange," he said. For about ten minutes Jeremy watched and snapped pictures of the beast. At no point did it drop down onto four legs, which led him to believe he was witnessing a hairy hominid.

Maryland is not a state where the average person would think that the elusive bigfoot would make its home, but according to the Bigfoot Field Researchers Organization, there have been a total of 35 alleged sightings in Maryland since 1970 and two of them have been in the Patuxent Research Refuge. The refuge, operated by the U.S. Fish and Wildlife Service, was created in 1936 by President Franklin Roosevelt and is "the nation's only national wildlife refuge established to support wildlife research." This could suggest that what Jeremy photographed was simply a bear that is comfortable walking on two legs instead of four. His girlfriend, who was with him during the sighting, prefers the more mundane explanation.

"I've driven by there hundreds of times and have never seen anything like it," Jeremy says. "I doubt I'll ever see something like this again." (June 9, 2016, washingtoncitypaper.com/news)

A report to the BFRO by a man in Missouri said that he had an encounter with a dark haired bigfoot on October 8, 2016 near Ellington, Missouri. Said the witness:

> My son and I was bow hunting in Reynolds County MO, and I decided to hunt a pond that deer were using consistently. To make a long story short, I got settled in a tree behind the pond where I could watch a hollower [trail with steep sides] leading up to the pond and a log road running past the pond as well. So around 5 pm I noticed how quiet the woods became. The squirrels I had been watching disappeared, the birds became silent, so I started to become concerned of human activity. So I began to search the woods to see if someone was in the area when this large black figure appeared walking down the other side of this hollower I had set up to watch. At first I thought this was a man. But as it kept walking I noticed how massive it was, and all of a sudden it stopped and took two steps backwards and turned and looked straight at me.

It was then I realized that this is not a man but a bigfoot. As this creature looked at me, I could clearly see its eyes and nose. I could see flesh around its eyes and cheeks and also see hair covering its face as well. It stood there looking at me for I guess a good fifteen or twenty seconds, then turned and walked on down the ridge and disappeared into the woods. Needless to say, I was scared out of my mind and refused to climb down the tree, but it was getting dark and I knew I had to meet my son back out on the main road. Finally I got up the nerve and came down. So I walked over to where I saw it and looked back to the tree I was in, and then it became clear that what I had seen could not have been a man, because he would not have been tall enough to have been seen over the underbrush. This creature was at least seven and a half or eight foot tall. When I met up with my son I asked him if he met or passed anybody or vehicles on his way to pick me up, and he said no; then I told him what I saw.

The witness added that it was broad daylight on a clear day and that bigfoot had been sighted in the area previously including in 2007 when a hunter told him he had seen a bigfoot eating a "deer gut pile."

### 2017: Bigfoot Causes Car Crash in Idaho

A story appeared on January 10, 2017 on the North Dakota television station KFGO about lifelong trapper Chris Bauer of Ellendale, North Dakota who "knows the outdoors and is now a reluctant true believer in bigfoot. He's certain the creature he recently tracked is none other than the legendary bigfoot, or sasquatch."

The story said that a woman attending a family holiday gathering at a rural homestead north of Ellendale said she witnessed a large hairy creature outside the house. Bauer knows the family, who contacted him about the sighting. So, the following day he went out to the property to have a look at the tracks the witness said were left behind. Bauer was stunned to find a set of impressively large footprints measuring 18 inches long, 8 inches wide, with a four-foot stride, leading away from the farm. The humanoid-looking barefoot tracks continued in the snow for seven miles! To my knowledge,

288

this is the longest bigfoot trackway ever documented.

Bauer claims that while he was following the trackway, he ran smack into a stench so severe he almost became nauseous. He also noted that when he was assaulted by the smell an "eerie" silence descended throughout the area. He couldn't hear any animals or birds, something the experienced outdoorsman noted was strange and rather disconcerting.

An enhancement of the 1967 Pattterson bigfoot.

When he was contacted, Dickey County Sheriff Chris Estes didn't bother to go out and investigate but he did view photographs of the tracks. He admitted that he was very surprised by what he saw. He says it's either "an elaborate hoax someone put a lot work into… or there may be validity to it." He noted that the effort it would have taken to hoax a seven-mile long trackway makes it seem highly unlikely to be a hoax. (Jan. 10, 2017, kfgo.com)

A story in the *Idaho State Journal* on April 3, 2017 concerned a recent bigfoot sighting and how the respected bigfoot researcher Jeff Meldrum thought that the sighting was credible. Said the article:

> A northern Idaho woman recently made national news after she blamed a car crash on a sasquatch. Now a noted local Bigfoot researcher is saying that her story seems credible on the surface. Dr. Jeff Meldrum, professor of anatomy and anthropology at Idaho State University, has been researching Bigfoot sightings for years, and he said the woman's claim is not out of the realm of possibility.
>
> According to an article in the *Moscow-Pullman Daily News*, the woman, a 50-year-old resident of the town of Tensed, told police she saw a sasquatch chasing a deer on the side of the road last Wednesday night while driving on

U.S. Highway 95 near the Idaho/Washington border. Then, she checked her rearview mirror to get a second look at what she described as a 7- to 8-foot tall "shaggy" creature. But when she looked up, the deer ran in front of her and she struck the animal with her Subaru Forester.

Even though Meldrum has not interviewed the woman making the claims, he said the story does seem credible due to how she handled the sighting in the aftermath of the crash. "It's intriguing because she sounds like a very credible witness," he said, noting that there is no suggestion that she was inebriated or delusional. "Her first response was to report it to the sheriff and not post it on Facebook."

Meldrum also said that the whole scenario seems plausible, especially considering the time of year and the location of the crash, which occurred near a heavily wooded national forest. "The most common places to see a Bigfoot is on a highway at night or adjacent to a body of water," he said. "The whole northern panhandle is prime habitat for a sasquatch. This is also the time of year you would expect a Bigfoot to be chasing deer, when it's malnourished at the end of winter."

A group called the Bigfoot 911 investigative team said they had a sighting on Friday, August 4, 2017. The team was out in a forested area in McDowell County, North Carolina when they witnessed a "creature." The sighting happened at about 11:00 p.m. They'd been placing glow sticks around the forest, hoping to gain bigfoot's attention, when something emerged from beyond the trees and began throwing rocks at them. One of the team members described the creature as "a large bi-pedal animal covered in hair." The creature's face, however, was "solid black," and completely hairless. The creature then ran off into the woods. (strangedimensions.com)

Fox News reported in October, 2017 that on October 8 that the same group headed by John Bruner had another encounter with bigfoot in McDowell Country. Bruner is based out of Marion, North Carolina. The Fox News report said:

After being spotted, the creature ran off, though Bruner

followed and spotted it again, this time where a tree had been broken in half.

"It's face was solid black no hair on it, the hair looked shaggy all over," Bruner added.

The creature ran off again, with Bruner saying he saw its buttocks flex with each step. After a short while, something threw rocks at Bruner's group while they were exiting the woods.

A BFRO report says a motorist saw a bigfoot at 4:45 a.m. on his way to work near Rochester, Illinois on September 16, 2017. Said the witness:

I was driving on Rochester Road getting close to the stoplight at Oak Hill Road when from the left side of the road a two legged creature ran across the road in front of me. It was still dark out and I had my lights on; the creature was just at the end of where my lights hit. It didn't seem to be extremely tall, but what caught my eye were the huge muscles on its legs and arms. It didn't appear to have much of a neck, like the head was sitting on the shoulders. I could see that it was not wearing any clothes, but also did not see long hair either. I would estimate it to be between 6'-6'5". It was a dark dirty black/grey color. It disappeared quickly into the cornfield. This all runs extremely close to the river. The area it came from always has multiple deer feeding and crossing the road. I always drive slowly and cautiously on this stretch of road.

## Hunter Sexually Assaulted by 8-Foot Bigfoot

A story at DailyZone.net on November 4, 2017 was about a hunter in Colorado named Darrel Whitaker who claimed he was sexually assaulted by a bigfoot! The story included a photo of Whitaker and said:

Darrel Whitaker, from Glenwood Springs in Colorado, claims a sasquatch attacked him and attempted to rape him while he was walking in the woods. The 57-year-old man

Colorado hunter Darrell Whitaker said he was assaulted by a bigfoot in Nov. 2017.

was walking to his hunting cabin on Sunday, to see if it had suffered any damage during the winter. All of a sudden, a large "gorilla-like" creature dropped from a tree in front of him and punched him in the face.

"It was at least 8-foot tall and its punches hurt like hell! I was knocked right out at the first blow!"

While Mr. Whitaker was trying to recover from the attack, the large humanoid creature began to tear his clothes while letting out some terrifying howls.

"When I regained consciousness, he had already torn my pants and was tearing through my underwear. I stabbed him in the shoulder with my hunting knife, and that made him run away."

Mr. Whitaker immediately reported the attack to both the Glenwood Springs Police Department (GSPD) and the Colorado Parks and Wildlife agency, and a joint investigation has been launched.

The police were not entirely convinced and suggested that Whitaker was assaulted by a large, hairy man rather than a sasquatch. However, it doesn't seem

Darrell Whitaker shows a large footprint.

that Mr. Whitaker has much to gain by making up a story like this and going to the police. He seems to have been genuinely assaulted, apparently by a sexual predator from Bigfoot Nation. The article produced an impressive photo of a very large footprint and ended with a tongue-in-cheek plea for anyone who had seen an 8-foot hairy man to call the Glenwood Springs Police Department:

> Darrel Whitaker is convinced that the creature who attacked him was a sasquatch, but the GSPD investigators say it's more probable that the attacker is simply a particularly large and hairy man. They are currently interrogating nearby residents to see if anyone noticed an individual corresponding to the description of the suspect.
>
> According to the victim, the attacker measure around 8-foot tall and is extremely hairy. He has brown hair, dark brown eyes and extremely large feet. If you possess any information concerning the suspect, please contact the Glenwood Springs Police Department or the Colorado Parks and Wildlife agency.

## 2018: Bigfoot Starts Lawsuit in California

In January of 2018 a man reported to the BFRO that he had seen a bigfoot on January 29 while driving southbound on I-35 just after 4 in the afternoon. The witness said he was traveling southbound, between Cameron and Holt, Missouri, in an area called Wallace State Park. Sunset was still nearly an hour away (5:36), and temperatures hovered near 30° F. As his truck entered a gradual highway curve to the left, his eyes locked on a large, tall, brown "mass" moving in front of a tree line ahead. For several seconds, as his truck came closer, he got an increasingly clearer view of this large mass that was standing on two legs and walking. He said it was almost like it was "marching," but with a bilateral bend at the knees. He said he reported the incident to the Missouri Highway Patrol.

In March 2017, Claudia Ackley claims she and her daughters witnessed a sasquatch while hiking near Lake Arrowhead, California. However, after reporting the sighting to local authorities, she was dismayed to find they didn't believe her, stating that it was

The relentless advertising campaign featuring bigfoot continues unabated.

likely just a bear. Their unwillingness to believe Ackley ultimately led her to file a lawsuit, demanding recognition of the species.

"Respondents are, or ought to be, aware that the State of California is home to a large wild indigenous mammal, considered to be a giant hairy vertebrate, hominoid or primate, commonly known as Sasquatch."

The lawsuit presents the case that sasquatch, or bigfoot, has a long history of sightings and evidence in California, and that the state is ignoring "one of the greatest discoveries of our time." It also states that bigfoot is "likely a species at risk" that "very well may pose a threat to the health and wellbeing of the citizens of the State of California." This story has been widely reported on Fox News, Huffington Post and other news sites. The case was withdrawn in March of 2018 by Ackley on the advice of her attorneys. They want to re-file in a form more likely to prevail in court. In Bigfoot Nation everyone is innocent until proven guilty by their peers. Let us hope that bigfoot himself does not end up in court anytime soon.

⚘ ──ⵗⵗⵗⵗ── ⚘

But, who knows what will happen, given the sordid history of Bigfoot Nation. It is a history that is still in the shadows. It is a history that includes kidnapping, harassment, murder (on both

**294**

sides), courageous acts, sexual assault, questionable and provocative antics, night stalking, trespassing and dumpster diving, plus spying on the enemy. There are bigfoot detectives out there sifting through the evidence and chronicling every detail of the crimes committed at various locations in Bigfoot Nation.

One could say that bigfoot is using a form of chemical warfare with his smelly-skunky antics, but who can blame him? Is there some kind of Geneva Convention with Bigfoot Nation? Hell no. But if a treaty were written, you would think that it would be signed on some First Nation's reservation in British Columbia or Washington State. We might have to sign a separate one with Skunk Ape Nation. Maybe in Tampa or Biloxi. The bigfoot representatives could put a giant handprint down on a huge page of the document. Everyone would love it.

Meanwhile, until that unlikely time, Bigfoot Nation continues to move forward as some unstoppable force no less powerful than bigfoot himself. Bigfoot Nation continues marching forward through pop culture with movies, television shows and a wide variety of products, none of which have been officially licensed by any bigfoot or his representative. Millions in advertising royalties are going uncollected. Bigfoot Nation lawyers completely ignore the problem. China is no doubt pirating all sorts of bigfoot movies and products. Who cares? Some people might say that bigfoot needs a good lawyer, not just the public defender that his sorry hide has now.

And what about the ridicule? This ridicule is aimed at bigfoot and at his experiencers. Often both have been traumatized by those sudden meetings on a lonely, wooded road or trail. "A bigfoot in the headlights" isn't just an expression (is it?). The bottom line is, these guys really don't care about the ridicule because they are tough woodsmen who just don't know how they fit in with modern civilization. Well, its because they don't.

This can lead to the occasional violence. Bad hunters shooting at things in the woods, and those crazy bigfoot hunters who can't wait to get a swamp ape in their redneck freezers. And maybe worse, as bigfoot is apparently capable of taking a few slugs from some old rifle with his matted hair and muscular body, it all just makes him mad and he suddenly rips some person limb from limb in a rage that

**295**

would make a grizzly bear run.

Somewhere, right now, a bigfoot is lurking in the shadows, keeping his eye on those who encroach on his territory, and any nearby dumpsters. He knows his place in Bigfoot Nation and it is a place in the shadows. For him its no big deal, the struggle for national sovereignty is over—except for the yelling and the screaming.

All I want to know is, "Have you seen this man?"

A fake hunting permit from Vermont. The war continues.

# BIGFOOT NATION

# Bibliography and Footnotes

1. *The Bigfoot Files*, Peter Guttilla, 2003, Timeless Voyager Press, Santa Barbara, CA.
2. *On the Track of Unknown Animals*, Bernard Heuvelmans, 1955, MIT Press, Cambridge, MA.
3. *The Bigfoot Casebook*, Janet & Colin Bord, 1982, Granada, London.
4. *The Bigfoot Casebook, Updated*, Janet & Colin Bord, 2006, Pine Winds Press, Oregon.
5. *Tom Slick & the Search for the Yeti*, Loren Coleman, 1989, Faber & Faber, Boston.
6. *There are Giants in the Earth*, Michael Grumley, 1974, Doubleday & Co., Garden City, NY.
7. *Sasquatch in British Columbia*, Christopher L. Murphy, 2012, Hancock House, Surrey, BC.
8. *Who's Watching You?,* Linda Coil Suchy, 2009, Hancock House, Surrey, BC.
9. *Abominable Snowmen: Legend Come to Life*, Ivan T. Sanderson, 1961, Chilton Book Co., New York. Reprinted 2006, Adventures Unlimited Press, Kempton, IL.
10. *The Bigfoot Book*, Nick Redfern, 2016, Visible Ink, Detroit.
11. *Strange Indiana Monsters*, Michael Newton, 2006, Schiffer Publishing, Atglen, PA.
12. *Raincoast Sasquatch*, J. Robert Alley, 2003, Hancock House, Surrey, BC.
13. *Still Living?,* Myra Shackley, 1983, Thames & Hudson, London.

**297**

14. *Things and More Things*, Ivan T. Sanderson, 1970, reprinted 2007, Adventures Unlimited Press.
15. *Bigfoot: The Yeti & Sasquatch in Myth & Reality*, John Napier, 1973, E.P. Dutton, New York.
16. *Do Abominable Snowmen of North America Really Exist?*, Roger Patterson, 1966, Franklin Press, Yakima, WA.
17. *Weird America*, Jim Brandon, 1978, E.P. Dutton, New York.
18. *The Field Guide to Bigfoot, Yeti, and Other Mystery Primates Worldwide*, Loren Coleman and Patrick Huyghe, 2006, Anomalist Books, New York.
19. *Bigfoot: America's Abominable Snowman*, Elwood Baumann, 1975, Franklin Watts, Inc., New York.
20. *Bigfoot: Man, Monster or Myth?*, Peter Byrne, 1975, Acropolis Books, Olympia, WA.
21. *Sasquatch/Bigfoot*, Don Hunter with René Dahinden, 1993, Firefly Books, Buffalo, NY.
22. *The Locals*, Thom Powell, 2004, Hancock House, Surrey, BC.
23. *Meet the Sasquatch*, Christopher Murphy, 2004, Hancock House, Surrey, BC.
24. *Mysterious Creatures*, 1988, Time-Life Books, Alexandria, VA.
25. *The Making of Bigfoot*, Greg Long, 2004, Prometheus Books, Amherst, NY.
26. *Buccaneers of America*, Alexander O. Exquemelin, 1678, reprinted 1967, Penguin Books, London and 2000, Dover Books, Mineola, NY.
27. *The Aquatic Ape*, Elaine Morgan, 1982, Stein & Day, New York.
28. *Yetis, Sasquatch and Hairy Giants*, David Hatcher Childress, 2010, Adventures Unlimited, Kempton, IL.
29. *Sasquatch: The Apes among Us*, John Green, 1978, Hancock House, Surrey, BC.
30. *Bigfoot*, Ann Slate & Alan Berry, 1976, Bantam Books, NY.
31. *The Bigfoot Film Controversy*, Roger Patterson and Chris Murphy, 2004, Hancock House, Surrey, BC.
32. *Sasquatch: Legend Meets Science*, Jeff Meldrum, 2006, Forge Books, New York.

33. "Gigantopithecus," E.L. Simons & P.E. Ettel, *Scientific American,* January 1970.
34. *The Mysterious Monsters*, Robert & Frances Guenette, Sun Classic, Los Angeles.
35. *The Beast of Boggy Creek*, Lyle Blackburn, 2012, Anomalist Books, New York.
36. *The Hoopa Project*, David Paulides, 2008, Hancock House, Surrey, BC.
37. *Missing 411: Western United States & Canada*, David Paulides, 2012, Create Space.
38. *Missing 411: Eastern United States*, David Paulides, 2012, Create Space.
39. *Missing 411: North America & Beyond*, David Paulides, 2013, Create Space.
40. *Missing 411: The Devil's in the Detail*, David Paulides, 2014, Create Space.
41. *Missing 411: Hunters*, David Paulides, 2015, Create Space.
42. *Missing 411: Off the Grid*, David Paulides, 2017, Create Space.
43. *Strange Abominable Snowmen*, Warren Smith, 1970, Popular Library, New York.
44. *The Historical Bigfoot*, Chad Arment, 2006, Coachwhip Publications, Darke County, OH.
45. *Big Footprints*, Grover S. Krantz, 1992, Johnson Books, Boulder, CO.
46. *Buffalo Bill* (Autobiography), William Cody, 1879, Frank Bliss Co., Hartford, CT, reprinted 1978, University of Nebraska Press.
47. *The Neandertals*, Erik Tinkaus & Pat Shipman, 1970, SBS, New York.
48. *The Mountain Gorilla*, George Schaller, 1963, Chicago University Press, Chicago & London.
49. *Men and Apes*, Desmond & Ramona Morris, 1968, McGraw Hill, New York.
50. *Sasquatch Research in America*, Frank D. Sobczak, 2011, Self Published, NC.
51. *In Search of Giants*, Thomas N. Steenburg, 2000, Hancock House, Surrey, BC.

52. *Stranger Than Science*, Frank Edwards, 1959, Bantam Books, New York.
53. *Strange World,* Frank Edwards, 1962, Bantam Books, New York.
54. *Encounters with Bigfoot*, John Green, 1980, Hancock House, Surrey, BC.
55. *On the Track of the Sasquatch*, John Green, 1980, Hancock House, Surrey, BC.
56. *Sasquatch/Bigfoot,* Thomas N. Steenburg, 1990, Hancock House, Surrey, BC.
57. *Rumors of Existence*, Matthew Bille, 1995, Hancock House, Surrey, BC.
58. *The Wilderness Hunter: Outdoor Pastimes of an American Hunter*, Theodore Roosevelt, 1893, G.P. Putnam's Sons, New York.
59. *Weird Arizona*, Wesley Treat, Mark Moran, Mark Sceurman, ed., 2007, Sterling Publishing, New York.
60. *Weird Florida*, Michael Newton, 2007, Sterling Publishing, New York.
61. *Bigfoot Memoirs*, Stan Johnson, 1996, Wild Flower Press, Newberg, OR.
62. *Lost Cities & Ancient Mysteries of the Southwest*, David Hatcher Childress, 2009, Adventures Unlimited Press, Kempton, IL.
63. *Desert Lore of Southern California*, Choral Pepper, 1994, Sunbelt Publications, San Diego.
64. *Mysterious California*, Mike Marinacci, 1988, Pan Pipes Press, Los Angeles.
65. *Cryptozoology: Science & Speculation*, Chad Arment, 2004, Coachwhip Publications, Darke County, OH.
66. *Bigfoot Encounters in Ohio: Quest for the Grassman*, Christopher Murphy, Joedy Cook and George Clappison, 2006, Hancock House, Surrey, BC.
67. *Legend Tripping*, Robert Robinson, 2016, Adventures Unlimited Press, Kempton, IL.
68. *Monsters Caught on Film*, Dr. Melvin Willin, 2010, David and Charles, Devon, UK.

69. *The Mogollon Monster, Arizona's Bigfoot*, Susan Farnsworth, 1996 (republished 2010), Southwest Publications, Mesa, AZ.
70. *More Mogollon Monster, Arizona's Bigfoot*, Susan Farnsworth and Mitchell Waite, 2011, Southwest Publications, Mesa, AZ.
71. *Wood Knocks, Volume One,* (Journal of Sasquatch Research), Edited by David Weatherly, 2016, Leprechan Press, Prescott, AZ.
72. *Wood Knocks, Volume Two,* Edited by David Weatherly, 2017, Leprechan Press, Prescott, AZ.
73. *The Yeti*, Odette Tchernine, 1970, Neville Spearman, London.
74. *Out of the Shadows*, Tony Healy & Paul Cropper, 1994, Macmillan Australia, Melbourne.
75. *Bhutanese Tales of the Yeti*, Kunzung Choden, 1997, White Lotus, Bangkok.
76. *My Quest for the Yeti*, Reinhold Messner, 1998 (Austria), 2001, St. Martin's Press, New York.

Have you seen this man?

# Get these fascinating books from your nearest bookstore or directly from:
## Adventures Unlimited Press
### www.adventuresunlimitedpress.com

## COVERT WARS AND BREAKAWAY CIVILIZATIONS
## By Joseph P. Farrell

Farrell delves into the creation of breakaway civilizations by the Nazis in South America and other parts of the world. He discusses the advanced technology that they took with them at the end of the war and the psychological war that they waged for decades on America and NATO. He investigates the secret space programs currently sponsored by the breakaway civilizations and the current militaries in control of planet Earth. Plenty of astounding accounts, documents and speculation on the incredible alternative history of hidden conflicts and secret space programs that began when World War II officially "ended."
**292 Pages. 6x9 Paperback. Illustrated. $19.95. Code: BCCW**

## THE ENIGMA OF CRANIAL DEFORMATION
### Elongated Skulls of the Ancients
### By David Hatcher Childress and Brien Foerster

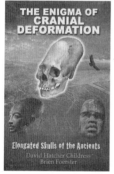

In a book filled with over a hundred astonishing photos and a color photo section, Childress and Foerster take us to Peru, Bolivia, Egypt, Malta, China, Mexico and other places in search of strange elongated skulls and other cranial deformation. The puzzle of why diverse ancient people—even on remote Pacific Islands—would use head-binding to create elongated heads is mystifying. Where did they even get this idea? Did some people naturally look this way—with long narrow heads? Were they some alien race? Were they an elite race that roamed the entire planet? Why do anthropologists rarely talk about cranial deformation and know so little about it? Color Section.
**250 Pages. 6x9 Paperback. Illustrated. $19.95. Code: ECD**

## ARK OF GOD
### The Incredible Power of the Ark of the Covenant
### By David Hatcher Childress

Childress takes us on an incredible journey in search of the truth about (and science behind) the fantastic biblical artifact known as the Ark of the Covenant. This object made by Moses at Mount Sinai—part wooden-metal box and part golden statue—had the power to create "lightning" to kill people, and also to fly and lead people through the wilderness. The Ark of the Covenant suddenly disappears from the Bible record and what happened to it is not mentioned. Was it hidden in the underground passages of King Solomon's temple and later discovered by the Knights Templar? Was it taken through Egypt to Ethiopia as many Coptic Christians believe? Childress looks into hidden history, astonishing ancient technology, and a 3,000-year-old mystery that continues to fascinate millions of people today. Color section.
**420 Pages. 6x9 Paperback. Illustrated. $22.00 Code: AOG**

## YETIS, SASQUATCH & HAIRY GIANTS
### By David Hatcher Childress
Childress takes the reader on a fantastic journey across the Himalayas to Europe and North America in his quest for Yeti, Sasquatch and Hairy Giants. Childress begins with a discussion of giants and then tells of his own decades-long quest for the Yeti in Nepal, Sikkim, Bhutan and other areas of the Himalayas, and then proceeds to his research into Bigfoot, Sasquatch and Skunk Apes in North America. Chapters include: The Giants of Yore; Giants Among Us; Wildmen and Hairy Giants; The Call of the Yeti; Kanchenjunga Demons; The Yeti of Tibet, Mongolia & Russia; Bigfoot & the Grassman; Sasquatch Rules the Forest; Modern Sasquatch Accounts; more. Includes a 16-page color photo insert of astonishing photos!
**360 pages. 5x9 Paperback. Illustrated. Bibliography. Index. $18.95. Code: YSHG**

## SECRETS OF THE HOLY LANCE
### The Spear of Destiny in History & Legend
### by Jerry E. Smith
*Secrets of the Holy Lance* traces the Spear from its possession by Constantine, Rome's first Christian Caesar, to Charlemagne's claim that with it he ruled the Holy Roman Empire by Divine Right, and on through two thousand years of kings and emperors, until it came within Hitler's grasp—and beyond! Did it rest for a while in Antarctic ice? Is it now hidden in Europe, awaiting the next person to claim its awesome power? Neither debunking nor worshiping, *Secrets of the Holy Lance* seeks to pierce the veil of myth and mystery around the Spear.
**312 PAGES. 6x9 PAPERBACK. ILLUSTRATED. $16.95. CODE: SOHL**

## THE CRYSTAL SKULLS
### Astonishing Portals to Man's Past
### by David Hatcher Childress and Stephen S. Mehler
Childress introduces the technology and lore of crystals, and then plunges into the turbulent times of the Mexican Revolution form the backdrop for the rollicking adventures of Ambrose Bierce, the renowned journalist who went missing in the jungles in 1913, and F.A. Mitchell-Hedges, the notorious adventurer who emerged from the jungles with the most famous of the crystal skulls. Mehler shares his extensive knowledge of and experience with crystal skulls. Having been involved in the field since the 1980s, he has personally examined many of the most influential skulls, and has worked with the leaders in crystal skull research. Color section.
**294 pages. 6x9 Paperback. Illustrated. $18.95. Code: CRSK**

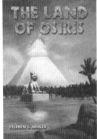

## THE LAND OF OSIRIS
### An Introduction to Khemitology
### by Stephen S. Mehler
Was there an advanced prehistoric civilization in ancient Egypt? Were they the people who built the great pyramids and carved the Great Sphinx? Did the pyramids serve as energy devices and not as tombs for kings? Chapters include: Egyptology and Its Paradigms; Khemitology—New Paradigms; Asgat Nefer—The Harmony of Water; Khemit and the Myth of Atlantis; The Extraterrestrial Question; more. Color section.
**272 PAGES. 6x9 PAPERBACK. ILLUSTRATED . $18.95. CODE: LOOS**

## VIMANA:
### Flying Machines of the Ancients
### by David Hatcher Childress
According to early Sanskrit texts the ancients had several types of airships called vimanas. Like aircraft of today, vimanas were used to fly through the air from city to city; to conduct aerial surveys of uncharted lands; and as delivery vehicles for awesome weapons. David Hatcher Childress, popular *Lost Cities* author, takes us on an astounding investigation into tales of ancient flying machines. In his new book, packed with photos and diagrams, he consults ancient texts and modern stories and presents astonishing evidence that aircraft, similar to the ones we use today, were used thousands of years ago in India, Sumeria, China and other countries. Includes a 24-page color section.
**408 Pages. 6x9 Paperback. Illustrated. $22.95. Code: VMA**

## HIDDEN FINANCE, ROGUE NETWORKS & SECRET SORCERY
### The Fascist International, 9/11, & Penetrated Operations
### By Joseph P. Farrell

Pursuing his investigations of high financial fraud, international banking, hidden systems of finance, black budgets and breakaway civilizations, Farrell investigates the theory that there were not *two* levels to the 9/11 event, but *three*. He says that the twin towers were downed by the force of an exotic energy weapon, one similar to the Tesla energy weapon suggested by Dr. Judy Wood, and ties together the tangled web of missing money, secret technology and involvement of portions of the Saudi royal family. Farrell unravels the many layers behind the 9-11 attack, layers that include the Deutschebank, the Bush family, the German industrialist Carl Duisberg, Saudi Arabian princes and the energy weapons developed by Tesla before WWII.
**296 Pages. 6x9 Paperback. Illustrated. $19.95. Code: HFRN**

## THRICE GREAT HERMETICA AND THE JANUS AGE
### By Joseph P. Farrell

What do the Fourth Crusade, the exploration of the New World, secret excavations of the Holy Land, and the pontificate of Innocent the Third all have in common? Answer: Venice and the Templars. What do they have in common with Jesus, Gottfried Leibniz, Sir Isaac Newton, Rene Descartes, and the Earl of Oxford? Answer: Egypt and a body of doctrine known as Hermeticism. The hidden role of Venice and Hermeticism reached far and wide, into the plays of Shakespeare (a.k.a. Edward DeVere, Earl of Oxford), into the quest of the three great mathematicians of the Early Enlightenment for a lost form of analysis, and back into the end of the classical era, to little known Egyptian influences at work during the time of Jesus.
**354 Pages. 6x9 Paperback. Illustrated. $19.95. Code: TGHJ**

## INVISIBLE RESIDENTS
### The Reality of Underwater UFOS
### by Ivan T. Sanderson

In this book, Sanderson, a renowned zoologist with a keen interest in the paranormal, puts forward the curious theory that "OINTS"—Other Intelligences—live under the Earth's oceans. This underwater, parallel, civilization may be twice as old as Homo sapiens, he proposes, and may have "developed what we call space flight." Sanderson postulates that the OINTS are behind many UFO sightings as well as the mysterious disappearances of aircraft and ships in the Bermuda Triangle. What better place to have an impenetrable base than deep within the oceans of the planet? Sanderson offers here an exhaustive study of USOs (Unidentified Submarine Objects) observed in nearly every part of the world.
**298 PAGES. 6x9 PAPERBACK. ILLUSTRATED. $16.95. CODE: INVS**

## THE FREE-ENERGY DEVICE HANDBOOK
### A Compilation of Patents and Reports
### by David Hatcher Childress

A large-format compilation of various patents, papers, descriptions and diagrams concerning free-energy devices and systems. *The Free-Energy Device Handbook* is a visual tool for experimenters and researchers into magnetic motors and other "over-unity" devices. With chapters on the Adams Motor, the Hans Coler Generator, cold fusion, superconductors, "N" machines, space-energy generators, Nikola Tesla, T. Townsend Brown, and the latest in free-energy devices. Packed with photos, technical diagrams, patents and fascinating information, this book belongs on every science shelf.
**292 PAGES. 8x10 PAPERBACK. ILLUSTRATED. $16.95. CODE: FEH**

## TECHNOLOGY OF THE GODS
### The Incredible Sciences of the Ancients
### by David Hatcher Childress

Childress looks at the technology that was allegedly used in Atlantis and the theory that the Great Pyramid of Egypt was originally a gigantic power station. He examines tales of ancient flight and the technology that it involved; how the ancients used electricity; megalithic building techniques; the use of crystal lenses and the fire from the gods; evidence of various high tech weapons in the past, including atomic weapons; ancient metallurgy and heavy machinery; the role of modern inventors such as Nikola Tesla in bringing ancient technology back into modern use; impossible artifacts; and more.

**356 pages. 6x9 Paperback. Illustrated. $16.95. code: TGOD**

## THE ANTI-GRAVITY HANDBOOK
### edited by David Hatcher Childress

The new expanded compilation of material on Anti-Gravity, Free Energy, Flying Saucer Propulsion, UFOs, Suppressed Technology, NASA Cover-ups and more. Highly illustrated with patents, technical illustrations and photos. This revised and expanded edition has more material, including photos of Area 51, Nevada, the government's secret testing facility. This classic on weird science is back in a new format!

**230 PAGES. 7x10 PAPERBACK. ILLUSTRATED. $16.95. CODE: AGH**

## ANTI–GRAVITY & THE WORLD GRID

Is the earth surrounded by an intricate electromagnetic grid network offering free energy? This compilation of material on ley lines and world power points contains chapters on the geography, mathematics, and light harmonics of the earth grid. Learn the purpose of ley lines and ancient megalithic structures located on the grid. Discover how the grid made the Philadelphia Experiment possible. Explore the Coral Castle and many other mysteries, including acoustic levitation, Tesla Shields and scalar wave weaponry. Browse through the section on anti-gravity patents, and research resources.

**274 PAGES. 7x10 PAPERBACK. ILLUSTRATED. $14.95. CODE: AGW**

## ANTI–GRAVITY & THE UNIFIED FIELD
### edited by David Hatcher Childress

Is Einstein's Unified Field Theory the answer to all of our energy problems? Explored in this compilation of material is how gravity, electricity and magnetism manifest from a unified field around us. Why artificial gravity is possible; secrets of UFO propulsion; free energy; Nikola Tesla and anti-gravity airships of the 20s and 30s; flying saucers as superconducting whirls of plasma; anti-mass generators; vortex propulsion; suppressed technology; government cover-ups; gravitational pulse drive; spacecraft & more.

**240 PAGES. 7x10 PAPERBACK. ILLUSTRATED. $14.95. CODE: AGU**

## THE TIME TRAVEL HANDBOOK
### A Manual of Practical Teleportation & Time Travel
### edited by David Hatcher Childress

*The Time Travel Handbook* takes the reader beyond the government experiments and deep into the uncharted territory of early time travellers such as Nikola Tesla and Guglielmo Marconi and their alleged time travel experiments, as well as the Wilson Brothers of EMI and their connection to the Philadelphia Experiment—the U.S. Navy's forays into invisibility, time travel, and teleportation. Childress looks into the claims of time travelling individuals, and investigates the unusual claim that the pyramids on Mars were built in the future and sent back in time. A highly visual, large format book, with patents, photos and schematics. Be the first on your block to build your own time travel device!

**316 PAGES. 7x10 PAPERBACK. ILLUSTRATED. $16.95. CODE: TTH**

## ANCIENT ALIENS ON THE MOON
### By Mike Bara
What did NASA find in their explorations of the solar system that they may have kept from the general public? How ancient really are these ruins on the Moon? Using official NASA and Russian photos of the Moon, Bara looks at vast cityscapes and domes in the Sinus Medii region as well as glass domes in the Crisium region. Bara also takes a detailed look at the mission of Apollo 17 and the case that this was a salvage mission, primarily concerned with investigating an opening into a massive hexagonal ruin near the landing site. Chapters include: The History of Lunar Anomalies; The Early 20th Century; Sinus Medii; To the Moon Alice!; Mare Crisium; Yes, Virginia, We Really Went to the Moon; Apollo 17; more. Tons of photos of the Moon examined for possible structures and other anomalies.
**248 Pages. 6x9 Paperback. Illustrated.. $19.95. Code: AAOM**

## ANCIENT ALIENS ON MARS
### By Mike Bara
Bara brings us this lavishly illustrated volume on alien structures on Mars. Was there once a vast, technologically advanced civilization on Mars, and did it leave evidence of its existence behind for humans to find eons later? Did these advanced extraterrestrial visitors vanish in a solar system wide cataclysm of their own making, only to make their way to Earth and start anew? Was Mars once as lush and green as the Earth, and teeming with life? Chapters include: War of the Worlds; The Mars Tidal Model; The Death of Mars; Cydonia and the Face on Mars; The Monuments of Mars; The Search for Life on Mars; The True Colors of Mars and The Pathfinder Sphinx; more. Color section.
**252 Pages. 6x9 Paperback. Illustrated. $19.95. Code: AMAR**

## ANCIENT ALIENS ON MARS II
### By Mike Bara
Using data acquired from sophisticated new scientific instruments like the Mars Odyssey THEMIS infrared imager, Bara shows that the region of Cydonia overlays a vast underground city full of enormous structures and devices that may still be operating. He peels back the layers of mystery to show images of tunnel systems, temples and ruins, and exposes the sophisticated NASA conspiracy designed to hide them. Bara also tackles the enigma of Mars' hollowed out moon Phobos, and exposes evidence that it is artificial. Long-held myths about Mars, including claims that it is protected by a sophisticated UFO defense system, are examined. Data from the Mars rovers Spirit, Opportunity and Curiosity are examined; everything from fossilized plants to mechanical debris is exposed in images taken directly from NASA's own archives.
**294 Pages. 6x9 Paperback. Illustrated. $19.95. Code: AAM2**

## ANCIENT TECHNOLOGY IN PERU & BOLIVIA
### By David Hatcher Childress
Childress speculates on the existence of a sunken city in Lake Titicaca and reveals new evidence that the Sumerians may have arrived in South America 4,000 years ago. He demonstrates that the use of "keystone cuts" with metal clamps poured into them to secure megalithic construction was an advanced technology used all over the world, from the Andes to Egypt, Greece and Southeast Asia. He maintains that only power tools could have made the intricate articulation and drill holes found in extremely hard granite and basalt blocks in Bolivia and Peru, and that the megalith builders had to have had advanced methods for moving and stacking gigantic blocks of stone, some weighing over 100 tons.
**340 Pages. 6x9 Paperback. Illustrated.. $19.95 Code: ATP**

## ABOMINABLE SNOWMEN:
## LEGEND COME TO LIFE
### The Story of Sub-Humans on Six Continents from the Early Ice Age Until Today
### by Ivan T. Sanderson

Do "Abominable Snowmen" exist? Prepare yourself for a shock. In the opinion of one of the world's leading naturalists, not one, but possibly four kinds, still walk the earth! Do they really live on the fringes of the towering Himalayas and the edge of myth-haunted Tibet? From how many areas in the world have factual reports of wild, strange, hairy men emanated? Reports of strange apemen have come in from every continent, except Antarctica.

525 PAGES. 6X9 PAPERBACK. ILLUSTRATED. $16.95. CODE: ABML

## IN SECRET MONGOLIA
### by Henning Haslund

Haslund takes us into the barely known world of Mongolia of 1921, a land of god-kings, bandits, vast mountain wilderness and a Russian army running amok. Starting in Peking, Haslund journeys to Mongolia as part of a mission to establish a Danish butter farm in a remote corner of northern Mongolia. With Haslund we meet the "Mad Baron" Ungern-Sternberg and his renegade Russian army, the many characters of Urga's fledgling foreign community, and the last god-king of Mongolia, Seng Chen Gegen, the fifth reincarnation of the Tiger god and the "ruler of all Torguts." Aside from the esoteric and mystical material, there is plenty of just plain adventure: Haslund encounters a Mongolian werewolf; is ambushed along the trail; escapes from prison and fights terrifying blizzards; more.

374 PAGES. 6X9 PAPERBACK. ILLUSTRATED. BIBLIOGRAPHY & INDEX. $16.95. CODE: ISM

## MEN & GODS IN MONGOLIA
### by Henning Haslund

Haslund takes us to the lost city of Karakota in the Gobi desert. We meet the Bodgo Gegen, a god-king in Mongolia similar to the Dalai Lama of Tibet. We meet Dambin Jansang, the dreaded warlord of the "Black Gobi." Haslund and companions journey across the Gobi desert by camel caravan; are kidnapped and held for ransom; witness initiation into Shamanic societies; meet reincarnated warlords; and experience the violent birth of "modern" Mongolia.

358 PAGES. 6X9 PAPERBACK. ILLUSTRATED. INDEX. $18.95. CODE: MGM

## MYSTERIES OF ANCIENT SOUTH AMERICA
### by Harold T. Wilkins

Wilkins digs into old manuscripts and books to bring us some truly amazing stories of South America: a bizarre subterranean tunnel system; lost cities in the remote border jungles of Brazil; cataclysmic changes that shaped South America; and other strange stories from one of the world's great researchers. Chapters include: Dead Cities of Ancient Brazil, The Jungle Light that Shines by Itself, The Missionary Men in Black: Forerunners of the Great Catastrophe, The Sign of the Sun: The World's Oldest Alphabet, The Atlanean "Subterraneans" of the Incas, Tiahuanacu and the Giants, more.

236 PAGES. 6X9 PAPERBACK. ILLUSTRATED. INDEX. $14.95. CODE: MASA

## SECRET CITIES OF OLD SOUTH AMERICA
### by Harold T. Wilkins

The reprint of Wilkins' classic book, first published in 1952, claiming that South America was Atlantis. Chapters include Mysteries of a Lost World; Atlantis Unveiled; Red Riddles on the Rocks; South America's Amazons Existed!; The Mystery of El Dorado and Gran Payatiti—the Final Refuge of the Incas; Monstrous Beasts of the Unexplored Swamps & Wilds; Weird Denizens of Antediluvian Forests; New Light on Atlantis from the World's Oldest Book; The Mystery of Old Man Noah and the Arks; and more.

438 PAGES. 6X9 PAPERBACK. ILLUSTRATED. BIBLIOGRAPHY & INDEX. $16.95. CODE: SCOS

# ANCIENT ALIENS & SECRET SOCIETIES
## By Mike Bara
Did ancient "visitors"—of extraterrestrial origin—come to Earth long, long ago and fashion man in their own image? Were the science and secrets that they taught the ancients intended to be a guide for all humanity to the present era? Bara establishes the reality of the catastrophe that jolted the human race, and traces the history of secret societies from the priesthood of Amun in Egypt to the Templars in Jerusalem and the Scottish Rite Freemasons. Bara also reveals the true origins of NASA and exposes the bizarre triad of secret societies in control of that agency since its inception. Chapters include: Out of the Ashes; From the Sky Down; Ancient Aliens?; The Dawn of the Secret Societies; The Fractures of Time; Into the 20th Century; The Wink of an Eye; more.
**288 Pages. 6x9 Paperback. Illustrated. $19.95. Code: AASS**

---

# THE CRYSTAL SKULLS
## Astonishing Portals to Man's Past
## by David Hatcher Childress and Stephen S. Mehler
Childress introduces the technology and lore of crystals, and then plunges into the turbulent times of the Mexican Revolution form the backdrop for the rollicking adventures of Ambrose Bierce, the renowned journalist who went missing in the jungles in 1913, and F.A. Mitchell-Hedges, the notorious adventurer who emerged from the jungles with the most famous of the crystal skulls. Mehler shares his extensive knowledge of and experience with crystal skulls. Having been involved in the field since the 1980s, he has personally examined many of the most influential skulls, and has worked with the leaders in crystal skull research, including the inimitable Nick Nocerino, who developed a meticulous methodology for the purpose of examining the skulls.
**294 pages. 6x9 Paperback. Illustrated. Bibliography. $18.95. Code: CRSK**

---

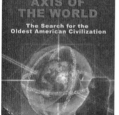

# AXIS OF THE WORLD
## The Search for the Oldest American Civilization
## by Igor Witkowski
Polish author Witkowski's research reveals remnants of a high civilization that was able to exert its influence on almost the entire planet, and did so with full consciousness. Sites around South America show that this was not just one of the places influenced by this culture, but a place where they built their crowning achievements. Easter Island, in the southeastern Pacific, constitutes one of them. The Rongo-Rongo language that developed there points westward to the Indus Valley. Taken together, the facts presented by Witkowski provide a fresh, new proof that an antediluvian, great civilization flourished several millennia ago.
**220 pages. 6x9 Paperback. Illustrated. References. $18.95. Code: AXOW**

---

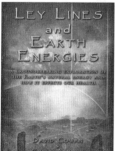

# LEY LINE & EARTH ENERGIES
## An Extraordinary Journey into the Earth's Natural Energy System
## by David Cowan & Chris Arnold
The mysterious standing stones, burial grounds and stone circles that lace Europe, the British Isles and other areas have intrigued scientists, writers, artists and travellers through the centuries. How do ley lines work? How did our ancestors use Earth energy to map their sacred sites and burial grounds? How do ghosts and poltergeists interact with Earth energy? How can Earth spirals and black spots affect our health? This exploration shows how natural forces affect our behavior, how they can be used to enhance our health and well being.
**368 PAGES. 6x9 PAPERBACK. ILLUSTRATED. $18.95. CODE: LLEE**

## SAUCERS, SWASTIKAS AND PSYOPS
### A History of a Breakaway Civilization
### By Joseph P. Farrell
Farrell discusses SS Commando Otto Skorzeny; George Adamski; the alleged Hannebu and Vril craft of the Third Reich; The Strange Case of Dr. Hermann Oberth; Nazis in the US and their connections to "UFO contactees"; The Memes—an idea or behavior spread from person to person within a culture—are Implants. Chapters include: The Nov. 20, 1952 Contact: The Memes are Implants; The Interplanetary Federation of Brotherhood; Adamski's Technological Descriptions and Another ET Message: The Danger of Weaponized Gravity; Adamski's Retro-Looking Saucers, and the Nazi Saucer Myth; Dr. Oberth's 1968 Statements on UFOs and Extraterrestrials; more.
**272 Pages. 6x9 Paperback. Illustrated. $19.95. Code: SSPY**

## LBJ AND THE CONSPIRACY TO KILL KENNEDY
### By Joseph P. Farrell
Farrell says that a coalescence of interests in the military industrial complex, the CIA, and Lyndon Baines Johnson's powerful and corrupt political machine in Texas led to the events culminating in the assassination of JFK. Chapters include: Oswald, the FBI, and the CIA: Hoover's Concern of a Second Oswald; Oswald and the Anti-Castro Cubans; The Mafia; Hoover, Johnson, and the Mob; The FBI, the Secret Service, Hoover, and Johnson; The CIA and "Murder Incorporated"; Ruby's Bizarre Behavior; The French Connection and Permindex; Big Oil; The Dead Witnesses: Guy Bannister, Jr., Mary Pinchot Meyer, Rose Cheramie, Dorothy Killgallen, Congressman Hale Boggs; LBJ and the Planning of the Texas Trip; LBJ: A Study in Character, Connections, and Cabals; LBJ and the Aftermath: Accessory After the Fact; The Requirements of Coups D'État; more.
**342 Pages. 6x9 Paperback. $19.95 Code: LCKK**

## THE TESLA PAPERS
### Nikola Tesla on Free Energy &
### Wireless Transmission of Power
### by Nikola Tesla, edited by David Hatcher Childress
David Hatcher Childress takes us into the incredible world of Nikola Tesla and his amazing inventions. Tesla's fantastic vision of the future, including wireless power, anti-gravity, free energy and highly advanced solar power. Also included are some of the papers, patents and material collected on Tesla at the Colorado Springs Tesla Symposiums, including papers on: •The Secret History of Wireless Transmission •Tesla and the Magnifying Transmitter •Design and Construction of a Half-Wave Tesla Coil •Electrostatics: A Key to Free Energy •Progress in Zero-Point Energy Research •Electromagnetic Energy from Antennas to Atoms
**325 PAGES. 8X10 PAPERBACK. ILLUSTRATED. $16.95. CODE: TTP**

## COVERT WARS & THE CLASH OF CIVILIZATIONS
### UFOs, Oligarchs and Space Secrecy
### By Joseph P. Farrell
Farrell's customary meticulous research and sharp analysis blow the lid off of a worldwide web of nefarious financial and technological control that very few people even suspect exists. He elaborates on the advanced technology that they took with them at the "end" of World War II and shows how the breakaway civilizations have created a huge system of hidden finance with the involvement of various banks and financial institutions around the world. He investigates the current space secrecy that involves UFOs, suppressed technologies and the hidden oligarchs who control planet earth for their own gain and profit.
**358 Pages. 6x9 Paperback. Illustrated. $19.95. Code: CWCC**

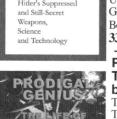

## HITLER'S SUPPRESSED AND STILL-SECRET WEAPONS, SCIENCE AND TECHNOLOGY
### by Henry Stevens

In the closing months of WWII the Allies assembled mind-blowing intelligence reports of supermetals, electric guns, and ray weapons able to stop the engines of Allied aircraft—in addition to feared x-ray and laser weaponry. Chapters include: The Kammler Group; German Flying Disc Update; The Electromagnetic Vampire; Liquid Air; Synthetic Blood; German Free Energy Research; German Atomic Tests; The Fuel-Air Bomb; Supermetals; Red Mercury; Means to Stop Engines; more.

**335 Pages. 6x9 Paperback. Illustrated. $19.95. Code: HSSW**

## PRODIGAL GENIUS
### The Life of Nikola Tesla
### by John J. O'Neill

This special edition of O'Neill's book has many rare photographs of Tesla and his most advanced inventions. Tesla's eccentric personality gives his life story a strange romantic quality. He made his first million before he was forty, yet gave up his royalties in a gesture of friendship, and died almost in poverty. Tesla could see an invention in 3-D, from every angle, within his mind, before it was built; how he refused to accept the Nobel Prize; his friendships with Mark Twain, George Westinghouse and competition with Thomas Edison. Tesla is revealed as a figure of genius whose influence on the world reaches into the far future. Deluxe, illustrated edition.

**408 pages. 6x9 Paperback. Illustrated. Bibliography. $18.95. Code: PRG**

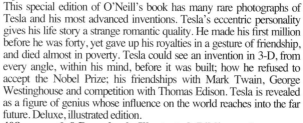

## HAARP
### The Ultimate Weapon of the Conspiracy
### by Jerry Smith

The HAARP project in Alaska is one of the most controversial projects ever undertaken by the U.S. Government. At at worst, HAARP could be the most dangerous device ever created, a futuristic technology that is everything from super-beam weapon to world-wide mind control device. Topics include Over-the-Horizon Radar and HAARP, Mind Control, ELF and HAARP, The Telsa Connection, The Russian Woodpecker, GWEN & HAARP, Earth Penetrating Tomography, Weather Modification, Secret Science of the Conspiracy, more. Includes the complete 1987 Eastlund patent for his pulsed super-weapon that he claims was stolen by the HAARP Project.

**256 pages. 6x9 Paperback. Illustrated. Bib. $14.95. Code: HARP**

## WEATHER WARFARE
### The Military's Plan to Draft Mother Nature
### by Jerry E. Smith

Weather modification in the form of cloud seeding to increase snow packs in the Sierras or suppress hail over Kansas is now an everyday affair. Underground nuclear tests in Nevada have set off earthquakes. A Russian company has been offering to sell typhoons (hurricanes) on demand since the 1990s. Scientists have been searching for ways to move hurricanes for over fifty years. In the same amount of time we went from the Wright Brothers to Neil Armstrong. Hundreds of environmental and weather modifying technologies have been patented in the United States alone – and hundreds more are being developed in civilian, academic, military and quasi-military laboratories around the world *at this moment!* Numerous ongoing military programs do inject aerosols at high altitude for communications and surveillance operations.

**304 Pages. 6x9 Paperback. Illustrated. Bib. $18.95. Code: WWAR**

# ORDER FORM

**10% Discount
When You Order
3 or More Items!**

One Adventure Place
P.O. Box 74
Kempton, Illinois 60946
United States of America
Tel.: 815-253-6390 • Fax: 815-253-6300
Email: auphq@frontiernet.net
http://www.adventuresunlimitedpress.com

## ORDERING INSTRUCTIONS

✓ Remit by USD$ Check, Money Order or Credit Card

✓ Visa, Master Card, Discover & AmEx Accepted

✓ Paypal Payments Can Be Made To:
info@wexclub.com

✓ Prices May Change Without Notice

✓ 10% Discount for 3 or More Items

## SHIPPING CHARGES

### United States

✓ Postal Book Rate { $4.50 First Item / 50¢ Each Additional Item

✓ POSTAL BOOK RATE Cannot Be Tracked!
Not responsible for non-delivery.

✓ Priority Mail { $6.00 First Item / $2.00 Each Additional Item

✓ UPS { $7.00 First Item / $1.50 Each Additional Item

NOTE: UPS Delivery Available to Mainland USA Only

### Canada

✓ Postal Air Mail { $15.00 First Item / $2.50 Each Additional Item

✓ Personal Checks or Bank Drafts MUST BE
US$ and Drawn on a US Bank

✓ Canadian Postal Money Orders OK

✓ Payment MUST BE US$

### All Other Countries

✓ Sorry, No Surface Delivery!

✓ Postal Air Mail { $19.00 First Item / $6.00 Each Additional Item

✓ Checks and Money Orders MUST BE US$
and Drawn on a US Bank or branch.

✓ Paypal Payments Can Be Made in US$ To:
info@wexclub.com

## SPECIAL NOTES

✓ RETAILERS: Standard Discounts Available

✓ BACKORDERS: We Backorder all Out-of-
Stock Items Unless Otherwise Requested

✓ PRO FORMA INVOICES: Available on Request

✓ DVD Return Policy: Replace defective DVDs only

ORDER ONLINE AT: www.adventuresunlimitedpress.com

**10% Discount When You Order
3 or More Items!**

---

Please check: ✓

☐ This is my first order     ☐ I have ordered before

Name
Address
City
State/Province                 Postal Code
Country
Phone: Day                    Evening
Fax            Email

| Item Code | Item Description | Qty | Total |
|---|---|---|---|
| | | | |
| | | | |
| | | | |
| | | | |
| | | | |
| | | | |
| | | | |
| | | | |
| | | | |
| | | | |
| | | | |
| | | | |
| | | | |
| | | | |

Please check: ✓

☐ Postal-Surface
☐ Postal-Air Mail (Priority in USA)
☐ UPS
(Mainland USA only)
☐ Visa/MasterCard/Discover/American Express

Subtotal ▶
Less Discount-10% for 3 or more items ▶
Balance ▶
Illinois Residents 6.25% Sales Tax ▶
Previous Credit ▶
Shipping ▶
Total (check/MO in USD$ only) ▶

Card Number:
Expiration Date:              Security Code:

✓ SEND A CATALOG TO A FRIEND: